Blood on Their Hands

Blood on Their Hands

How Greedy Companies, Inept Bureaucracy, and Bad Science Killed Thousands of Hemophiliacs

ERIC WEINBERG

DONNA SHAW

RUTGERS UNIVERSITY PRESS

NEW BRUNSWICK, CAMDEN, AND NEWARK, NEW JERSEY, AND LONDON

LIBRARY OF CONGRESS CATALOGING-IN-PUBLICATION DATA

Names: Weinberg, Eric, 1955– author. | Shaw, Donna, 1951– author.
Title: Blood on their hands : how greedy companies, inept bureaucracy, and bad
    science killed thousands of hemophiliacs / Eric Weinberg and Donna Shaw.
Description: New Brunswick, New Jersey : Rutgers University Press, 2017. | Includes
    bibliographical references and index.
Identifiers: LCCN 2016050297| ISBN 9780813576220 (hardcover : alk. paper) |
    ISBN 9780813576237 (e-book (epub)) | ISBN 9780813576244 (e-book (web pdf))
Subjects: LCSH: Biological products—Law and legislation—United States. | Blood—
    Transfusion—Complications—United States. | Products liability—United States. |
    Blood banks—United States.—Quality control. | Hemophilia—Law and
    legislation—United States—Criminal provisions. | Hemophiliacs—Legal status,
    laws, etc.—United States. | Hemophiliacs—Infections—United States. | Weinberg,
    Eric, 1955–
Classification: LCC KF3894.B5 W45 2017 | DDC 343.7307/86161572061—dc23
LC record available at https://lccn.loc.gov/2016050297

A British Cataloging-in-Publication record for this book is available from the
British Library.

∝ The paper used in this publication meets the requirements of the American
National Standard for Information Sciences—Permanence of Paper for Printed
Library Materials, ANSI Z39.48–1992.

www.rutgersuniversitypress.org

Manufactured in the United States of America

For our families: Diane, Jake, Arnie, Mike, and Noah;
Walt, Matt, Terri, and Mom

CONTENTS

PREFACE AND ACKNOWLEDGMENTS

Joe Salgado's funeral in 2008 was on one of those rare August days when New Jersey was pleasantly warm instead of suffocatingly hot. Saint Joseph's Church in Raritan was packed, so his old friend, Eric Weinberg, stood in back. The priest and Joe's children told the mourners how Joe had gotten on his knees every morning to thank God for His blessings. He was only fifty-nine, but they were grateful for the time they had together. It was, after all, years longer than Joe's family had expected. The irony of that hit Weinberg: somehow, all that Joe had been through had enriched his life in ways his friend could only try to understand.

Later, standing at his graveside in Sacred Heart Cemetery, on a rise above the Millstone River, Weinberg remembered how, some twenty-five years earlier, Joe had joked about Weinberg joining the softball team for the Somerset County Prosecutor's Office, where they had worked together as lawyers. Jews can't play softball, Salgado ribbed him, and they stuck Weinberg in the outfield. It was true—Weinberg was more of a basketball guy—but that year, they made it to the final four of the law enforcement state softball tournament, and, in a key game against the state police, Weinberg hit everything they threw at him. You were hot as a firecracker, a retired detective reminded him at the cemetery. It felt good to laugh a little and reminisce, as if Joe were there with them, listening.

Joe was just a little older than Weinberg when they met in 1980, but it was only a few months after Weinberg's father had died, so Joe became his mentor. He was the one who encouraged Weinberg when he failed the bar exam the first time around, the one he could talk to about anything. Joe was serious and tough but also kind and funny, and he loved fishing almost as much as he loved his wife and kids. His obituary said he died peacefully at home, but Weinberg knew about the lifetime of pain that had led up to that day, even though they had not talked much about it.

The day Joe finally told Weinberg he was sick was in 1993, during lunch at a Chinese restaurant. He said what Weinberg already pretty much knew, since by then, Weinberg had been representing similar clients for two years: Joe was born with hemophilia, a rare bleeding disorder that usually is hereditary and found in males, and he had been infected with the AIDS virus and hepatitis from using contaminated blood-clotting products. Then Joe asked him to be his lawyer, too, saying it had taken him years to realize that his suffering was not an act of God—as the drug industry liked to call it in legal pleadings—but of man.

The years passed. Weinberg spent them on Joe's case and hundreds of others like it. Just before Joe died, Weinberg wanted to visit, but his friend didn't want people to remember him that way. His faith and his family had sustained and enriched him. Illness was part of his life, but Joe never let it define who he was.

Joe was a piece on a global chessboard, one that included patients, doctors, researchers, not-for-profit organizations, and four major pharmaceutical companies, along with health officials and politicians from many nations. But this was no game: it was, and is, one of the largest public health disasters in modern history.

And it isn't over.

How many victims are involved? In the United States alone, government agencies and hemophilia activists have estimated that in the late 1970s to mid-1980s, between six thousand and ten thousand hemophiliacs— about half of the country's total, and as many as 90 to 95 percent with severe hemophilia—were sickened from tainted clotting products. An additional twelve thousand Americans are believed to have received HIV-infected blood transfusions. Another, unknown number—so poorly defined and studied that for years, officials could put it only at somewhere between one hundred thousand and two hundred thousand—were infected with hepatitis C from blood and plasma products.

Many thousands more were stricken in Canada, Central and South America, Europe, Asia, and Australia—in other words, on every continent and in every nation where the products were used. Those countries are still coping with the aftermath, struggling to assist families that can never be made whole, and to ensure that such a tragedy never happens again.

Most were infected before anyone knew of the existence of HIV, although that was no excuse, since industry and government regulators had been aware for decades that plasma could, and did, carry dangerous viruses like hepatitis. Other patients, especially overseas, were sickened later, by older products dumped in their countries after safer medicines were available in the United States.

In 1991, with his solo law practice in New Brunswick, New Jersey, thriving, Weinberg found himself drawn into this international tragedy, in which he would help to represent a community of thousands infected with HIV and hepatitis by these hugely profitable medicines. The litigation took a decade, and many of his clients got sicker and died before it was over. Some are still ill and dying today. With advances in medicine, others are doing better, considering what they've been through.

Several years have passed since most of the lawsuits have ended, and Weinberg has come to understand that the case, and the medical outrage it represented, didn't affect just his clients, but him as well. He was a participant whose actions would push the litigation in certain directions, but in turn he also would be pushed, as a lawyer, husband, father, and man. Inevitably, he came to feel like part of the community he represented—not one of them, but one who was deeply affected by them.

This is the story of a brave and resilient community. It is also about a powerful industry, and institutions of government and civil justice, invented and refined to protect life and basic freedoms. It is about the worth of advocacy in the face of harm.

So this is Weinberg's story, but even more it is the story of his clients. He was thirty-five when the litigation started and forty-five, married with four young sons, when those cases that involved him concluded in 2001. Circumstances he never could have imagined drew him in and eventually resulted in more than a billion dollars in settlements, from the companies and the U.S. government combined, to thousands of devastated, sick, and dying Americans. The cases consumed and gutted his law practice, but after years of work, and as much as it could be under the circumstances, partial justice was achieved.

This book is dedicated to the memory of Joe Salgado (which, at the request of his widow, is not his real name), and to the thousands of others who have suffered the inconceivable pain and heartbreak of the tainted-blood era. So many of them, and people close to them, have provided us, the authors, with advice, information, photos, and documents, and have shared their deeply personal stories. Their courage, determination, and spirit are awe inspiring. Among those who deserve special thanks, in alphabetical order, are Ken Baxter, Elena Bostick, Michael Gillard, Bill Horn-McGinnis, Andrea Johnson, Jaime Johnson Kern, Dana Kuhn, Terry MacNeill, Denise Maloney, Jeffrey Moualim, Marilyn Ness, Michael Rosenberg, Richard Vogel, Christina Wilson, and Joanne Womboldt.

We are indebted as well to the many sources, colleagues, associates, friends, and family members who have helped us on the journey.

Jane Dystel, our agent, from Dystel, Goderich & Bourret LLC, and Peter Mickulas, our editor at Rutgers University Press, provided invaluable expertise, support, and encouragement, as did other members of the Rutgers staff.

Our reviewer, Douglas Starr, codirector of the Science Journalism Program at Boston University, has award-winning expertise from his own years of writing and publishing about the blood supply and its history. His comments heartened us and helped us hone our manuscript.

Many of the lawyers involved in the case offered advice, support, and/or permission to quote them. In alphabetical order, they include Charles Goodell, James Holloran, Rob Jenner, Judy Kavanaugh, Charles Kozak, Robert Limbacher, Thomas Mull, Robert Parks, the Honorable Joel Pisano, Robert Sachs, Wayne Spivey, and Cage Wavell.

Donna Shaw's former editors and colleagues at the *Philadelphia Inquirer*, as well as her current colleagues at the College of New Jersey, unfailingly offered support, advice, and the motivation required to complete the research and writing.

Finally, this book would not exist were it not for the love and support of our spouses, children, and parents. We missed far too much time with all of you, but you stuck by us. We promise to make up for it.

NOTE ON TEXT

The dialogue and quotations in this book come from a variety of verbal and written sources, including one-on-one conversations, formal interviews, sworn testimony, court transcripts, published studies, personal journals, and notes taken contemporaneously to or shortly after the events described, as well as an enormous trove of other court, government, and corporate documents. Certain dialogue is reconstructed from interview notes, journals, or recollections of conversations. In addition, we have changed the names of some people to protect their privacy.

Blood on Their Hands

1

Liquid Gold

Delano Boudreaux woke to the sound of men cursing and the smell of wet, stale sweat. He didn't want to open his eyes. Just a few more seconds, he said to himself. A few more seconds and I'll get up, before the guards come.[1]

He rolled over on his flimsy mattress, straightening out to flatten his body against the cool concrete wall along his bunk. This will have to last me all day, he thought. Soon I'll be out in the goddamn sun, boiling my hide, getting bitten by the Louisiana state bird better known as the mosquito. I'll be bent over, sweat running up my spine, goose-picking grass from around the fences, and weeding around the flowers. As if the damn flowers made the prison look good.

Not that Boudreaux, who arrived there in 1979, had it as bad as most of the other inmates at the Louisiana State Penitentiary at Angola, America's largest maximum-security prison. Located northwest of Baton Rouge, at the end of state Highway 66, Angola is a nineteenth-century plantation transformed after the Civil War into an 18,000-acre prison farm. The dormitories, which a map on the prison website says can hold up to 5,295 inmates,[2] spread across its rich bottomland and are surrounded on three sides by an alligator-infested stretch of the Mississippi River. The fourth side is swamp, with more gators and the world's biggest, baddest rattlesnakes. At least that's what the inmates—most of them violent offenders and lifers—are told. "The Farm," as it is dubbed, has been used continuously for agriculture for more than two hundred years, and

most of the inmates, except for those on Death Row, work the fields, growing cotton, soybeans, corn, and other vegetables.

Today, Angola is perhaps best known for its rodeo, an annual extrava-
ganza that every October draws thrill-seeking tourists by the thousands to
gawk at inmates clad in black-and-white stripes as they ride bulls and
broncos. On the prison's separate rodeo website, longtime warden Nathan
Burl Cain, who resigned in 2016, boasted that it was "the most unique
show or performance you'll see in this country or maybe in the world."
One purpose, Cain said, was to take selfish men and teach them to worry
about others.[3]

But when Boudreaux first got there, the prison had more of a reputation as a corrupt and violent hellhole whose murder rate sometimes challenged that of inmate deaths by natural causes. Angola was a place full of
evil men, murderers, rapists, and the worst of the worst. Most would die
in that wretched place, one way or another.

Boudreaux, of course, was innocent. He insisted so. Convicted of
armed robbery—his brother, he said, was the only one with a gun—he
drew a sentence of sixty years. Eventually, in 1999, he would be released
after serving twenty-one years.

But that was years away, little more than a ridiculously distant dream
on that clammy, muggy morning, as he reluctantly climbed from his bunk
for another day's work. It would be hot, of course, but worse for those
inmates who toiled in Angola's broad, open fields. Boudreaux would not be
among them, for he had a bit of a scam going: he'd conned the prison medical department into believing he had a bad shoulder. That's how he got
assigned to weed-pulling duty, and while he hated it, it was a lot better than
the harder labor of the farm.

He was almost ready to leave for work when he remembered something that made him smile. He wouldn't be yanking weeds today after all.
No scalding sun, no mosquitoes. No, sir.

It was bleeding day.

Twice a week, an inmate could get a "call out" from work for the whole
day just by spending an hour with a needle in his arm, donating blood
plasma that then was sold and used for who-knows-what. Cosmetics for
ladies, somebody said. Plasma was the secret ingredient in those fancy
brands they sold at department stores, the inmates had heard.

The plasma center operated conveniently in a tin and cement-block structure on Angola's grounds. The center contained a holding cell, restrooms, a bleeding area, and storage freezers. Like others of its kind, it was operated not by the local hospital or the Red Cross but by a for-profit company whose owner paid the state handsomely for the right to set up shop at the prison. The profits for the company, Louisiana Biologics, were even greater; by the early 1980s, they were in the millions of dollars, according to documents later produced in lawsuits. Louisiana Biologics ran half a dozen or so facilities at prisons in Louisiana, Tennessee, and Florida. Many similar civilian centers, owned by other companies, operated in cities and towns across America, usually in neighborhoods where down-on-their-luck types needed quick and easy cash.

At Angola, inmates helped run many of the day-to-day operations. It wasn't unusual for a donor to arrive at the center and have fellow inmates assist as someone recorded his name, swabbed his arm, stuck him with a needle, drew the blood, spun it in a centrifuge to separate out the watery plasma, and then reinfused the donor with his red blood cells. Each donor gave two units per visit, one plastic bag at a time, and because he was getting back his red cells, could be bled twice per week without fear of anemia.

The bags would quickly be slant-frozen—suspended at an angle—the better to preserve the precious blood proteins. Then they were boxed and placed on pallets, with bills of lading and invoices attached to track their every move.

Corporate documents and witness depositions reveal that, at the height of Angola's productivity, a large shipment of human plasma would be picked up every two weeks from the penitentiary, loaded into tractor trailers, and delivered to a major international pharmaceutical company, Baxter Healthcare Corporation's Hyland Division, at its manufacturing facility in Glendale, California. In the early 1980s, between 20 and 25 percent of Glendale's plasma came from prisons, according to the documents.[4]

Once at Glendale, the frozen plasma bags would be taken to a processing room and slit open, and the precious contents dumped, thousands of units at a time, into huge vats. Rotating paddles would agitate and liquefy the plasma as it thawed. From there, the proteins would be extracted and sent on for further processing.

In industry parlance, the stuff of life could be cracked into separate and distinct components. These blood proteins, called fractions, were the raw material not for cosmetics, as some inmates believed, but for several lifesaving and often breathtakingly expensive medicines, serums, and vaccines. Manufactured at the time primarily by Baxter and three other large pharmaceutical firms, also known as fractionators, these products brought in billions of dollars globally in annual sales.

In late 1993, as part of a lawsuit filed by a patient who claimed he had contracted the AIDS virus from blood products, the manager of Baxter's plasma operations testified about the safety of the process. The plasma, he insisted in sworn testimony, came from "a completely wholesome, diverse group of donors, including college students, housewives and folks that had jobs who would come in before work or after work, some folks who had part-time jobs and some people that were unemployed."

Like Rumpelstiltskin spinning straw into gold, Angola's facility churned out this yellowish plasma, opening its doors to donors early in the morning and bleeding them into the night. It had metal tables for the inmates to lie on, some so beaten up that a table once collapsed underneath a guy getting bled. Boudreaux, who took a paralegal course in prison and wasn't one to pass up an opportunity, promptly filed a grievance on behalf of his fallen comrade.

Yes, Boudreaux and the other inmates loved what they called "the bleeding," and not just because it was considered a day's work. "Donate" wasn't precisely the right word for what they did. They were paid between five and fifteen dollars per donation, as much as thirty dollars per week if they were bled twice. That compared very favorably to the four cents per hour they received for working in the fields, or twenty cents for working in the laundry.

So there wasn't much a man wouldn't say or do to stay on the donor list.

The blood money went into a commissary account, which an inmate could spend on cigarettes, peanut butter, sugar, coffee, and personal items. Ironically, he also might use those goods, especially the cigarettes, to bribe his way back into the plasma center, should somebody suddenly decide a certain guy's blood was no longer fit to sell. Under federal safety regulations, donors were supposed to be excluded permanently if they had a history of hepatitis, and the potentially dangerous liver infection was common in prisons—places, after all, where high-risk activities like homosexual sex, intravenous drug use with shared needles, and homemade tattoos all were rampant. That, at least, was the rule.

But at Angola, for example, there was an inmate named Shorty who specialized in tattoos. He had fashioned a tattoo gun from the motor of an old cassette player, the barrel of an ink pen, and a guitar string. He used that contraption over and over on men throughout the prison. Still, if you slipped two cartons of cigarettes to a worker at the plasma center, he might look the other way about tattoos or needle tracks, even if he knew you'd just had sex on the prison bus, or in the honeymoon suite better known as the plasma center's bathroom. Some inmates even had sex in the holding cell as they waited to give their blood. That cell was a social center in a rough world, where prisoners housed in distant barracks could also meet, talk, fight, or shoot drugs.

Indeed, in all the years that Boudreaux was a donor—until the last remnants of the nation's prison plasma machine were dismantled because by then nobody, not even those gullible foreigners who trusted everything American, wanted inmate blood anymore—he estimated that he'd seen a real, honest-to-God doctor at the plasma center maybe once. The exam, he said, went something like this:

DOCTOR: How you doing? You hurting anywhere?
BOUDREAUX: No.

End of exam.

So at a time when the screening tests performed on donated blood and plasma were insufficient, when health experts including those from the United Nations were warning that prisons were "often ideal breeding grounds" for HIV,[5] when thousands or even tens of thousands of plasma units were combined into a single industrial vat for the sake of saving on manufacturing costs, Boudreaux wasn't asked if he was having sex with other inmates, consensual or otherwise. He wasn't asked to remove his shirt so somebody could check for needle marks, tattoos, piercings, or blood-brother ritual cuts. If anybody did ask, he'd deny engaging in such behaviors. For the eighteen dollars he made each week, who wouldn't?

Not long after he got out of prison in 1999, Boudreaux was diagnosed with hepatitis C, a potentially deadly form of the virus that causes liver cancer in some patients. He claimed not to know when or how he got it.

He certainly wasn't the only one. In the 1980s, there were about a dozen plasma operations in U.S. prisons, mostly in southern and western states, on average paying between $5 and $8.50 per donation. Between 30 percent and 60 percent of all inmates were donors.[6] Besides Angola, other centers were in places like Raiford State Penitentiary in Florida and Tennessee State Penitentiary in Nashville. Many were operated by businesspeople with ties to local politicians.

So in the 1970s and early 1980s, just before HIV was discovered, if 20 to 25 percent of the industry's raw plasma came from prisons, what about the rest? Much of it, according to corporate and government documents, was collected not at Red Cross blood drives or community or hospital facilities, but at commercial plasma centers. Many if not most of these centers were located in lower-income communities as well as skid-row neighborhoods, including areas frequented by IV drug abusers, alcoholics, homeless people, prostitutes, and illegal immigrants, populations at higher risk for infectious diseases. Maybe these donors were motivated by the desire to help one's fellow man, but most simply needed the money.

So the for-profit plasma centers thrived not just in prisons but in areas close to transient hotels, homeless shelters, and social services. Court exhibits and depositions included numerous examples. There were centers in Texas border towns, where impoverished Mexicans came across the Rio Grande River and sold their blood. They were in neighborhoods like the one in Akron, Ohio, where in 1974, city health officials determined that at least fifty people with hepatitis had sold their plasma, and lawyers representing hemophiliacs learned that women hired to draw blood there were poorly trained, with some of them moonlighting as go-go dancers at a nearby bar. And they were in places like Johnson City, Tennessee, where the center's manager told FDA inspectors in 1984 that some donors were so poor he would lend them shoes so they would be in compliance with the state health code.[7] He quickly added that he refused to lend anyone his shirt.

Except for the prisons, much of that network still exists today.

Blood centers also operated in several poor regions of the Caribbean, Central and South America, Asia, and even sub-Saharan Africa, believed to be the birthplace of the AIDS virus. Corruption was not unusual, and these centers rarely if ever were inspected by the U.S. Food and Drug Administration. In 1978, a center in Nicaragua was burned down by towns-people angry with its owners—dictator Anastasio Somoza and his business partner—who were believed to have helped plot the assassination of a local newspaper publisher.[8] Somoza later fled the country and was assassinated in 1980; his partner also left Nicaragua, and reentered the plasma business with the wife of a politician in Belize. Another center, in South Africa, was found to be smuggling plasma out of the country by deliberately mislabeling it as an animal product, then relabeling it as human blood when it reached its destination: the European factory of a major U.S. blood-products supplier. The ruse wasn't discovered until after the product had been manufactured and sold. The suburban Philadelphia company involved, Rhone-Poulenc Rorer Inc., and its Armour subsidiary, called themselves the victims, saying they thought the plasma came from Canada. But they did not issue a product recall, and patients continued to use it without knowing of its origins.[9]

Even some of those who sold their plasma for more altruistic reasons unwittingly took part in what would become a public-health nightmare. Some plasma centers, for example, recruited heavily for donors in the gay communities of large cities, especially among men who had been infected with hepatitis B. Ads in newspapers targeted at the gay community proclaimed, "We need a few good arms!" and "Do your share!" and "Help stamp out hepatitis B!" and "Donors urgently needed!" These plasma donations, the ads said, not only would earn them as much as thirty-one hundred dollars per year but "at the same time, you'll be helping to contribute to the health and welfare of other gay men and women." And this was true, because their hepatitis antibodies and antigens were used in research and production of lifesaving vaccines and serums. But instead of discarding what was left after extracting these valuable materials, the companies—with the full knowledge of the FDA—poured the remainder into the same plasma pools used to make other medicines. The FDA decided this didn't violate federal standards, despite its rule about excluding people with a history of hepatitis. "You can argue that it wasn't wise," a high-ranking FDA official told a reporter in 1996. "But to argue that it was violative is inaccurate. That doesn't mean that people couldn't have done better."[10]

So it wasn't as if the manufacturers or the government were unaware of the dangers. Indeed, from the very start of mass production of hemophilia medicines in the late 1960s, some plasma vats were so disease-laden that the newest employees were deliberately assigned to what every other worker knew was the worst job at the plant: slashing open the plasma bags and dumping the contents into the vats. At one company, fourteen workers who had been in the plasma-processing area for eighteen months or less contracted hepatitis between 1968 and 1971, and blood tests showed that most of their fellow employees also had been exposed, according to a government-funded study published in the prestigious *Journal of the American Medical Association.*[11] The authors didn't identify which company was involved, leaving readers to figure it out based on the authors and geographic clues in the article. Not long afterward, the companies took to dressing their employees in protective moon suits, like so many earthbound astronauts.

Two decades later, the former president of one major blood-products manufacturer, a man whose conscience apparently bothered him enough that he became a consultant for hemophilia activists, would admit in an interview: "It was sort of accepted that all of the workers in our plant were positive for hepatitis B, and so were all the hemophiliacs, and it was accepted that all the hemophiliacs would probably die of hepatitis at some time in their lives."[12]

In 1976, British journalist Michael Gillard investigated the use of plasma drawn from drug addicts, homeless people, and alcoholics, and in a televised series he reported what he had seen in America while tracing the source of the plasma used to make clotting medicines for his countrymen. Gillard visited a dozen plasma centers and each time, despite providing false identification, was allowed to sell his blood. His work sparked the obligatory investigations and proclamations of outrage, but nothing changed enough to prevent HIV from entering America's blood supply, and hemophilia products, a few years later.

Men and boys with hemophilia and their families knew little or nothing of any of this, of course. (The most common form of the condition is genetic and occurs primarily in males.) Neither did many of their physicians, although some had their doubts and refused to prescribe the commercial products, sticking instead with more inconvenient, less effective, blood and plasma transfusions. But the pressure on them was intense, because the freeze-dried clotting medicines were a revolutionary advance in the treatment of hemophilia. They came in tiny vials and could be self-administered, so even people with severe hemophilia could travel, hold jobs, marry, and have children instead of enduring painful deaths in their youth. Nearly everyone—doctors, patients, and advocacy organizations—embraced them. And so clotting medicines emerged as standard therapy across America and through much of the industrialized world.

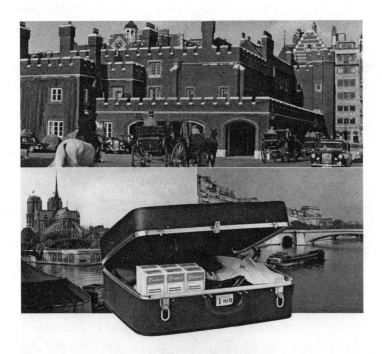

PASSPORT TO FREEDOM
for the hemophiliac

FIGURE 1.1. This early magazine advertisement for Factor VIII products emphasized one of the most desirable attributes of the medicines: portability. They also could be self-administered.

Credit: Marilyn Ness.

There was some understanding of the potential dangers, especially when patients started getting sick. But hepatitis, they were told, was the price they had to pay, because scientists didn't know how to cleanse the clotting concentrates. Indeed, while much of the manufacturers' plasma was rendered germ-free before reaching consumers who used other products, the more fragile clotting proteins used in hemophilia medicines were not. Impossible and too expensive, the industry said, and the lapdog government regulators went along. Until a foreign competitor began heat-treating its hemophilia medicines to kill viruses, none of the major fractionators that purchased plasma from prisoners or other high-risk sellers followed suit.[13] Even after such methods were added to the process, some companies continued to sell off their older products, especially overseas, with clusters of cases springing up in previously uninfected patients.[14] In internal documents, executives talked about not wanting to lose revenue, contracts, or market share. That would upset the shareholders.[15]

So while it certainly horrified those who used these medicines, it shouldn't have surprised the manufacturers or the government when tens of thousands of patients worldwide were stricken. First was hepatitis. Then came HIV. Most people with severe hemophilia who regularly infused commercial clotting drugs between 1980 and 1985 contracted the AIDS virus. Thousands died. So did some of their spouses and children, infected through sex or childbirth before the men were aware they were ill.

There was David, a handsome, blue-eyed software designer forced to leave his Silicon Valley job when AIDS struck.

There was Michael, a deputy attorney general for the state of Pennsylvania and onetime president of the National Hemophilia Foundation.

There was Evan, an American University senior who excelled in tennis and French and was majoring in peace and conflict studies when he died at age twenty-two.

There was eleven-year-old Roger, a loyal Mets fan from New Jersey, who ended his days blind and strapped into a wheelchair, able to think and moan but not speak.

And there were those left behind when their loved ones died.

There was Judith, a literate, well-educated beauty who lost her
   only child and descended into near madness, losing her looks
   and her job, chain-smoking as she wrote daily letters of
   outrage to then-president Bill Clinton, undoubtedly getting
   herself placed on some Secret Service watch list for her
   trouble.

There was Ethel, who lost all three of her sons, a daughter-in-law,
   and a brother. After spending all of her savings on them, the
   formerly middle-class mother and grandmother from
   Baltimore was left destitute, struggling to survive on Social
   Security, while other family members took on the task of
   raising two orphaned children left behind.

There was Fern, frail and soft-spoken, whose depression at losing
   her only child was so deep that she could not function and
   was evicted from her home on Christmas Eve.

If one were to try to conceive of a way to kill a vulnerable population
of innocent human beings, it would be difficult to find a more effective
and cruel way to do it. People with hemophilia were devastated by the very
medicine that was supposed to ease their pain and lengthen their lives.
Children were injected by well-meaning parents who would forever blame
themselves.

Few involved in the devastation were willing to accept responsibility,
some because they knew they were culpable, others because they were in
denial. It must be noted here, however, that many honorable, well-
meaning people who worked for these companies—some of whom had
dedicated their lives to helping the hemophilia community, some of
whom had hemophiliacs in their own families—were just as unaware,
especially of the plasma sources, as were patients and physicians.

Equally as anguished were many government scientists who watched
as their bosses appeared to kowtow to Big Pharma. Then and now, the FDA
had a revolving door between itself and drug companies, with many officials either coming from or eventually going to high-paying industry jobs.

So it was that generations of children, teenagers, and adults with
hemophilia fell victim to one of the worst medically induced epidemics in
the history of modern medicine.

2

Beginnings

From the start of his career, Eric Weinberg had the notion that he would be the kind of lawyer who made a difference. Fresh out of Boston University School of Law in 1980, he vowed that there would be no corporate fat-cat clients for him. He would help regular people with real problems.

But several years later, as a small-town lawyer working from a Victorian-era house in a modest section of New Brunswick, New Jersey, he had another thought: be careful what you wish for. For here he was in a Newark courtroom, facing a less-than-sympathetic-looking jury, trying gamely to convince them that Peter, his young Nigerian client, who was in the United States on a student visa, had been set up by older Nigerians involved in a cocaine deal and was completely innocent of any wrongdoing. To make matters worse, this wasn't just a legal strategy— Weinberg was sure the kid was innocent.

Peter's stricken parents sat quietly behind them in the courtroom every day, wearing colorful Nigerian garb, watching Weinberg's every move. They had come to the United States thinking they would see their son's college graduation. They arrived to find him in a dingy cell, awaiting trial, a federal prosecutor demanding a life sentence.

The judge in the case had a reputation as a liberal on social issues but tough when sentencing convicted defendants. Now the prosecutor had a complaint, and asked for a sidebar conference. The judge agreed, and the lawyers approached the bench.

"Your Honor," the prosecutor said, "I have some concerns about the defendant's parents."

"What are your concerns, counselor?" asked the judge.

"I don't know if you can hear from the bench, judge, but the defendant's mother is constantly murmuring and making sounds."

"I have not heard her, but I'll take your word for it. Do you have some concern that the jury is being distracted?"

"Yes, your honor. But I think it's more than that. It sounds to us like she's trying to chant some spells or something, some kind of incantation, to jinx the government's case."

The judge stared at her for a moment, and then turned to Weinberg.

"Mr. Weinberg, is your client's mother trying to put a hex on the government?"

At this point in the trial, Weinberg was pretty sure he was shredding the prosecution's case.

"I wouldn't know, your Honor. I think I'm doing OK on my own."

"I will address the parents, counsel. Please return to your seats," the judge said.

He leaned forward and spoke in an even voice to the parents.

"Sir and madam, do you understand English?"

They both nodded yes.

"Good. I understand that you are here in support of your son. However, in our system of laws, it is very important that we maintain a quiet courtroom, so that the jury can see and hear all of the evidence. It is important for all of the parties. So please do not speak, or make any sounds, during the trial. You are free to leave the courtroom and talk outside if you must, or wait until the jury is out, and we are in recess. Do you understand?"

"Yes, your Honor," they said.

After two weeks of trial, the case went to the jury. They reached a verdict in a few hours: Peter was not guilty. His co-defendant was guilty. Peter and his parents hugged Weinberg who, after congratulating his colleagues, took the elevator to the ground floor, found a pay phone, and called his office. As he spoke to his secretary, several of the women jurors walked past, smiled, and waved. Behind them, the juror Weinberg had been most concerned about during the trial was walking alone. He was a big guy, probably in his forties or fifties. He had sat in the back row of the jury box, in the middle, and Weinberg could never figure out what he was thinking during the trial. He saw Weinberg at the telephone and walked over. The lawyer put the phone down.

"You did a great job for your client," the juror said.

"Thanks. I was a little worried when you came back with a question," Weinberg said.

"We decided your guy was innocent in the first five minutes. He was lucky to have you as his lawyer." The man smiled and shook Weinberg's hand.

Well, there was a lesson learned. You never know about juries. But truth be told, Weinberg had been on something of a roll lately.

It started in August 1980, two months after he had graduated from law school, when he was hired by the Somerset County Prosecutor's Office in Somerville, the county seat. He had lived in that part of New Jersey since he was seven years old. The job, though, came only six months after the worst time in his life, when his father died at the age of forty-eight. Weinberg had wanted to stay in Boston after law school and work there, but as the eldest of three children, he felt he had to go home and be near his mother, who had developed multiple sclerosis. He knew the toll of his father's death would further drain her strength. He was worried, too, about his brother and sister, who were having a hard time adjusting to the shock.

Weinberg started out as the sole legal assistant for a small staff consisting of the prosecutor, David Linett; the first assistant prosecutor, Leonard Arnold; and eight other assistants. It was a great office. Linett and Arnold were both smart, Harvard-educated lawyers and had put together a very competent staff of attorneys and detectives. It was the kind of job Weinberg had craved since his second year of law school, when he tried his first case as part of a clinical program at Boston University. The starting salary—$13,500—was ridiculously low, but once he passed the bar, he would be promoted.

Weinberg shared an office with Joe Salgado, who had about five years of experience as an assistant prosecutor and quickly took to the role of mentor. Joe was good at what he did and knew his way around the courtroom. He had an easygoing manner, with a sarcastic streak that took a while to recognize as innocent and grounded in a deep-seated sense of humor about life in general. Joe, married with two kids and a devout Catholic, enjoyed having fun.

A few days after Weinberg moved into the office, Joe got up from his desk and stretched his legs. Weinberg noticed he did this every time he stood.

"Did you have a knee injury?" he asked.

"Nah, just early arthritis. Come here," said Joe, gesturing to the large windows overlooking the intersection below. He reached into his desk and took out a pair of binoculars, then limped to the window and began to scan the street.

"What is it?" Weinberg thought maybe there was some investigation going on right beneath their office.

"Hmm," said Joe, his head pivoting left to right and back. "Okay, here we go."

He passed the binoculars to Weinberg. A couple of pretty women in summer dresses were walking down the street. Weinberg had to laugh.

But he was still an emotional wreck when he took the New Jersey bar exam, and when the results came in the mail just before Thanksgiving, Weinberg took one look at the envelope and knew by the color that he had failed. "The Board of Bar Examiners is sorry to inform you," the letter began. Failing was a terrible blow, layered on what had already happened in his life that year. He had always been a successful student, near the top of his class, always in the top two or three percentiles on standardized tests, and usually without really trying. To fail the most important test of his life was embarrassing. But there was nothing to do except study harder, so he enrolled in two bar exam preparatory courses and got back to work.

Weinberg took the exam again in February 1981, and when he learned in May that he had passed, he cried—partly from relief, partly because of his deep sadness that his father would never know. Loss of a loved one could actually cause physical pain.

For the next two and a half years, he worked as an assistant prosecutor. He loved the job and felt good about what he was doing: Somerset County was small enough, with a population of 250,000, to have serious crime without a sense of futility in dealing with it. He felt part of a system of justice that seemed to work. He had the power to charge; he could listen to police officers or state troopers and decide whether the charges they brought had merit. He learned about the importance of allegiance to a system of laws. Best of all, Weinberg had interesting cases.

Len Arnold taught him that a good trial lawyer could tell a jury what a case was about in a few sentences. Arnold knew criminal law as well as any lawyer in New Jersey. He had literally written the book, a text on criminal law. He was a great trial lawyer, a Jewish cowboy in central New Jersey who favored cowboy boots and a sardonic air, which he pulled off because he was always completely prepared to try his cases. He worked closely with the detectives, always visiting scenes of crimes or other places where critical actions had happened, and he taught the younger lawyers that there was no substitute, ever, for that kind of legwork.

Watching Arnold try a case was like being at the theater. To him, these were interesting stories with plots that had to be built piece by piece. Arnold knew what he needed to prove, and structured his case to prove every element, saving some good evidence to use as zingers when the defense attorney cross-examined his witnesses.

Dave Linett was more formal and reserved, his personality in stark contrast to that of Arnold. Linett was a very capable administrator and a visionary in terms of how technology would impact the practice of law; he had their office designated as the pilot program for implementing computer technology statewide into all twenty-one prosecutors' offices. Linett also understood the strengths and weaknesses of his staff, including himself. He delegated responsibility for the trial functions to Arnold, and they worked well together.

But when Tom Kean, a Republican, was elected governor of New Jersey, Linett, a Democrat, was a goner. And Arnold, although a Republican, was not a politician. So almost everyone in the office, including Weinberg and Joe Salgado, was fired.

To Weinberg, perhaps the worst part was that he had just been assigned his first murder prosecution. *State of New Jersey vs. William Grunow* was a great, gory love triangle of a case in which a wealthy businessman, Grunow, was charged with bludgeoning and stabbing his secretary's husband to death.

Weinberg had been the on-call prosecutor when the secretary called the police to report her husband missing. Two detectives brought her in for an interview. She was distraught, perhaps more than she should have been over a husband who had been away only a couple of days. She confessed that she and Grunow had been carrying on a tempestuous affair for years, before and after her marriage. Two detectives went to Grunow's house, and when they arrived, he was in his garage, spray-painting a hacksaw and hatchet with orange paint. They got a search warrant and, along with Weinberg, went back to the house.

By then, it was dark. A long driveway led to a courtyard between the house and the garage. A backhoe was parked in the woods nearby. The detectives searched the property as two police dogs walked through the woods, trying to find a scent they had taken from a piece of the husband's clothing. It was a long night of work. At one point Weinberg nodded off on a couch in the house. Grunow covered him with a blanket.

As the sun came up, Weinberg was in the garage talking to a detective. They walked toward the driveway and noticed what appeared to be human tissue and hair in the gravel. A detective found a freshly turned plot of earth not far from the backhoe. They got a second warrant, this one to bring their own backhoe to the property and start digging. After an hour, there was a loud clang. The backhoe had torn a hole into a steel drum, and through the hole they saw the husband's body.

Grunow then confessed. He said that, using a different name, he had called the husband, a contractor, and had asked him about doing a construction job. Grunow said that when the husband arrived at their meeting site, Grunow revealed the affair and tried to reason with him, but the husband became enraged and, according to Grunow, attacked him. He said he struck the husband in self-defense with an iron pipe wrapped in newspaper, then panicked, loaded him into the back of a van, and drove to his own house.

As an appeals court later would dryly observe, "The victim did not survive the encounter."[1]

Grunow said he knew his rival was dead, but his body was hissing, so he stabbed him several times in the chest with a garden pick, sawed off his limbs, folded him up, and dropped him into the fifty-five-gallon drum. Then he topped off the drum with motor oil, sealed it shut, and buried it in his yard with the backhoe.

It was a case any lawyer would want to try, but the new prosecutor, Nicholas Bissell, took it over. Bissell, a Somerville lawyer, was extremely ambitious and aggressive. He had been cultivating political connections for several years and had friends in the right places. Weinberg didn't. He cleared out his office and typed up a résumé. Grunow was convicted of aggravated manslaughter. He appealed and won a new trial, but in a plea bargain, pled guilty and was sentenced to twenty years in prison. He was paroled in 1990.[2]

For a while, Weinberg hunkered down in his apartment, writing a screenplay based on a shooting incident he had come across while researching a case. He even went to California for a few weeks, hoping to develop some Hollywood connections. It didn't happen. So it wasn't long before Weinberg came back to Somerset County and, thanks to a lead from a friend, was hired by a small insurance defense firm called Franchino, Lenahan, and Cross, in Raritan Township, just west of Somerville. Sal Franchino was senior partner of the firm and Tom Lenahan was the second in command.

Weinberg liked Franchino, who was frugal, funny, clever, and good to work with. Lenahan was one of the better lawyers in the insurance defense bar, not too much older than Weinberg. The third partner was Gene Cross, a good lawyer and laconic, easygoing guy who was happy working modest hours and spending time with his young children. They hired Weinberg for twenty-two thousand dollars a year, and he was glad to have the work. He even had a company car, which was a nice perk, since he tried cases in courtrooms all over New Jersey. Weinberg's big black Labrador retriever, Spike, loved to ride in the backseat. But Franchino was a neat freak and Spike drove him crazy—Franchino would check the car windows in the parking lot and then come to Weinberg's office to complain that the rear passenger windows were smudged with obvious residue of dog nose, so there had to be dog hairs on the back seat as well. If Weinberg walked from the office kitchen with a cup of coffee and a muffin, Franchino would pick the crumbs off the carpet and neatly place them on a napkin to show him what a slob he was. But Weinberg liked working there and learned a lot about civil litigation.

It was while he was there that he became engaged to Diane Santoro, and they were married in March 1984. By that summer, Weinberg knew he wanted to be his own boss, and Diane was secure in her job as a microbiologist at a major pharmaceutical company. They purchased a two-family house in Highland Park and carried the mortgage on her salary while he built up his practice. They had no children yet, only Spike, and the time seemed right. So Weinberg took the three real-estate cases he had to his name, worked briefly with another lawyer, then opened his own practice in New Brunswick. In 1987, he purchased an old Victorian house on Livingston Avenue, once the town's most elegant thoroughfare but by then past its prime. The city was home to Rutgers University as well as to the Johnson & Johnson healthcare company, and extensive redevelopment plans were in the works that would, in time, make New Brunswick a model for urban renewal. Weinberg took on some personal-injury cases, had some successes, and his practice began to grow.

In 1988, he was hired for his first case involving a product regulated by the U.S. Food and Drug Administration. The clients were the parents of twins Lindsey and Sean, born prematurely, and little Lindsey was the first to come home, along with a prescription for an apnea monitor. The device was supposed to monitor her breathing and heart rate, and sound a loud alarm if she was in distress. Her parents were trained in CPR in case the alarm went off. The mother put Lindsey to bed at 2 A.M. At 7:40 A.M., she went to the baby's room and found her head wedged between the crib mattress and bumper pads; the monitor was making a soft beeping sound, and all the lights were flashing green. Frantically, the mother started CPR. When police arrived they also tried to revive the baby, and as one officer removed the belt that attached the monitor's LCD leads to the child, the alarm finally sounded, loud and clear. But Lindsey was gone. The grief-stricken parents asked Weinberg to find out what had gone wrong, especially fearful lest Sean come home from the hospital with the same prescription.

Weinberg's first child, Jake, was ten months old at the time, and he and Diane were expecting Arnie, who would arrive that October. So he understood how deeply these parents were hurt and wanted to help them find answers. The parents' story was confirmed by the police report; the responding officer had been explicit in describing the malfunction of the machine. Still, Weinberg accepted the case knowing it would be difficult— after all, the FDA had approved the monitor, and the agency was and is considered the gold standard worldwide.

But by the time the trial date neared, Weinberg had learned from Cage Wavell, a Texas lawyer with some similar cases, that the manufacturer had received numerous complaints from doctors whose tiny patients had died despite the monitor. The company called these events suspicious and did not report them to the FDA, although it did keep what it referred to as a "death list," which included about two dozen names. Its argument was that the monitor had not failed, and so under the law it did not have to tell the FDA. Instead, the company often blamed the parents, suggesting that they had been drinking and had failed to respond to the alarms.

Weinberg flew to Corpus Christi to meet with Wavell, a colorful character who had survived several gunshots, apparently linked to a romance gone wrong. He gave Weinberg a tour of his office—the scene of the shooting—and pointed out a couple of bullet holes still in the molding around a door. Given that experience, Wavell had a deep appreciation for life. Wavell and Weinberg worked on the case for several hours, then went for Mexican food and beer at a place where men openly wore their guns. Then they drove over to South Padre Island, walked on the beach, and talked about how to prove their cases. After three days of work, Weinberg had a better sense of what it was about.

The case made headlines across the country, and by 1989 federal officials were investigating the company. Reporters interviewed Weinberg and his clients, and, as often happens when publicity is involved, a congressional investigation soon followed. When the case went to trial in 1992, the company knew it was in trouble and settled for a handsome sum. But the experience was an eye-opener. Wavell and Weinberg became catalysts for change, and Weinberg learned that rules and regulations could not always protect consumers from an outlaw business. He also learned that a company, even one regulated by the federal government, could control the release of critically important health information about its products.

In May 1991, Weinberg went to trial in another major case. His client, an airline pilot named Patrick, had become a quadriplegic after diving headfirst into the deep end of a friend's in-ground pool. Again, the manufacturer had known of design flaws in its product; many people had suffered paralyzing injuries. The diving end had dangerous, sloping shallows, but rather than fix the design, the company had issued warning labels that owners were supposed to stick on their pools. Nobody had labeled the pool where Patrick was injured. His head struck bottom even before his feet entered the water. After three weeks at trial, the defendants settled for $1.6 million, enough so Patrick could provide for himself for the ten more years he would live.

Both cases involved products that were inherently dangerous in their design. In both cases, the manufacturers knew of the defects and failed to fix them or adequately warn consumers. The cases demonstrated the basic principle of U.S. product-liability law: if a company sells a defective product and people are injured, it must compensate them.

By then, Weinberg's practice was doing well enough that he and Diane made a decision. She felt strongly that she should be at home with the boys, for their benefit and hers. She was doing regulatory work, an important specialty within the drug industry, and leaving her career after twelve successful years wouldn't be easy, but she felt it was time. Weinberg was pleased, but they both had concerns about money. He would need to take on a lot of new cases.

That summer, the Weinbergs vacationed for a week on Sanibel Island in the Gulf of Mexico. A few days after returning home, Weinberg got a telephone call from a potential new client. His professional and personal lives were about to change.

3

How Could It Happen and Nobody Did Anything Wrong?

It was June 21, 1991, at exactly 1 P.M., when Andrea Johnson and her daughter, Jaime, walked into Weinberg's life.

As he went to his office foyer to greet them, he saw that Andrea relied on a cane and her teenage daughter's arm for support. Andrea looked almost too frail to handle the few stone steps outside his office.

She was young and pretty, her face nearly perfect, symmetrical and fine like a porcelain doll. As she stood, Weinberg saw that she could not straighten up to her full height. Andrea and Jaime introduced themselves and went to his conference room, Andrea sitting down heavily, Jaime next to her. He could see they were apprehensive.

"I'm sorry to be so clumsy," Andrea said. "It's this darned multiple sclerosis I have on top of everything else."

She looked at Weinberg closely, made strong eye contact, and spoke without a hint of self-pity. He immediately liked her.

"I was thinking that was what you have," Weinberg said. "My mother has MS."

"Really? Where does she go?"

"Robert Wood Johnson Hospital. Dr. LePore."

"That's my doctor. He's terrific," Andrea said.

"It really is a small world," Weinberg agreed.

"Sure is."

"Well, if you're a friend of Joe, you have my sincerest sympathies," Weinberg joked, referring to Joe Salgado, his former colleague who had referred her to him.

"He's a good person," she said, smiling. "He told me you might be interested in what happened to my husband, and I guess to me. I asked him if there was a legal case and he said to talk with you."

"Why don't you tell me everything you think I should know, Andrea? Just so you know, before you came here today, I did a little reading about hemophilia and HIV. Just take your time and walk me through everything," Weinberg said.

From talking to her on the phone, he already knew a key fact: Andrea had contracted HIV from having sex with her husband, before they knew he was infected.

"I don't really know where to start," she replied.

"Tell me about Clyde."

"He was a good father," Andrea said, looking at Jaime for affirmation. Jaime smiled.

Weinberg thought of his own father, and knew something about Jaime's pain in that moment. His sons were quite young. He imagined what it had meant to her, having to watch as her father died, slowly and agonizingly. For this young woman to know her mother might suffer the same kind of death seemed unbearably unfair.

"He shouldn't have died the way he did," Andrea said. "I don't understand why it happened, and I need to know if someone was responsible—you know, if it had to be the way it was. Did Clyde have to die from AIDS?"

There was nothing in Weinberg's experience to prepare him for what had happened to this family.

Clyde, a diesel mechanic with a good job, had died of AIDS complications in August 1989. Before that, the Johnsons had been living a good, middle-class life, with one exception. Clyde was born with hemophilia Type A, a hereditary disorder of the blood that meant he had less than the normal amount of a clotting protein called Factor VIII.[1] It made him highly susceptible to internal bleeding following even minor bumps and bruises. Sometimes he would have bleeding episodes spontaneously, seemingly for no reason at all.

Andrea pulled a family portrait—Clyde, Andrea, and Jaime, smiling and looking happy in formal clothes—from her handbag and placed it on Weinberg's conference table.

"Clyde and I started dating in high school," she said. "He was a really funny person, and I just fell in love with him. He told me he had hemophilia and he had to take blood sometimes, because of the bleeding. So it was a part of our lives but not so much, because he just dealt with it. He was good with cars and engines. He always wanted to be a mechanic, and he was a good one. At the garage he was one of the best."

"How was he able to do that with his hemophilia?" Weinberg asked.

"See," Andrea said, "that's what people don't understand about hemophilia. It's not so much getting cut that's the problem. He never had any real problems with that kind of thing. It was internal bleeding that happened when he would fall down, bump himself hard, something like that. So he took the factor, and it would stop the bleeding, and he could work."

"The factor"—Factor VIII clotting medicines—had transformed the lives of hemophiliacs like Clyde, starting in the late 1960s and early 1970s.[2] Before that, during his childhood and teen years, Clyde's life sometimes was a living hell, full of pain and crude, inefficient treatments that relied on transfusions of blood, plasma, and a plasma product called cryoprecipitate. But then scientists invented the world's first freeze-dried blood-clotting concentrates. They were made from human plasma and sold in tiny glass vials that came boxed with sterile saline and syringes. Clyde learned how to mix the precious powder with the saline, draw the mix into a syringe, and infuse himself in response to bleeding episodes, or when he felt them coming on.

Suddenly, Clyde and other men and boys with hemophilia were able to live relatively normal lives. Factor VIII concentrates did not require refrigeration, meaning patients could move freely, no longer tied to hospital emergency rooms or doctors' offices or home freezers. It gave them choices in life that most people take for granted, allowing Clyde to go to technical school and get a good job, taking those little glass vials with him.

"How often would he need the factor?" Weinberg asked.

"Pretty much every day," she replied. "The doctors told us he could take it whenever he felt a bleed coming on. Clyde didn't really like to take medicine, so he would wait until he got like a tingling or something, and he would know a bleed was coming."

"How did he manage before there was clotting factor?"

"Clyde got through it, you know? But he didn't really complain about too much. Even at the end, he never said much about how he was hurting, nothing like that. I ought to just stop talking. Jaime, I told you to tell me when I was talking too much."

"No, I'm listening carefully to you," Weinberg said.

What Clyde and Andrea didn't know was that a blood-borne disease, a virus that later would be named the human immunodeficiency virus, or HIV, was lurking in those little bottles. Sometime in 1981 or 1982, Clyde was infected. He was only twenty-eight years old. Jaime was five. But Clyde wasn't diagnosed until September 1986. By then, he'd also contracted hepatitis B and C, and infected his wife.

As Weinberg would learn, scientists had known for decades what could go wrong with plasma products. There was no doubt that they were lifesavers, but they also carried significant risk.

The Johnsons knew nothing of this history. Neither did thousands of other patients.

In the three years after his diagnosis, until he died, Clyde was hospitalized thirteen times. He was in the hospital for Christmas 1988, the last Christmas he would see. His body was wracked with AIDS complications—diseases with exotic names like candida esophagitis and severe recurrent herpes simplex—as well as multiple bouts of pneumonia, encephalitis, and wasting syndrome. He also contracted diabetes, a side effect of the medicines that treated his pneumocystis carinii.

Andrea cared for her husband as best she could while waiting for the disease to consume her as well. By then Jaime was entering her teens and got to watch as her young father wasted away and died.

Weinberg turned to Jaime. She was growing up to be as pretty as her mother.

"What do you think about all this?" he asked.

"I think if they did something wrong, somebody should say so. Do you think you could find out if they did something wrong to my father and mother?"

Life had pushed Jaime hard, and she was asking for help but challenging him, too. Would he be true to the job, to really getting to the bottom of it?

"Jaime, Joe is going through the same thing as us," Andrea said. "He wouldn't have sent us to Mr. Weinberg if he didn't think he was the one who could help us."

Weinberg was stunned. He had known Joe Salgado for more than a decade, but until Andrea Johnson called, had never suspected that Joe had hemophilia, much less AIDS. Andrea had assumed that Weinberg knew, so he tried not to show his shock. For a moment, he lost track of the conversation—was he dreaming this meeting?—and then recovered.

Andrea showed him a letter written by Joe. He was president of the Hemophilia Association of New Jersey (HANJ), an advocacy group. Joe had written to the four major manufacturers of the clotting-factor concentrates, suggesting that they fund a compensation program to pay expenses for hemophiliacs infected with HIV. Andrea said the companies had refused. The hemophilia community was at a loss for what to do next. But now, in the summer of 1991, it was clear to these families that HIV was sweeping through them, and that many would die.

Weinberg had won some difficult cases, but this one was different. What Andrea was describing was not a single case. He would be taking on an influential multibillion-dollar industry, one with government backing, and armies of top-notch lawyers and experts.

He had many more questions. What were their lives like before AIDS? What did they know about the risks of the products in the 1970s, when Clyde was using them even though there was an epidemic of hepatitis among hemophiliacs?

"We really didn't know about hepatitis then," Andrea said. "Clyde was like most of the hemophiliacs—they needed the doctors and the hospitals, so they trusted them and never really asked too many questions. The clotting factor came out and it made our lives easier. There really wasn't any other choice."

"How old was Clyde when he died?"

"Thirty-five."

"How much was he earning before he got sick?"

"About thirty thousand, and he never missed a day's work until he got real sick."

"Now I have to ask this: What do you think I'll be able to do for you?"

Andrea looked closely at the tall young lawyer with the serious demeanor, taking his measure. Although calm, her anger was palpable now.

"I was expecting you to ask me that question," Andrea said. "Some people over at the Hemophilia Association of New Jersey have been talking about it. Basically, nobody thinks anything can be done. The companies claim it was nobody's fault. I don't believe that, Mr. Weinberg. They say there are ten thousand hemophiliacs with AIDS in this country, just like my Clyde, and they all got it from the factor. The more I think about it, the more I wonder, how could it be? How could it happen and nobody did anything wrong?"

"Andrea, if you want the presidents of these companies to go to jail, I understand that feeling but I can't do anything about it," Weinberg replied. "All I can do is try to get you some answers and some money."

"I know," she replied. "But what bothers me is how they could invent heat-treated clotting factor so soon after AIDS came along, when they had all those years before that to do something to kill those viruses, and they didn't do anything even though they knew Clyde and the others were getting hepatitis. What took them so long is what I'm saying."

Weinberg already had written that question on his legal pad. What *had* taken so long? From the background he had collected before Andrea's appointment, he knew the companies had started using heat to kill viruses in clotting concentrates in the early to mid-1980s—using technology developed in the 1940s to kill hepatitis in other plasma products—after they realized that clotting factor was contaminated with HIV. If the companies had the ability to develop these processes sooner, when people with hemophilia were getting sick from hepatitis, then the case, he thought, could be won.

Andrea had another question. She had heard from other members of the hemophilia community that a German company had figured out how to sterilize the clotting medicines in the late 1970s, before HIV was discovered, but that the four major companies who made the drugs had rejected the process because they didn't own it. They didn't want to pay another company for it. Could that be true?

If so, it would be key to Weinberg's legal strategy. And by the end of the meeting with Andrea and Jaime, he had other questions written on his pad. How could the U.S. Food and Drug Administration, considered the world's leading drug regulator, have approved these products for sale? And why did the medical community accept the risk—knowing that pooled blood products could easily be tainted—and not demand that they be made safer? Were hemophiliacs just supposed to accept that they were canaries in the coal mine for the rest of the world?

"So, will you take our case?" Andrea asked after almost two hours in his office.

"Yes," Weinberg replied. "We are going to have to file soon, though, because the clock is ticking. There's a statute of limitations to deal with."

Andrea Johnson signed a retainer agreement, with Weinberg accepting the case on a contingency basis. He would cover all expenses. If they won, he would collect a percentage of any award. Otherwise, he'd get nothing.

Andrea and Jaime walked out into the bright, warm sunshine of that early summer afternoon, Andrea leaning heavily on her daughter for support. For the rest of the day, Weinberg could not stop thinking about them. He kept coming back to the family portrait that Andrea had taken from her purse.

The photograph was from the mid-1980s, with Clyde standing tall, a big man, bearded and robust. His wife stood beside him, and their pride in the moment was evident. They were a handsome family, well dressed for a special day. Jaime stood in front of and between them. They were looking into the camera, smiling. It reminded Weinberg of a rotogravure of another family stricken with hemophilia—the Russian royals, Tsar Nicholas, his wife, Alexandra, and their children, posing some years before the revolution of 1917 and the family's eventual execution. Their youngest child, heir to his father's title, was a hemophiliac. What was striking was their gilded ignorance of death soon to come.

A photograph can be a haunting thing. When it is revisited years later, it is layered over with life experience. The viewer knows far more than the subjects did at the moment the flash exploded and the images were captured. Clyde and Andrea Johnson weren't Russian royalty, yet their pride and dignity seemed noble.

The Weinbergs had rented a shore house on New Jersey's Long Beach Island that summer, and they spent long weekends there with their little boys. Through July and August, Weinberg took warm nighttime walks with Spike and thought about hemophilia and AIDS. He talked the case over with Diane. She thought it was a great case and, with her expertise in regulatory work, was outraged by it.

Clyde Johnson and Joe Salgado were ordinary men who had overcome hemophilia. In certain ways, their lives had not been so different from his. They had all grown up within fifteen miles of one other, at around the same time, and Andrea reminded Weinberg of a girl he had known in high school—pretty, friendly, and kind. Then Clyde got AIDS and died, knowing he'd given it to his wife. Weinberg thought about his old friend Joe and wondered if his faith had been shaken after he was infected.

Up to that time, much of what Weinberg knew about hemophilia and HIV came from news media reports about Ryan White, a teenager with hemophilia. Ryan, a middle-class kid from Kokomo, Indiana, had been diagnosed with HIV in December 1984 by a surgeon who had removed part of his lung as a treatment for pneumonia. After learning of the diagnosis, the school board, teachers, and principal in Ryan's district voted to expel him from school, saying they feared for other students. Eventually, he won the right to return, but he and his family were shunned by former friends and neighbors. At church, no one would shake his hand. In testimony before the President's Commission on AIDS, he said he had been subjected to "Ryan White jokes," as well as rumors that he bit people, spit on food, and urinated on bathroom walls in attempts to infect others. Some restaurants threw away his dishes after he left. Students vandalized and wrote obscenities on his school locker; someone fired a bullet into his home. Eventually, he and his family moved to Cicero, Indiana, where pop star Michael Jackson had purchased a home for them. More information was available about AIDS by then, and the community in Cicero was more supportive. Ryan died in April 1990 at the age of eighteen, when the magnitude and scope of what was happening to the hemophilia community was still neither well understood nor in the public consciousness.

Even though the Johnsons' case was compelling, Weinberg knew he faced serious obstacles. The history of similar litigation had been completely unfavorable to the plaintiffs. Eleven cases involving infected hemophiliacs had been tried to verdict, and the companies had won ten of them. The eleventh case was won by the plaintiffs but reversed and dismissed on appeal. The plaintiffs had argued that they should have been warned of the risks, but the juries had disagreed. Most of the victims had been infected before anyone even knew there was such a thing as AIDS.

There were other difficulties. The law provides a specific time frame, under a statute of limitations, within which an injured person can sue for damages. In personal-injury cases, the limit is two years from the date a plaintiff knew or should have known of the injury. Clyde was diagnosed with HIV in 1987, so four years passed before Andrea came to see Weinberg.

Another extremely difficult problem would be proving what lawyers call causation. Clyde Johnson, like many other patients, had infused multiple products, made by several different companies, at different times. It might be impossible to pinpoint which one had first infected him with HIV.

There were other risks, not the least of which was the difficulty Weinberg would confront in trying to prove that an entire industry and several governments had done wrong. Consider: There were four global pharmaceutical companies involved in the production of clotting-factor concentrates in the early 1980s, but there also were national plasma-processing services in several industrialized countries, including England, Scotland, France, and Belgium. None of those government operations had produced virus-free products until the mid-1980s, too late to save the hundreds of thousands worldwide already infected with HIV and hepatitis C.

To win the Johnson case, Weinberg not only would have to establish the negligence of a powerful, well-connected industry with what at the time was about four billion dollars in sales at stake, but he would have to explain why government scientists and regulators had failed as well.

Still, he felt he had to try. He filed the suit on behalf of Andrea Johnson individually and on behalf of Clyde Johnson's estate versus the four companies: Baxter Healthcare Corp., Bayer Corp., Rhone-Poulenc Rorer Inc., and Green Cross Corp. Filing that single case would be a catalyst to the eventual certification years later, by a federal judge, of class-action litigation against the companies. Weinberg, the small-town lawyer, was about to enter a whole new level of practice.

When word got out, others in the hemophilia community began phoning him. As hopes dimmed in the lives of so many, they and their survivors wanted answers, too.

At the same time, people with hemophilia would become activists in their own right, forming advocacy groups like the Committee of Ten Thousand (COTT), named for the number of hemophiliacs, from infants to adults, estimated to have been infected in the United States alone.

The hemophilia community soon learned that its health and welfare was in the hands of a regulatory system incapable of protecting it—a system made up of public health officials who were often dedicated but undertrained, underfunded, and overmatched, with some bosses seemingly more interested in helping Big Pharma than in protecting consumers.

That system continues, to this day, to fail the American public.

Weinberg knew this would be his most important case ever. Beginning that summer, and for most of the decade that followed, he would research and discuss the case with experts, regulators, and industry executives. He would review more than a million pages of internal company documents and government reports. He would spend the better part of his professional life—and a good part of what should have been his personal life—on the case. This unprecedented tragedy, in which FDA-approved products shot death into the veins of most of those who used them, would test him in the most extreme ways that a lawyer could be tested for passionately pursuing a client's cause.

4

A History Ignored

By the fall of 1991, Weinberg had three hemophilia-related clients. After Andrea Johnson came Ron Niederman, a married father of two sons. Niederman owned an electronics repair shop in Milltown, not far from Weinberg's office. He had suffered the debilitating effects of severe hemophilia, including frequent bleeding in his knee and elbow joints and the resultant arthritis, and walked with a limp common to hemophiliacs of his generation. When the clotting drugs had become available, Niederman, like Clyde Johnson, had embraced them with enthusiasm.

But as the risks became more apparent, Niederman got involved with the Hemophilia Association of New Jersey. Unlike Andrea Johnson, Ron Niederman was openly angry. He had been exposed to HIV, hepatitis B, hepatitis C, and some other viruses.

"The question I have is whether you think this case can be won," he asked Weinberg.

"I do," Weinberg replied. "I can't guarantee a result. But I think the companies could and should have done better, and that you should not be HIV-positive. That's the bottom line."

Niederman was still working every day in his repair shop, providing for his family, sharing a life with his wife and sons. As they talked, Weinberg began to understand that Niederman's perspective on life was typical of many people with hemophilia. When you're born with a serious genetic disorder, you can either give in and seek pity or deal with it and live as normal a life as possible. Ron Niederman had chosen the latter course.

He thought that his hepatitis infection might have been unavoidable, but he could not accept what he saw as the industry's delay in responding.

The third client was Sallie Weiss, who had survived her husband, Marty, and was raising their son alone. Marty Weiss was born and died within a month of Clyde Johnson. Sallie had saved folders full of her husband's medical information. Marty had become quite ill in 1987, two years before his death, and as Weinberg went through Sallie's materials, he could see that she and Marty had been on a desperate search for answers. She, too, had turned to the Hemophilia Association of New Jersey for help. HANJ was a refuge, and Weinberg made a mental note to speak with someone there. Clearly, there were going to be many other affected families.

Weinberg was beginning to wonder if he could handle these cases along with his non-hemophilia clients. He had begun to accept the fact that the hemophilia litigation would require far more resources. From the end of 1991 on, most of his new clients were people with hemophilia or their survivors. He wasn't doing as many of the little things it took to generate other business.

As Weinberg saw it, there were two primary questions he needed to answer. First, why did the manufacturers not cleanse their clotting drugs until after HIV came along? Second, why did the government permit the products to be sold?

Weinberg had never taken a single science class during his four years at Rutgers, but as a lawyer he had learned how to do basic library research. That experience guided him as he studied hemophilia, blood-borne illnesses, and HIV.

For the first year of the case, he visited libraries nearly every week, spending long hours poring through medical journals, books, and lay magazines as well as Medline, the database of the National Library of Medicine. In this way, time consuming as it was, he began to accumulate a substantial collection of medical literature, which he indexed and highlighted. He was learning the science, forming the basis of legal arguments, and identifying potential experts who could testify in his cases.

One of his first lessons was that, long before HIV entered the blood supply, blood products were known to pose a serious risk of hepatitis. This was important because it meant that even before there was a blood-products industry, scientists had known of the risks of pooling large numbers of plasma units.

Although research began much earlier, the for-profit blood business has its modern roots in World War II. It was an amazing, historic achievement by scientists from academia, business, and government. Working together, they learned how to use blood and its components, particularly plasma and a purified plasma protein called albumin, to save thousands of wounded soldiers suffering from shock and blood loss.

In 1940, with the war raging in Europe, a New York researcher named Dr. Charles Drew, an expert on mass production of plasma, was appointed medical director of a "Plasma for Britain" project that collected, processed,

FIGURE 4.1. During World War II, blood plasma was airlifted to numerous war fronts. Plasma saved an untold number of lives.

Credit: U.S. Farm Security Administration/Office of War Information Photograph Collection, Library of Congress.

and transported liquid plasma to England for use by civilians and soldiers wounded by German bombs. At the same time, as it became apparent that the United States would enter the war, the military started planning for its own battlefield casualties. In 1941, Dr. Drew, an especially remarkable man for that era as he was African American, was asked to supervise an American Red Cross pilot program similar to Plasma for Britain.[1] It produced freeze-dried plasma, which lasted longer than liquid and wasn't as fragile. Doctors needed something that could survive the trip to faraway war zones, and a dried product "can be packaged under vacuum and preserved for years, without refrigeration and without being affected by extremes of heat and cold," according to an Army medical history.[2]

In 1941 and 1942, military records show, several commercial businesses, including Armour and Company (then known primarily as a meat-packing firm), were hired to produce freeze-dried plasma.

Key to these efforts was Harvard researcher Edwin Cohn, who worked with the military to refine his process of separating albumin from plasma, using a method called alcohol fractionation. Ultimately, this groundbreaking research would result in methods of separating every blood component for a variety of medical uses. Dr. Cohn's breakthrough came none too soon. In his 1998 book, *Blood: An Epic History of Medicine and Commerce*, Douglas Starr describes the scene in which Dr. Cohn's staff learned of Japan's attack on Pearl Harbor in December 1941. They immediately sent fifty bottles of albumin—at that point, the world's entire stock—to Dr. Isidor Ravdin, a surgeon being flown to Hawaii by the navy. Dr. Ravdin administered the albumin to seven severely burned servicemen, and all of them, he reported, "showed general clinical improvement," including one who was in such critical condition that "other doctors questioned whether it was worth transfusing him at all."[3]

But it wasn't long before military doctors began to report that plasma products were causing jaundice, or hepatitis. The earliest major incident occurred in 1942, when an estimated 330,000 people, including 50,000 soldiers, were infected with hepatitis from yellow fever vaccine.[4]

More reports involving wounded soldiers came from Allied doctors like U.S. Army Captain Emanuel M. Rappaport at Schick General Hospital in Clinton, Iowa. Many of his patients, he reported, were suffering from homologous serum jaundice, a viral inflammation of the liver. The men

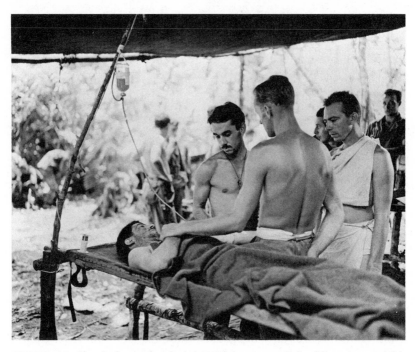

FIGURE 4.2. Blood plasma is administered to a wounded soldier at a portable hospital in New Guinea during World War II.

Credit: U.S. Farm Security Administration/Office of War Information Photograph Collection, Library of Congress.

had served in different theaters but had one thing in common: battlefield transfusions.

In 1945, Dr. Rappaport published his findings in the *Journal of the American Medical Association* and made the explicit connection between the size of the plasma pools and the risk of hepatitis.[5] He concluded that "pooling of plasma probably increases considerably the incidence of jaundice (hepatitis) among the recipients." In a larger study a year later—which the War Department asked *JAMA* not to publish, saying it contained material that was "not truly based on general Army experience"[6]—he proposed more stringent screening of donors and urged immediate research on ways to kill viruses in blood products. "It is likely that this syndrome will be encountered . . . more frequently in the future," he wrote.[7]

In 1962, the U.S. Army's Office of the Surgeon General acknowledged that "numerous" wartime cases of homologous serum jaundice had resulted from transfusions. By late 1945, "pooled plasma was indicted as the vehicle," the report states. It went a crucial step further, concluding that "a single transfusion of blood is likely to cause jaundice in only a small percentage of the recipients. When, however, blood is pooled, as it is when plasma is processed, the chances of contracting jaundice are correspondingly increased."[8]

The army was referring to pools of only about fifty units.

Solutions were sought and then abandoned when experiments with human volunteers from the military, prisons, and state hospitals showed that plasma-induced hepatitis "carried a high risk of mortality" or illness, including liver damage, other studies said.

But by the time the war ended, doctors had adopted a better albumin product, developed by Dr. Cohn. It was heat-treated at 60 degrees centigrade (140 degrees Fahrenheit) for ten hours in a water bath to kill viruses, with a sugar coating that stabilized and protected precious proteins. The method was so efficient at killing viruses that albumin is processed today in essentially the same way.

But scientists also concluded that heat killed most of the blood-clotting proteins needed for the treatment of hemophilia.

Interest in the research was renewed in 1950 when an army-funded team led by J. Garrott Allen, then of the University of Chicago, reported that prolonged heating could kill hepatitis in plasma. But Dr. Allen's method still killed too many blood-clotting proteins. He kept working on it.

In 1964, hemophilia treatment was revolutionized. Stanford University scientist Judith Pool, who had studied under Dr. Allen, and her colleagues discovered that when frozen human plasma was thawed slowly, at controlled temperatures, the clotting proteins sank to the bottom in a fibrous paste. They called this stringy residue cryoprecipitate, and found that it could easily be infused into patients.[9] It came from a single donor or a small number of donors, not a large pool. For the first time, hemophiliacs could treat their disease at home, keeping cryo in their freezers.

A few years later came the next major stride: Baxter Healthcare Corporation's Hyland division further refined cryoprecipitate to make the world's first freeze-dried blood-clotting concentrates.

Dr. Allen, though, was infuriated. In 1969, he warned that clotting concentrates were being manufactured not with the plasma of traditional donors but with plasma from paid donors from "skid row." But the government had already approved the medicines for sale.

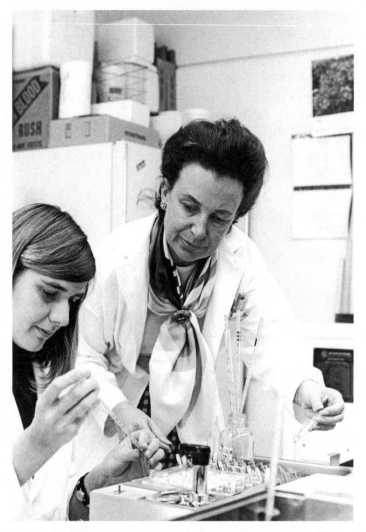

FIGURE 4.3. Dr. Judith Graham Pool revolutionized the treatment of hemophilia in 1964, when she and her research team at Stanford University Medical Center developed cryoprecipitation, a method of separating clotting proteins from blood plasma.

Credit: Stanford Medical History Center.

In 1970, researchers from the National Institutes of Health warned that just one unit of hepatitis-contaminated plasma could contaminate an entire pool. Diluted ten million times, it still was infectious.

In 1972, the Nixon administration began work on a National Blood Policy that sought to eliminate paid donors. In fact, transitioning to an all-volunteer blood system was identified as one of the best ways to reduce risk. The task of drafting the document was assigned to Dr. Ian Mitchell, a transplanted Canadian who was an official with the U.S. Department of Health, Education, and Welfare. Dr. Mitchell gathered an impressive amount of information and tried to formulate a policy that would encourage the entrenched interests to agree. He found resistance from nearly every corner.

In 1974, during the debate, Dr. Pool wrote to federal health officials, warning them against the continued use of paid donors. The proposed policy, she said, "assumes a continuation of the dangerous, expensive, wasteful and unethical purchase of plasma by pharmaceutical houses."[10] She and the World Health Organization advocated the all-volunteer system.

The National Blood Policy, enacted in 1974, urged a transition away from paid donors but did not forbid them. It did call for more research into the types of viruses that might contaminate blood.

In 1977, the World Federation of Hemophilia called on the makers of clotting concentrates to kill viruses in their products for the sake of "future generations of persons with hemophilia."[11] The organization repeated its message in 1979, urging more speed.

One of the key presentations at the 1977 meeting was by a team that included Dr. David Van Thiel, a gastroenterologist and hemophilia treater from the University of Pittsburgh School of Medicine, and the Central Blood Bank of Pittsburgh. He and his colleagues reported that they were seeing persistent signs of hepatitis in patients treated with clotting-factor concentrates, even those who had developed antibodies to hepatitis B. This was a very worrisome development, because it meant there were other, unknown hepatitis viruses in the products. They called for the immediate development of a product free of viruses. Their study was published in the *New England Journal of Medicine* in 1978.[12]

The government decided that blood bags should be labeled "paid" or "volunteer."[13] But already, it was acknowledging problems in trying to enforce the National Blood Policy, a job that had been left to the blood bankers themselves to avoid creating a new bureaucracy. Perhaps, officials conceded in a 1978 report, the policy did need to be backed up by "a legislative or regulatory approach" after all.

STANFORD UNIVERSITY MEDICAL CENTER

STANFORD, CALIFORNIA 94305 • (415) 321-1200

Stanford University School of Medicine
Department of Medicine

April 30, 1974

Dr. Chas. C. Edwards
Assistant Secretary for Health
Department of Health, Education and Welfare
330 Independence Avenue, SW
Washington, D.C. 20201

Dear Dr. Edwards:

In response to the request for comments in the Federal
Register issue of March 8, 1974, I would like to submit the
following:

The hemophilic patients of our nation are estimated to
require the Factor VIII extracted from the following numbers
of pints of blood for optimal (but not prophylactic) care:

2,331,500 if a high-yield process (blood bank
          cryoprecipitation) is used;
6,475,000 if a low-yield process (pharmaceutical frac-
          tionation) is used.*

Since 7,835,700 units of whole blood were collected from
volunteer donors in the U.S.A. in 1971,** it follows that the
raw material for safe and ethically acceptable Factor VIII
supplies is already available.

My concern with the proposed Implementation Plan for a new
National Blood Policy is that it in no way requires or even en-
courages the use of volunteer blood for this purpose but assumes
a continuation of the dangerous, expensive, wasteful, and unethical purchase of plasma by pharmaceutical houses to provide
such therapeutic material.

Sincerely yours,

Judith G. Pool, Ph.D.
Professor of Medicine

*NHLI's Blood Resource Studies
   Vol. 3, June 30, 1972
** NHLI's Blood Resource Studies,
   Vol. 1, June 30, 1972

JGP/mva

FIGURE 4.4. In 1974, Dr. Pool wrote a letter to the government in which she
denounced the practice of using plasma from paid donors for hemophilia medicines, calling it "dangerous, expensive, wasteful and unethical."

It was too late. In July 1982, the U.S. Centers for Disease Control
announced the first three cases of AIDS in hemophiliacs.[14]

To Weinberg, it seemed more and more obvious that, with all that science had known about hepatitis for the past half century, the companies

had a legal, moral, and ethical duty to research methods of killing viruses. And Dr. Cohn's work, decades earlier, was critical to the case. His alcohol fractionation methods were the foundation of the industry.

Weinberg found particularly sobering a 1962 book he found, written by a Nobel laureate, Sir MacFarlane Burnet, who prophetically said: "The diseases which we may have to face in the future will be those that are capable of initiating infection in minimal dose. And since bacterial infections are, with unimportant exceptions, amenable to treatment with one or other of the new drugs, our real problems are likely to be concerned with virus diseases . . . it is possible, even probable, that one new virus capable of producing symptoms emerges each year."[15]

What might come next, Weinberg wondered, after HIV?

It's hard to imagine that anyone would take medicines they thought could sicken or even kill them, until one understands what the hemophilia community faced before cryoprecipitate and Factor VIII concentrates. In 1964, Clyde Johnson and Marty Weiss were eleven years old, Joe Salgado was thirteen, and Ron Niederman was fourteen. Until that time, the life expectancy of a person with hemophilia was only about thirty-five years at best, with many succumbing much sooner. Patients were infused in hospitals with large amounts of whole blood or plasma, putting them at risk of vascular overload and heart failure. By the time a hemophiliac with a bleeding episode could be taken to a hospital or physician's office, crippling puddles of blood might have accumulated in his joints. So when Dr. Pool developed cryoprecipitate, the benefits were profound.

Early in the Factor VIII years, though, some people inside the hemophilia community began to see what it would mean to give industry, rather than blood bankers and hospitals, the lead. One was the historian and Pulitzer Prize–winning author Robert Massie, who with his wife, Suzanne, wrote about raising a son with hemophilia.[16] To them, Factor VIII concentrates were a dream come true. Robert Massie had high hopes that the American Red Cross, the nation's largest supplier of blood and blood products, would produce them.

But multiple interviews with researchers and officials made it clear to Massie that this would not happen. The profit motive was too strong to allow such a miraculous medicine to be handed over to the not-for-profit sector, and the commercial scale-up required investment that the pharmaceutical industry was better prepared to handle. Massie was very concerned.

In July 1968 a meeting was arranged so he could talk to Hyland president Fred Marquart; University of North Carolina hemophilia researcher Dr. Kenneth Brinkhous, whose team had pioneered the process; and representatives of the Red Cross and the National Hemophilia Foundation.

Also in attendance was Dr. Edward Shanbrom, a Southern California physician hired by Marquart as his medical director. It was Dr. Shanbrom who, after calling upon Judith Pool to learn about her process, led Hyland in developing the first commercial Factor VIII product. Before meeting her, Hyland had been throwing away the residual plasma that contained clotting proteins.

On the day of the meeting, "I hoped that they were there to announce the release of Red Cross concentrates, either free, or at a far lower price than Hyland's," Massie wrote in his book.[17]

Instead, Massie said, Marquart produced data that showed how expensive it was to make Factor VIII concentrates using paid donors. They would not lower their prices. And the Red Cross—which had favored a National Blood Policy that eliminated paid donors—said it would not get into the clotting-factor business. Instead, it would sign an "interim" contract and ship its plasma to Hyland. The means and methods of production were up to the company.

"To my surprise," Massie wrote, "Mr. Marquart's presentation was received with understanding nods by everyone but me . . . this was the odd way our dialogue went; he was talking about sales, I was talking about . . . crippled joints."[18]

The meeting ended with Massie feeling defeated.

"The Red Cross, supposedly the alternative to Hyland, was going to produce AHF through Hyland," he wrote. " . . . And the top two leaders of the National Hemophilia Foundation, who should have been arguing and pleading and pounding the table with me on behalf of the nation's hemophiliacs, had simply sat there, acting as mediators."[19]

A month later, the Massie family moved to France, where they soon qualified for the national health plan.

In the timeline of human existence, the modern corporation is a relatively new invention. But in recent decades, there has been some remarkable research, and other examples that shine a light on corporate culture and behaviors. Among the questions they raise: What leads seemingly decent, honorable people to make unethical morally or socially irresponsible decisions as managers? Is it some fault in their personal makeup, some gap in their training, some lapse in parental guidance?

One of the best-known studies, particularly among countless MBA students, is the Panalba role-playing case.[20] Written in 1976 by Wharton School marketing professor J. Scott Armstrong, it goes like this: Students are put into groups and told by their professor to pretend they are high-ranking officials on the board of directors of a pharmaceutical company in crisis. One of its most profitable medicines is killing people. Should they withdraw it from the market, stop production but sell the remaining stock, stop all advertising but keep providing the drug to doctors who request it, continue marketing until the drug is banned, or fight to keep selling it? To add to the pressure, students are told to assume that the board's consumer representative is media savvy, implying that person may leak the company's decision to the nearest journalist.

In Armstrong's study, none of the fifty-seven groups voted to remove the drug from the market, and 79 percent "took active steps to prevent its removal." (In one Ivy League MBA classroom in which this exercise was used in the 1990s, the students decided to have the consumer representative murdered before he or she could talk to the media.)

There are many other well-known examples that bring into question how executives—and even government officials—decide the balance between safety and profits. One in particular involved the Ford Pinto, a subcompact car sold in the 1970s whose gas tank was behind the rear axle, making it prone to explode after rear-end collisions. The government eventually attributed twenty-seven deaths and twenty-four burn injuries to that design. In 1978, a jury awarded millions of dollars to the victims.

What that case really highlighted, however, was the little-known fact that the federal government had written standards for the value of a human life, and that industry could use those calculations to compare product costs to the intrinsic worth of the dead and injured.

In a 1972 report, the National Highway Traffic Safety Administration put the value of a life at $200,725 (about $1.15 million in 2015, adjusted for inflation). In a memo a year later, Ford rounded that down to $200,000 (plus $67,000 for each serious burn injury) to calculate that for all cars and light trucks with rollover and fuel-leakage issues, it would cost the U.S. auto industry a total of $137 million, or $11 per vehicle, to fix the defects, compared to the $49.5 million value of the people who were killed or burned. Although the Ford memo focused on fuel leakage after rollovers, not Pintos or rear-end collisions, the public didn't see the distinction. It was a public relations disaster.

In an influential 1990 article, UCLA law professor Gary Schwartz said the Pinto case "shows how disturbed the public can be by corporate decisions that balance life and safety against monetary cost." He also suggested that, while the Pinto was not nearly as bad as its detractors said, manufacturers ought to be required "to advise consumers of non-obvious hazards that remain in products' designs" even though it probably meant they would have to be "excessive and even counterproductive" in their warnings.[21]

That standard—benefits outweighing risks—has long existed for prescription medicines as well, including those for hemophilia.

It seems logical that such products are sold, at least until you are one of the unlucky few who is injured. It seems illogical when one learns that thousands of people—including the majority of those who used clotting drugs in the early to mid-1980s—contracted HIV and hepatitis. It means that somebody squeezed the benefit-risk analysis until it screamed for mercy.

In what would become the worldwide blood-product scandal, industry, physicians, even the National Hemophilia Foundation, repeatedly told hemophiliacs that the benefits of clotting drugs outweighed the risks. And when the lawsuits started, there was another, more cynical, calculation at work: the companies knew that, because most hemophiliacs used multiple products from different manufacturers, it would be nearly impossible for them to prove exactly which products had infected them.

In health economics, the risk-benefit analysis is sometimes calculated using the QALY, or quality-adjusted life year. It can be used to determine the amount of time that will be added to someone's life if they get a certain medicine, and is adjusted depending upon the risk of the treatment doing some harm.

As the number of HIV-infected hemophiliacs who were filing lawsuits was on the rise, an industry conference on blood safety and screening in

Washington in 1994 tackled the issue of safety, cost, and QALYs. One pre-
senter, Dr. James AuBuchon, then of Dartmouth-Hitchcock Medical Center
in New Hampshire, put it in blunt, real-world terms: "Zero-risk" blood
products were not attainable. A respected expert in analyzing cost effectiveness and safety, Dr. AuBuchon told the crowd that life had inherent
risks and you couldn't do everything to protect everybody. You did your
best, but it came with a price.

How much? One of AuBuchon's papers, published in 2004, found that
a new blood test would prevent an estimated 37 cases of hepatitis B, 128
cases of hepatitis C, and 8 cases of HIV. The net cost: $154 million to save
a cumulative 53 years of life and 102 QALYs.[22]

That kind of analysis might horrify people. But consider it in a different context: Cheerios would be unaffordable if each box was produced
individually, from one bunch of grain at a time. The same principle is true
of blood products.

Even so, whether it's cars, medicines, or breakfast cereal, if society
concedes that all products carry some risk, who gets to decide how far to
push the safety envelope? Will it be the executives whose careers, salaries,
and stock options depend on the financial success of their companies?
Will it be scientists and design experts, many of them with ties to industry? Consumer representatives? The government?

In the mid-1990s, asked whether the plasma products industry should
have been more careful in protecting the hemophilia community, a company spokesman replied in personal and clearly heartfelt terms about his
colleagues. You need to remember, he told a journalist, that many executives took a very deep interest in their jobs. Some were hemophiliacs, or
had children or brothers or other family members with hemophilia. Many
volunteered to work in summer camps for children with hemophilia. They
genuinely cared about the patients, and were in agony over the HIV
disaster. In creating these medicines, "they thought they were doing God's
work," he said.

How does one reconcile that perspective with the research of
Armstrong and others, where "good" people go to extreme lengths to protect the bottom line or follow an authority figure, even if they have reason
to believe that innocents will suffer?

Is it that simple—that, in a moral conflict between the individual and the corporation, the corporation usually wins unless procedures are in place to prevent it?

In the years leading up to the discovery of HIV, the demand for and profits from blood products continued to rise. Companies bought and pooled ever growing quantities of human plasma, fanning out across the globe to identify new sources. Once it was determined that the government would not compel them to stop using paid donors, companies resorted to increasingly inventive measures. They were revealed as the hemophilia litigation progressed, more corporate documents were handed over, and more sworn statements were taken by lawyers like Weinberg. For example:

- Bayer's Cutter Laboratories had a written policy of buying plasma from admitted intravenous drug abusers, if employees believed the donor hadn't injected illegal drugs within the previous six months. The policy remained in effect until 1981, when California regulators told the company that it violated state and federal law.
- It wasn't until 1995 that the federal government recommended that plasma no longer be collected from inmates or the recently incarcerated. By then, the industry had halted most such collections on its own.
- Even as AIDS was spreading worldwide, some international traders tried to open additional plasma collection centers in sub-Saharan Africa. Those efforts were stymied in part by the World Health Organization, which opposed the plasma hunters and encouraged less-developed nations to evict them.

Through those years, scientists like Drs. Allen and Pool, who complained so long and loudly about paid donors and large pools, were marginalized.

In 1975, a year after she had tried once again to point out the dangers of paid donors by writing directly to the U.S. Secretary of Health, Education, and Welfare, Dr. Pool died of cancer. But Dr. Allen carried on. In a sworn statement in 1987, taken as part of a Kentucky lawsuit, he said, "No medical, economic or social reason could justify ever using . . . unheated, pooled plasma or its clotting products. Large pools are highly profitable, but they are medically bankrupt."

5

Digging In

By the end of 1991, Weinberg had filed three separate lawsuits—on behalf of the Johnsons, Niedermans, and Weisses—in Middlesex County, New Jersey, his home county. Middlesex was a good place for a plaintiff's lawyer. Juries were typically blue-collar and included people of color, both known to be favorable to plaintiffs. The bench was a good mix of liberal and conservative judges, and Weinberg had tried cases before several of them. He knew the hemophilia cases probably would end up before one judge, and was comfortable with the notion that whatever judge was assigned, his clients would get a fair shake.

The blood-product companies had other ideas. They thought federal courts were a more favorable place for corporations. This is generally true, although why is not entirely clear. It might be that the federal bench tends to be more conservative, or that federal procedural rules are more onerous and therefore more difficult for plaintiffs to handle. In addition, federal juries tend to be from a broader and more well-to-do social spectrum, and therefore are likely to be more conservative. Whatever the reasons, the companies exercised their prerogative to remove the cases from state court, and they were transferred to the U.S. District Court in Newark.

Weinberg's three cases were assigned to Magistrate Judge Joel Pisano, who recently had been appointed to the federal bench. Judge Pisano had been a trial lawyer in private practice. Magistrate judges are typically younger than district court judges. They are essentially junior-grade federal judges and serve two basic functions. One, they handle minor cases from start to finish. Two, they handle preliminary issues in major cases, but when the cases are set for trial, they are transferred to a district court judge. So the magistrate judge must make sure that the parties comply with the rules of "discovery"—that is, the exchange of documents, the taking of sworn statements, and the choosing of expert witnesses.

Judge Pisano, in his early forties at the time, was assigned to the discovery issues in Weinberg's cases, all of which in turn were assigned to different district judges. These were the first hemophilia-HIV cases to be filed in New Jersey. There was a small body of case law involving infectious diseases transmitted by blood, but it was not helpful, as those cases involved hospitals that used whole blood or red blood cells, not for-profit companies that made plasma products.

The first case management conference took place at the federal courthouse in Newark on a cold day in February 1992. To Weinberg, it seemed clear that Judge Pisano was not impressed with his theory of liability. He seemed unreceptive to arguments that the commercial manufacturers should be considered different from hospitals. Weinberg had the sense that the judge didn't like him very much, either. In addition, Weinberg's adversaries were all from large firms that represented a wide array of corporations, and they spent far more of their time in the federal courthouse than he did. From the outset, Judge Pisano's orders imposed most of the burdens of discovery on the plaintiffs—Weinberg's clients.

Among the issues he listed was the identification of the product that had caused each client's HIV infection, which was going to be difficult since most had used more than one brand. Weinberg argued that the burden of proving which product was to blame should be borne by the defendants—that each should have to prove another company was to blame. He tried his best to convince the court that wide-ranging discovery was essential to his cases—and that for starters, he needed corporate documents that would identify plasma sources.

The industry lawyers were smart and tough—dozens of them and their support staff, from major law firms with huge resources—and they fought back on every issue. They knew Weinberg's cases were potentially just the tip of a very damaging iceberg, and their legal strategy was to be as difficult and aggressive as possible, to keep him from making any progress.

And so he was inundated with all manner of demands for discovery, with the approval of the court.

Weinberg was at another disadvantage. Most of the corporate lawyers had been defending their clients for several years. They knew the issues, the history of the products, and the evidence that had been developed. Defendants are always in control of the information they own. While they are required to be responsive, they can decide what is or is not responsive. They can construe a plaintiff's request as narrowly as possible.

Conversely, there had been little coordination on the plaintiffs' side. Although a dozen cases had been tried in various other states, there was no single repository of documents and sworn statements that Weinberg could use. He was sure, given the disjointed nature of the cases thus far, that the industry had produced just a small percentage of the documents it possessed.

Even if there had been a repository, however, he was taking a different approach. In almost all of the previous cases, the plaintiffs had argued that the industry knew about the risk of HIV and had failed to warn anyone. Those cases, then, had been premised on a legal theory called "failure to warn."

So when did the scientific community first understand that HIV was blood-borne, and that clotting products could transmit it? The issue was very controversial. It is always difficult to say when something as amorphous as the "medical community" has "knowledge" of what is medically possible. Plaintiffs bear the burden of proof, which is defined as a preponderance of the evidence—that is, it is more likely so than not so. In the cases thus far, plaintiffs had been required to show when there was consensus on HIV. Losing that difficult argument had resulted in their claims being rejected repeatedly.

The plaintiffs also had to prove when they were infected, but many could not. It made for an easier case if hemophiliacs could show they were sickened after HIV was determined to be transmitted by blood. But the majority had likely been exposed much earlier.

So in developing his theory of the case, Weinberg looked instead for evidence that the industry could have killed the viruses in its products sooner. Since the companies had known for decades that they carried hepatitis, he could argue they had a duty to do this earlier, especially if the emergence of new viruses was foreseeable. He could argue that their products had a design defect, just as he had in the swimming-pool and baby-monitor cases. To him, it was a simple and logical theory, especially once he found out about the high-risk paid donors.

Under this theory, there seemed to be the obvious potential for a national class-action lawsuit.

Shortly after Weinberg's three cases had been moved to federal court, the lawyers for Baxter and Bayer called. They wanted to talk, and everyone agreed to meet in the courthouse after their next case management conference. The meeting included about half a dozen company lawyers and Weinberg.

The two lawyers who did most of the talking for the companies were Bob Limbacher, a partner at Philadelphia's Dechert Price & Rhoads, and Charlie Goodell, the senior partner in the Baltimore firm of Goodell, DeVries, Leech & Dann. Limbacher was about Weinberg's age, well-dressed, with a confident manner and a shock of thick black hair. Goodell was about ten years older, tall, and with the bearing of an athlete, laid back but highly focused and serious on the job.

"You know, Eric, we've been down this road before," said Limbacher. "There really isn't much new in these cases that we haven't already seen."

Goodell agreed. "These will be expensive to prosecute and the track record in this litigation is not good for your side."

He was right, of course.

"But it's not a no-pay case," Limbacher said. "If your clients are willing to release all of the manufacturers, we can talk about putting some money in their pockets. Something you should definitely consider, Eric."

"What kinds of settlements are you proposing? Because these are not whiplash cases," Weinberg said. "I'm representing people who were infected with HIV."

"Well, we don't think we did anything wrong," Goodell said. "So given that, but also considering the time and expense of defending these cases, they would be nominal settlements. Maybe ten thousand dollars for each case. But consider the alternatives. If you don't take a reasonable settlement now, then we have to fight you, and once we go down that road, there won't be any settlements, and we will win. So think about what is in your clients' best interests."

The federal courthouse in Newark is an imposing edifice. With its tall, stately columns, coffered ceilings, and marble floors, it looks like a place for justice to be done.

Weinberg was worried, but hoped the other side didn't see how much. He wasn't surprised by the position they took. He had been thinking about how he would respond to a lowball offer when it came, and he had prepared a little speech for them.

"You're wrong," he said. "I've looked at what's been done before and this is different. There is no blood shield statute in New Jersey, so these are strict liability cases. We're talking about design defect and manufacturing defect, and if I'm right, then every person with hemophilia who was infected with HIV would have a case, and that means there is a strong possibility that this litigation will become a class action. Then you'll be dealing not only with my clients, but thousands of others just like them. That's what I think. So your offer makes no sense to me."

The defense lawyers looked uncomfortable. The issue regarding the blood shield statute was an Achilles heel. In the 1950s and 1960s, forty-seven states had passed blood shield statutes that declared blood and plasma products were services, not products at all, thus limiting the rights of people to sue.[1] Blood bankers and health care providers had convinced lawmakers that human blood was unavoidably unsafe. But New Jersey was not one of those forty-seven states. Weinberg knew he had struck a very sensitive nerve.

"Look," he continued, "I appreciate that your experience is telling you that you should play hardball with me. I don't blame you for that and I don't take it personally. But this is just the beginning. The right thing to do is to contemplate a national settlement, with money set aside for the victims and their medical expenses. That will bring the litigation to an end, and your clients will have done the right thing."

The defense lawyers stared at Weinberg as if he were speaking in tongues. The silence was uncomfortable.

Finally, Limbacher said, "You know, our clients really made very little profit on the sale of clotting-factor concentrates. They were essentially doing a public service for the hemophiliacs. It isn't practical to talk about the profits."

Limbacher and Goodell seemed like nice guys; they were both smart, and they were doing their jobs. Weinberg would come to know both of them very well, and develop a deep respect for them, and even profes-sional friendships with them. But he understood perfectly. There would be no settlements. They had set a price—ten thousand dollars—and it was his job to change their thinking, to raise their sense of exposure. Ten thou-sand dollars for infection with deadly viruses obviously was not remotely acceptable. Auto accident cases with no permanent injuries were settling for ten thousand dollars in New Jersey.

But every lawyer at that meeting knew Weinberg couldn't do it alone. He didn't have the resources. Already, his law practice was suffering because of the time he was spending on this case. He also had two young sons, and in another year would have another, and did not have enough time with his family. Weinberg liked challenging these companies, but that wouldn't get the job done.

IN DECEMBER 1969, Dr. Herbert Ley, who had just been forced out of his job as commissioner of the U.S. Food and Drug Administration, was quoted in the *New York Times*: "The thing that bugs me is that the people think the FDA is protecting them. It isn't. What the FDA is doing and what the public thinks it is doing are as different as night and day. The real solu-tion is to isolate the FDA functions from political pressures, to give the agency the national leadership and support that will allow any Commissioner to act responsibly and solely in the public interest."[2]

Not much had changed since then.

The FDA, Weinberg decided, was going to be a central issue in his hemophilia cases. If the agency was there to protect consumers, then why were entire generations infected with HIV? Why did Clyde Johnson and Marty Weiss die slow and painful deaths? Why was Ron Niederman forced to live and work through the ravages of illness?

The FDA had approved clotting-factor products for infants, children, and adults with hemophilia, and had approved every single word on the product labels. This was the industry's primary defense. If everything had FDA's stamp of approval, how had the manufacturers done anything wrong?

From the baby-monitor case, Weinberg had developed a good working knowledge of how to maneuver through the regulatory system. Once, he had traveled to Washington for a congressional subcommittee hearing that focused on the manufacturer's failure to report nearly fifty infant deaths to the FDA. The subcommittee chairman had been astounded to learn not only that the company had withheld those reports but that it would argue that federal regulations didn't require it to report them.

To Weinberg, the lesson of that case was that Dr. Ley was right. In fact, the FDA still lacks the resources to monitor the safety of drugs in the marketplace, according to the Institute of Medicine, the nonpartisan health arm of the National Academy of Sciences.[3] The FDA's total budget for 2015 was $4.7 billion, for both food and drug regulation.[4] Compare that to the level of corporate spending: members of the Pharmaceutical Research and Manufacturers of America, the industry's primary trade association, spent an estimated $51.2 billion in 2014 to discover and develop new medicines. Since 2000, more than five hundred new medicines have been approved by the FDA, and more than seven thousand medicines and treatments are in development globally, about half of those in the United States.[5] The FDA cannot possibly know the details of every product the way manufacturers do.

There's also the long-standing problem of the FDA bowing to pressure from the drug industry—which contributes heavily to the politicians who vote on the FDA budget. And there's something of a revolving door between the FDA and drug companies, with high-ranking officials frequently leaving government for better-paying industry jobs.[6]

In the baby-monitor case, the truth was revealed only because the victims' parents sued, and lawyers uncovered information the FDA had never seen. So when Andrea Johnson, and then the Weiss and Niederman families, came to Weinberg, he knew that FDA approval was not the end of the story. A system that didn't protect premature babies was hardly in a position to do better for hemophiliacs.

In early 1992, two leads generated critically important information that would shape Weinberg's approach to the hemophilia litigation for the next decade. Ron Niederman told him about a hemophiliac named Michael Rosenberg who had a science background, was HIV-positive, and had been doing his own dogged research into the history of clotting factor. Over the next year and a half, Weinberg would speak at length with Rosenberg several times. He was smart and angry, and like many in his community had become deeply suspicious of authority.

FIGURE 5.1. Hemophilia activists Todd Smith, in wheelchair, and Ken Baxter, wearing a death mask, protest outside a Bayer plant in Berkeley, California. Smith also traveled to Germany to read a statement at Bayer's 1998 shareholder meeting.

Credit: Christina Wilson.

Rosenberg and others were building their own grassroots groups, convinced that the National Hemophilia Foundation was more interested in protecting the companies than its members. He and another activist, Dick Valdez, led the Hemophilia HIV/Peer Association, which worked with another organization called the Committee of Ten Thousand, named for the number of U.S. hemophiliacs believed to be HIV-positive. COTT was cofounded in the Boston area by a successful businessman, Jonathan Wadleigh, and a social worker, Tom Fahey. COTT, in turn, had spread across the country, where Californians Corey Dubin and Leo Murphy founded COTT West. These and other activists, hemophiliacs including Greg Haas and Matt Murphy, Leo's brother, would be powerful forces in the political and legal battles to come.

The first time they spoke, Rosenberg told Weinberg he did not like lawyers. But Rosenberg came to accept him and educated Weinberg about a German company called Behringwerke AG, which had developed a method to cleanse clotting factor far earlier than the four major fractionators had done. Weinberg decided to go to Germany to learn more about Behringwerke.

FIGURE 5.2. Todd Smith, a hemophilia activist from California, prepares to infuse Factor VIII clotting medicine. He was infected with HIV and hepatitis C from blood products and died in 2012.

Credit: Christina Wilson.

The other lead came from two related documents Weinberg found in early 1992 on the shelves of the Library of Science and Medicine of New Jersey. He had been trying to understand the regulatory system for blood products, from the time Judith Pool discovered cryoprecipitate through the HIV infection of the hemophilia community. It was a twenty-year span, from 1964 to 1984.

The documents helped explain what went wrong and why. One was a report, more than one hundred pages long, written after a March 1976 conference sponsored by government health agencies and the National Hemophilia Foundation. The report, *Unsolved Therapeutic Problems in Hemophilia*, made it clear that even in 1976, scientists understood that it was crucial for blood-clotting products to be virally inactivated lest patients get hepatitis B or worse. One of the coeditors of the publication was an FDA scientist named Dr. David Aronson, who by the time of Weinberg's discovery had retired as the agency's point man for blood products and had been hired by the fractionators to testify against HIV-infected hemophiliacs.

The other document was the transcript of a May 1972 Senate subcommittee hearing chaired by Senator Abraham Ribicoff, a Democrat from Connecticut. The hearing had focused on the failures of the Division of Biologics Standards, the predecessor of the FDA's Bureau of Biologics. In particular, it addressed the regulation of vaccines that, like clotting drugs, contained human plasma. Before the hearings, biologic products were regulated by National Institutes of Health, not the FDA. The NIH had repeatedly approved vaccines that failed government safety standards, resulting in successful lawsuits against the manufacturers and the government. This was a remarkable event, since regulators generally cannot be sued. But key government officials—who later became managers of the very drug firms they once regulated—ignored government standards, meaning the agencies didn't have their usual immunity.

Ribicoff had concluded that the NIH had been either ineffective or incompetent. A consensus was reached that the NIH was a good place for scientific discovery but was neither designed nor intended to be a regulatory agency. So, even though Ribicoff wanted even stronger measures, the Division of Biologics Standards was renamed the Bureau of Biologics (BoB) and was taken over by the FDA, although it remained on the NIH campus, with much of the same staff. Dr. Harry Meyer, who was named its first director when the BoB was formed in 1972, retired fourteen years later to become president of the medical research division of American Cyanamid, a maker of vaccines. Like Dr. Aronson, Dr. Meyer, too, would later emerge as a witness against the hemophiliacs.

Weinberg had begun to appreciate the fact that the dramatic evolution in the treatment of hemophilia, resulting from Dr. Pool's discovery, followed a timeline that paralleled these changes in the regulatory system, along with emerging knowledge of blood-borne viruses. But these documents crystallized, in his mind, what actually had gone wrong, and why the regulatory system was so horribly inept at precisely the wrong time for users of blood products.

It is not comforting for juries to accept the notion that no one is safe from dangerous drugs because the government hasn't done its job. While the great majority of approved health care products are relatively safe and effective, a small but still significant number have caused widespread injury and death. In many instances there is evidence, but it is overlooked.

For example, one of the key defendants in the hemophilia cases, Cutter Laboratories, in 1955 manufactured polio vaccine that mistakenly contained live virus, resulting in nearly two hundred cases of paralysis and ten deaths. In what became known as the "Cutter incident," it was determined that the company had not processed the virus well enough to kill it.[7] Investigators later concluded that the NIH had been warned in advance by one of its own staff members but had done nothing. Several administrators eventually lost their jobs as a result, but the event also revealed what could happen when regulators were ill trained or reluctant to take on an industry whose employees they viewed as colleagues, not adversaries.

So, as Weinberg was learning, his HIV-infected clients were severely impacted by a perfect storm of events: the commercialization of blood products, the emergence of a deadly virus, and a regulatory system too weak to handle them.

Eventually, the government would come to agree.

In 1993, then-FDA commissioner David Kessler told a House subcommittee that his agency had erred in its relationship with the blood industry. The FDA's reliance upon industry's voluntary compliance with government rules, he testified, was "emblematic of our collegial approach to regulated industry at that time." He tried to reassure Congress, adding, "Those days are behind us."[8]

Kessler volunteered, though, that when his wife had recently undergone surgery, she had stored her own blood in advance—just in case.

In 1996, the Institute of Medicine would be far more critical of the FDA, calling what happened to the hemophilia community "a failure of leadership."

A decade later, in 2006, yet another report, this one by the Government Accountability Office, would identify a continuing weakness in the regulatory structure.[9]

During years of litigation, the companies would continue to maintain that what happened to the hemophiliacs was "an act of God." Andrea Johnson was right: God had very little to do with it.

6

Reaching Out

Weinberg called Joe Salgado in February 1992, not long after telling the corporate lawyers to stick their ten-thousand-dollar settlement offers, and briefed him on what was happening. Salgado was president of the Hemophilia Association of New Jersey (HANJ), which was among the best organized, independent, and forward thinking of the state hemophilia advocacy groups. Its executive director, Elena Bostick, was a highly competent woman and well respected by the membership. Bostick was supported by a good board of directors, most of whom were people with hemophilia or who had hemophilia in their families. HANJ also was sophisticated in the political arena, and Bostick had recruited several key legislators to be on her board. They were successful at fund-raising and suspicious of the National Hemophilia Foundation's agenda and motives. HANJ guarded its independence closely.

Since Salgado had been rebuffed when he wrote to the companies, urging them to compensate hemophiliacs on a voluntary basis, he knew the only way the community would see any money was through the courts. He was at heart still a trial lawyer.

"My sense is the case can be won and should be litigated," Weinberg told him.

"You're going to need help," Salgado replied.

"No question. There are law firms that might get involved," Weinberg said. "I'm going to talk to some because this will be a vast project, far too difficult for just me to handle."

"Why would big law firms get involved in this?" Salgado asked. "They're going to look at the track record of the litigation and be skeptical, Eric, don't you think?"

"Yes, I agree. That's why the litigation needs a new direction."

"How many clients do you have?" Salgado asked.

"I've been contacted by about a dozen families. Ten have signed retainers, and the others will."

"Do you think more would help?"

"You mean would firms see opportunity if there were more clients?" Weinberg asked. "They just might."

Salgado took a leap.

"I think you should meet with Elena Bostick, the executive director," he said. "If Elena feels comfortable with you, she will introduce you to the HANJ board. That would help spread the word about your work to the New Jersey hemophilia community. Once you've got entrée to the community, it would probably mean more families would retain you."

"I'm agreeable to that," Weinberg said. "I'm committed to this litigation, Joe."

"Let me call Elena," Salgado replied. "I'll tell her what I'm thinking, and get back to you."

A day later, Salgado called with Bostick's number. Weinberg contacted her immediately, and they had a brief and somewhat guarded conversation. She agreed to meet him at her office in East Brunswick, about ten minutes from him, on a day in February 1992.

The HANJ offices were on the first floor of a drab two-story office building off Route 18, a cluttered highway running through East Brunswick and eventually toward what once were the farmlands of Middlesex and Monmouth Counties. The main office was a large room with a half dozen desks arranged in rows. A few smaller offices lined the back wall. One was Bostick's and another belonged to the agency's social worker, Julie Frenkel. As Weinberg walked in, Salgado greeted him and led him to Bostick and Frenkel.

"We've heard nice things about you from Andrea, Ron, and Sallie," Bostick said.

"That's good to hear," Weinberg replied.

"So tell us why you're here."

"Bottom line? What happened to your community is an extraordinary case. I've been investigating it since last summer," Weinberg said. "This is hard, but I win hard cases. I'm not afraid of them. And I think the community needs me. There aren't a whole bunch of law firms knocking down the doors to get in. I'm focused on proving something wrong happened here, and the fractionators should pay."

"How can you help? Aren't you in practice by yourself?"

Weinberg heard the anxiety in Bostick's voice and understood. She was responsible for the interests of people who were just now waking up to the awful dimensions of an epidemic. The New Jersey community felt betrayed by the drug companies, with whom they had developed what they thought were strong relationships. They knew the company representatives, so the dynamic was complicated.

"I'm working on putting together a team," Weinberg said. "I've got a new approach and I think it will work. I believe the companies are legally responsible for the damage they've caused. Would you like to hear how I've framed this out?"

Bostick nodded. Neither she nor Frenkel had hemophilia in their families, but within minutes it was obvious to Weinberg that they were a deeply committed team. Bostick was strong willed and tough, a natural and determined leader of people of whom she was fiercely protective. She had great presence.

Weinberg told them what he had learned, laying it out logically, without emotion, because he knew they needed a clinical analysis of the case.

As he left HANJ and drove back to his office, he decided he could definitely work with them, if they would accept him.

Bostick would become Weinberg's best ally, a friend and confidante, and in his own times of despair the only one, other than his wife, he could talk to frankly about the seemingly impossible task he had taken on. Julie Frenkel would be her right hand in these efforts. She had a great capacity to listen and respond in ways that gave her constituents hope. These women would be an inspiration to Weinberg. They worked for a community that needed a lot from them, from basic information to attending funeral after funeral. Yet, to his eye, their resolve never wavered.

The day after their initial meeting, Salgado called again.

"You passed the audition," he said. "Elena and Julie liked what you had to say and want to arrange a meeting of HANJ members specifically to discuss potential legal action. You will be invited to speak."

"Just tell me when, and I'll be there," Weinberg said.

The news amazed him, especially given HANJ's working relationship with the companies. But that relationship was unraveling.

"Timing is everything," Salgado said. "They see this legal case as inevitable."

Weinberg was asked to speak at an April 1992 forum at the Ramada Inn in East Brunswick. In the days before the meeting, he spent hours fine-tuning his notes and getting advice from Diane. She understood the issues well, with her expertise as a scientist who had worked on new drugs and then had handled regulatory matters for her company, including meeting with FDA officials to discuss labeling and other issues. On the evening of the HANJ meeting, Weinberg showered and dressed; kissed his sons, Jake and Arnie, goodnight; got a good-luck kiss and a vote of confidence from Diane; and drove to the Ramada.

The hotel was on Route 18, less than a mile from HANJ headquarters, with meeting rooms that were decent though by no means elegant. Weinberg entered through the lobby and walked to the room Bostick had reserved for the event. It had already begun to fill, and she was waiting for him in the anteroom.

She was nervous; this was all new to her and her agency. Plus, she had vouched for him, this young lawyer with an idea and passion but perhaps not much else.

"We're going to have a good crowd," she said. "They want to know what to do. They've all heard about you."

"Good," he said. "That will make it easier for me to talk to them."

Weinberg climbed onto the dais and sat next to Joe Salgado. He made a point of looking at the audience, making eye contact with as many people as possible, just as he did with juries. This crowd included hemophiliacs suffering from HIV and AIDS; spouses who had unwittingly been infected by their husbands; survivors of many who already had died; and parents, children, and friends of HANJ members. They reflected the diversity of New Jersey, as would be expected given that hemophilia affects all cultures, religions, and races. In the audience were whites and African Americans; people with Irish, Italian, Middle Eastern, and Hispanic-sounding names. They were young, old, middle-aged, Christian, Jew, and Muslim.

Salgado stood to introduce his old friend.

"Tonight," he said, "we've come to hear from an attorney about legal issues related to hemophilia and HIV infection. I would like to introduce Eric Weinberg. I've known him since 1980, when we worked together in the Somerset County Prosecutor's Office. Eric and I shared an office and after we left, we kept in touch. Since last summer, Eric has been investigating the HIV situation, and he has been retained by several families to represent them. He's going to tell you what he's been doing, what he's learned, and what he thinks about these cases. After he's finished we'll have a question-and-answer session, and then I think Eric has agreed to hang around if you want to talk to him one-on-one."

Weinberg stood to speak. The audience was completely focused on him. They were scared and angry, and nobody was answering their questions—not their doctors, priests, or rabbis, not their friends or advisers. HIV was looming, large and dark and threatening.

"Let me start by telling you that I think there is a legal case with merit here," he said. "I can't predict how long it will take. I can't tell you that we'll win. But I have learned enough to say that the fractionators failed to do what needed to be done."

He paused for a moment, then continued.

"So why has other litigation been such a failure? Why have they won every case, at trial or on appeal?"

Another pause.

"It's a medical fact that the vast majority of those of you with HIV were infected before the medical community, the CDC, the FDA, and the industry knew that HIV was in the blood supply and in the clotting-factor products," Weinberg said. "So it's simply not possible to argue that the fractionators failed to warn of the risk. That is a legal theory that for the most part will not work. So the question is, what legal theory will work?

"This is where I have focused my research. I believe the fractionators failed in their duty of care. Let me explain: They failed you long before HIV.

You know better than anyone about the trade-off. You were told years ago that the risk of hepatitis was acceptable, because clotting factor gave you freedom. It changed your life, allowed you to be mobile, allowed you to go to school, to camp, to work, to travel.

"But what if the trade-off was a lie? What if the fractionators could have made their products safer much sooner? Based on what I've learned, I think they could have done this, but there is far more work to be done."

Weinberg saw hope in some of the faces. After he was done speaking, many lined up to talk to him. He hoped he had been clear and had not created expectations that were too high.

And now, he had to come through. A dozen more families contacted him after the Ramada meeting, so he had to move faster to find another, larger law firm, with more resources, to partner with him. At the top of his list was one from East Brunswick, not far from HANJ headquarters, called Garruto, Galex & Cantor.

Bryan Garruto, Richard Galex, and Jane Cantor were all capable, respected trial lawyers, and their firm had garnered several impressive victories in complex, high-profile cases. Garruto and Galex agreed to meet Weinberg for lunch at the best restaurant in New Brunswick, The Frog and the Peach. Both seemed intrigued; this case would put them in the forefront on a novel theory of product liability and foreseeability, with potentially large damages. They told Weinberg to keep them posted. He was encouraged.

A month later, he flew to Miami to meet with Bob Parks, a well-known products liability attorney who had represented the Ray brothers—Ricky, Robert, and Randy, three children with hemophilia and HIV who lived in Arcadia, Florida, at least until someone burned down their home. Their civil case against the industry had been tried twice, once ending in a mistrial and then a hung jury, and then they had settled out of court. Parks invited Weinberg to go through the Ray file. Weinberg let Garruto know and said he would contact him upon his return to New Jersey.

Weinberg decided to stay in South Beach, which was just beginning to be reinvented. The South Beach he remembered from visits to his elderly aunts and uncles in the 1970s was decrepit and peopled mostly by retirees of modest means. By 1992, that had changed, and he took a room in the newly renovated Ritz Hotel, built in the art deco style familiar in Miami Beach. Most of the other guests were Europeans, and there were fashion photographers doing shoots by the pool overlooking the Atlantic Ocean. The room next to his was full of models.

After breakfast, Weinberg drove to Parks's office. His files practically filled a conference room. Parks had built his case carefully on the failure-to-warn theory. For any lawyer trying to understand a case, having the opportunity to go through another lawyer's trial files is enormously helpful.

Toward the end of the second day, Weinberg and Parks sat down to talk. Parks was in his fifties, with close-cropped hair and a beard. He was in good shape and carried himself with the confidence of a ball-player. He was direct in his manner and answered Weinberg's questions straight on. The more Weinberg got to know Parks over the next few years, the more he trusted him, even though they did not always see eye to eye.

Parks said he had considered the product-defect theory but had felt the facts of the Ray case, and his jury pool, were better suited to failure-to-warn. The defect theory had the disadvantage of requiring a jury to hold an entire industry responsible. He had not wanted to take on that burden. But Parks urged Weinberg to keep at it.

Parks's associate told Weinberg about some successful hemophilia litigation in Australia and referred him to Anne Marie Farrell, whose firm had handled most cases there.

Weinberg returned to New Jersey and contacted yet another lawyer who was involved in hemophilia litigation, Rob Jenner, from Bethesda, Maryland. Jenner chaired the AIDS litigation group of the Association of Trial Lawyers of America (ATLA) and had tried—and lost—a hemophilia case in Alaska. He, too, offered to share information and files, so Weinberg drove to Maryland.

Weinberg was learning about these cases by osmosis, from his own research, and from others who had gone before. He learned about the technologies involved in product sterilization and heat treatment, and about the business of blood. He definitely would need to prove that it had been possible to manufacture untainted clotting factor before his clients had been infected. Weinberg thought back to what Michael Rosenberg had told him about Behringwerke and knew he had to look into it further.

He also began examining the close working relationships among the industry, hemophilia doctors, and the National Hemophilia Foundation. The NHF ostensibly was dedicated to the interests of the families but, like many not-for-profit patient groups, it depended on the pharmaceutical industry for part of its funding. Many prominent hematologists received industry money as well. Whether those ties influenced the physicians' opinions was debatable, but it was beyond dispute that some doctors had told their patients that their HIV infections were unavoidable. And industry lawyers had retained some leading hemophilia doctors and NHF executives as expert witnesses.

In August 1992, the Weinbergs loaded their boys into the family car and drove to Washington, D.C. The ATLA AIDS litigation group was meeting for several days, and Weinberg wanted to listen and ask questions. The family checked into their hotel and Diane and the children, ages three and five, stayed at the swimming pool while he headed for the meeting. There were about eighty lawyers there.

Rob Jenner chaired the meeting with Wayne Spivey, a highly regarded lawyer from the Philadelphia firm of Shrager McDaid Loftus Flum & Spivey. Spivey and the senior partner, David Shrager, had represented several Canadian hemophiliacs, most of them children, who had been infected with HIV as late as 1987, by insufficiently heated clotting-factor concentrates manufactured by Armour Pharmaceutical Co., of suburban Philadelphia. Company memos had revealed that Armour had known the product was underheated, with live AIDS virus still present, yet had decided to sell it anyway. Each Canadian client had received a seven-figure settlement, but there was a catch: the company had insisted those embarrassing documents be sealed from public view. Sealing the documents, while not unusual in such a case, was an act that apparently even the judge had found distasteful: in a handwritten note on the margin of his formal order, he wrote that the company should not come back to him if someone violated it.

By the time of the ATLA meeting, it was generally accepted that hemophilia-AIDS cases were unwinnable if the victims were infected before 1983. This dogma was so established that the agenda for the meeting did not even include discussion of early HIV infections. This was precisely the issue Weinberg wanted to raise.

After about three hours of presentations, audience members were invited to speak. When his turn came, Weinberg stood, introduced himself, and said he wondered why there had been no discussion about whether the industry could have developed a safer product sooner. From what he knew, Weinberg said, there was a German company called Behringwerke that had invented a heating process in 1979 and had patented it in early 1981, but the American companies had not seriously worked on anything similar before 1982. This lack of corporate initiative, he said, was described in the medical literature and corporate documents.

The response was tepid. To him, it was as if a consensus had been reached, without any underlying rationale. But nobody made a convincing argument against his theory, so Weinberg felt somewhat encouraged.

After the meeting, Weinberg was chatting with two other lawyers, including Anne Marie Farrell, who had been tackling hemophilia-AIDS cases in Australia, when a man who had been standing in the back of the room approached them. Weinberg recognized him from his picture, which he had seen frequently in ATLA materials: David Shrager, from Philadelphia.

Shrager was in his late fifties, slim and balding, just shy of six feet tall. He was dignified and imposing, yet spoke with a distinctive Philadelphia accent. His handshake was firm. Shrager had been president of ATLA and was a major supporter of the organization. He also had a reputation as a top litigator, and later would be voted a "Legend of the Bar" by the Philadelphia Bar Association. Having won those Canadian cases, he and Spivey had the kind of firm and the background which Weinberg craved.

"Hey Eric, I'm David Shrager," he said. "Can I talk to you for a minute?"

"Sure," he said.

"I'm interested in what you had to say in there," Shrager said. "Tell me more about what you've been up to. Do you have many clients?"

"I do, and some of them couldn't find a lawyer in that room to represent them."

"You're right, unfortunately," said Shrager. "Why don't you give me your business card, and we'll meet soon. I think your theory may have merit."

FIGURE 6.1. David Shrager, of Philadelphia, was lead counsel for the U.S. hemophilia-AIDS litigation.

Credit: Shrager, Spivey & Sachs.

FIGURE 6.2. Wayne Spivey was one of David Shrager's partners and a key player in the U.S. hemophilia case. Earlier, he and Shrager also represented Canadian children who contracted AIDS from tainted clotting drugs.

Credit: Wayne Spivey.

They exchanged cards, with Shrager moving a little closer to Weinberg, as if they were coconspirators. Weinberg would learn that Shrager had a familiar style when he wanted to be friendly, but a completely different style when he was at war. For now, friendly was the rule of the day.

"We've been thinking, Wayne and I, about how we might get involved in other cases. Would you send me some things to read?" Shrager asked. "I just want to do some due diligence."

"When I get back to New Jersey, I'll put a package together for you," Weinberg promised.

"Great. You have my address. Nice meeting you," Shrager said, and left.

Weinberg hung around for a while, talking with other lawyers. He had accomplished what he had come to Washington to do: get someone powerful, with more resources, interested in his ideas. He went back to the swimming pool and gave Diane a summary of what had just happened. They were both pleased; the trip had been worthwhile. It was a beautiful summer day in Washington, and they took Jake and Arnie to the National Zoo.

Shrager certainly was interested but, over the next decade, his vision of the case would sometimes be at odds with Weinberg's. As a result, their relationship would become difficult and often contentious. Yet they managed to work closely together. Weinberg often turned to Shrager for help, regarding the older lawyer as selfish and arrogant at times, but at other times as a mentor and confidant. It was complicated.

Back in New Jersey, Weinberg did some research on Shrager. He learned that he was one of the most successful and respected personal-injury attorneys in Philadelphia. He had some high-profile clients, and a long history of success in medical malpractice cases. Shrager was pure Philly; he had graduated in 1957 from the University of Pennsylvania, where he had been an All–Ivy League fencer, and in 1960 from the University of Pennsylvania Law School.

Shrager's most publicized case had been his representation of Michael Moses Ward, a young boy whose mother had belonged to a radical cult called MOVE that for years had been at odds with its neighbors and Philadelphia police. In 1985, after repeated complaints about MOVE members brandishing guns (they had killed a police officer during a confrontation in 1978) and refusing to send their children to school, police dropped a bomb on the roof of the MOVE house in an attempt to destroy a home-made bunker. It caught fire, and rather than flee as the flames spread, first through their house and then the neighborhood, most of the MOVE members stayed inside and died. Ward's mother and ten other MOVE members were killed, and he suffered extensive burns. Shrager won a settlement with the city that provided for Ward for life.

Weinberg spent some time organizing materials to send to Shrager and Spivey. Although he still hoped to partner with Garruto and Galex, it was heartening that a nationally known and highly successful lawyer like Shrager would be interested. Weinberg mailed the package.

7

Help Wanted

Weinberg met with Garruto and Galex a couple of times in July 1992 to update them on his research and, he hoped, develop a preliminary partnership agreement. He kept them informed of the progress he was making in signing up clients and identifying expert witnesses. To Weinberg, their discussions felt comfortable, but August came and went with no agreement.

Then another opportunity arose. Weinberg had played basketball in an adult recreation league in Princeton for a couple of years, until he tore a knee ligament that required surgery. One of the other players was an Edison lawyer who had been a year ahead of Weinberg at Rutgers and had attended law school with one of his fraternity brothers. He worked at a large personal-injury firm, Levinson Axelrod, in Middlesex County. During the baby-monitor trial, he and Weinberg had chatted in the hallway of the Middlesex County Courthouse, and Weinberg had mentioned the hemophilia litigation. The Edison lawyer, in turn, had said that he would talk to his firm about the cases.

So, as sometimes happens, when one door seems to be closing, another opens. Weinberg got a call from Ron Grayzel, a partner at Levinson Axelrod. Weinberg knew him casually. Grayzel wrote frequently in the *New Jersey Law Journal* and was an emerging thought leader on New Jersey product-liability issues. They arranged to have lunch at Doll's Place, a favorite hangout of courthouse regulars in New Brunswick.

When Weinberg got to Doll's, Grayzel was already at a table. The lunch crowd was typical for a weekday; Weinberg knew at least a dozen of the customers, mostly lawyers, court staff, and judges. Gossip is an integral part of a court system, and he knew the courthouse buzz later that afternoon would be that Grayzel and Weinberg were having lunch. They were both fairly well known lawyers in Middlesex. There would be speculation, and Weinberg enjoyed the feeling.

Weinberg told Grayzel about the hemophilia case. By then he had about ten clients and was hearing from families in New Jersey and beyond pretty much on a weekly basis. Weinberg told Grayzel about his interest in finding a litigation partner.

Grayzel listened and then asked about other cases, and the experts that Weinberg thought would be needed. He wanted to know how many clients Weinberg thought might potentially retain them if they worked together. He asked about the success of the litigation to date, and what Weinberg thought the prospects were for success. He asked if they could file cases in state court and keep them there instead of being transferred to federal court. They were all good questions. The two talked for about an hour.

But Grayzel called a couple of weeks later to say his firm had decided not to get involved. There had been some changes at the firm, he said, and some other cases they had recently taken would require a lot of time and resources. He was gracious about it. Weinberg was disappointed but understood.

By late fall of 1992, he had been retained by thirteen hemophilia families and had heard from another couple of dozen, but he was hesitant to sign up more clients. The three filed cases—Johnson, Niederman, and Weiss—were in federal court, and the magistrate seemed to be losing patience. Weinberg thought his theories made sense, but he had yet to identify experts to support them. The industry lawyers were inundating him with information requests—they wanted, and were entitled to, medical records, infusion histories, lab reports, proof of employment, and loss of income records. They demanded to know when he contended his clients had been infected with HIV. They wanted to know who his witnesses were, who his experts were, and what they were going to say. In turn, Weinberg demanded information from the companies, but Judge Pisano did not seem impressed with his position that he needed documents from the defendants in order to establish the facts of his cases. He, too, pressed

Weinberg to produce the medical files and the information the companies sought.

So Weinberg continued to chase down evidence. He always carefully developed a case before filing a lawsuit, but this one required more speed because of the statute of limitations.

Weinberg had filed Andrea Johnson's case within two years of Clyde's death because of the statute; he had filed the Weinberg and Niederman cases so the court would understand there were thousands of people affected. Yet, by doing so, he had put himself in a difficult situation, and the court was putting the screws to him.

In the middle of this work, Weinberg's third son, Michael Dominic, was born on October 9, 1992. He was chubbier than his two brothers, a handsome, healthy baby and, despite all the pressures he faced, Weinberg counted his blessings once again.

That same month, Weinberg was contacted by Corey Dubin, the California activist who was one of the leaders of the Committee of Ten Thousand. COTT was interested in aggressively pursuing cases in court. Dubin had heard about Weinberg from Ron Niederman. Dubin was smart, energized, and doggedly pursuing justice for the hemophilia community; a news reporter would nickname him "Bull" in recognition of his tenacity. He and Weinberg talked for a couple of hours, and Dubin urged him to get in touch with Anne Marie Farrell, the Australian lawyer that Weinberg had met in Washington that summer.

The following week, Weinberg wrote to Farrell and said he was interested in her research on the German company Behringwerke. He offered to come to Australia, but she did not respond.

Weinberg also decided to try once more with Richard Galex, Bryan Garruto's partner. Their conversation was brief: the firm had decided not to work with him on the hemophilia litigation. Now, at least he knew for sure.

The following week, Elena Bostick called.

"I wanted to ask if you knew a lawyer from East Brunswick," she said. "His name is Bryan Garruto."

"I do," Weinberg said. He had kept Bostick updated on the case and had let her know that he was looking for a larger firm to join forces with him, but he had not discussed anyone in particular. He had intended to tell her about Garruto if a deal was cut. "I actually met with Bryan and his partner about working together in the hemophilia litigation. I thought we had the makings of a deal, but they decided against it. Why do you ask?"

"Bryan Garruto contacted us last week, to say he was involved in blood-products litigation," Bostick said. "He's offered to sponsor a meeting for potential clients, to hear his plan for litigating the cases."

Weinberg was surprised. "We talked about an agreement and I shared my theories, but I'm pretty sure that anything Bryan knows about this case, he's learned from me," he said.

"He told me he has a working arrangement with an Australian firm that handled the cases there," Bostick replied. "He said they would be working with them on the New Jersey litigation."

It had to be Farrell's firm, Weinberg thought to himself. Now he understood why she hadn't replied to him. Garruto evidently wanted to get involved in the case—just not with Weinberg. They must not have liked his approach to it.

"Well, what do you want to do?" Weinberg asked.

"He is offering to pay for an informational meeting, and the community wants information," Bostick said.

"I understand," Weinberg said, and he did.

Bostick said she would discuss the situation with her board, and get back to him. Within a day, she called back.

"Here is what we'll do," she said. "The Hemophilia Association of New Jersey will accept Garruto, Galex and & Cantor's offer to sponsor a seminar on one condition: that any lawyers who have been involved with hemophilia litigation in New Jersey are invited to participate."

"I'm the only one," Weinberg said.

"I know," Bostick said. "So they would have to agree that you can come, sit on the dais, and make a presentation."

Weinberg was disappointed, but he could see it from their point of view.

The meeting was scheduled for December 1992, and Garruto's firm launched an advertising campaign for hemophilia clients in the larger newspapers in central New Jersey.

The meeting was held at the Ramada. Weinberg prepared an outline of his presentation and some notes for the meeting but really didn't need them. He felt that he knew the case better than anyone. He had friends and clients in the community. Three clients—Ron Niederman, Richard Vogel, and Richard Johnson—had called him in the days leading up to the meeting to say they would be in attendance and ready to make the necessary inquiries of all of the lawyers who were present.

When Weinberg arrived, Garruto was talking to a small group, with Farrell at his side. Garruto barely acknowledged him; Farrell nodded and smiled uncomfortably. As the meeting began, Garruto and Farrell sat together at the dais. Weinberg sat alone, on the other side.

Elena Bostick and Joe Salgado made brief presentations and introduced the lawyers to the audience of about one hundred people. When the presentations began, Garruto went first. He talked about the history of hemophilia HIV litigation to date; he referred to the time in late 1982 into early 1983, when public health authorities first concluded that HIV was blood-borne, and then he introduced Farrell, who spoke about the Australian litigation. Their pitch, in essence, was that the best cases, the cases they wanted to lead with, were for people who were infected after 1983.

As soon as they were finished, Weinberg knew the evening was his. Most people with hemophilia were infected with HIV before 1983, and had been exposed to hepatitis B and hepatitis C even earlier.

What he knew was that, at the Hemophilia Treatment Center of the Robert Wood Johnson University Hospital in New Jersey, Dr. Parvin Saidi, the chief of hematology, and her colleagues had been tuned into the virus problem long before HIV. As early as 1979, they had made it a practice to draw blood from their hemophilia patients and store it in freezers, labeling each vial with the date of the draw. They also had done a "look back" study in 1985, when the FDA approved the first test for the virus, to see how many of those vials were HIV-positive. There were samples from hundreds of patients. These would be critical scientific and legal evidence, at least for patients from central New Jersey, including many of Weinberg's clients.

Most of these patients had not talked to their doctors about when they were infected, but for the majority, it was before 1982. Some were as early as 1979; most had been infected in 1980 or 1981. For these people, Garruto's approach offered little hope, Weinberg thought.

It was Weinberg's turn. He gathered his notes, took a deep breath, and looked at the audience.

"What you have heard here is interesting," he said, "because this has been the mistake made time and time again. Very few people in this community were infected with HIV in 1983 or 1984. Nine out of ten of you, maybe more, were infected earlier. The cases that have been tried were lost because the lawyers tried to argue later infection, but the evidence was simply not in their favor. So this approach will not work, which is why I've taken a different approach. If I'm right, then every one of you with HIV has a viable case. This simply should not have happened to anyone."

The floor was opened for questions, and several people lined up at the microphone. The first question was directed to Garruto, and it was on the minds of most of the audience: Will you accept cases of hemophiliacs who were infected before the AIDS virus was identified?

Garruto replied by explaining the strength of a later infection case versus the weakness of an early case. His strategy, he said, would be to lead with stronger cases, so the companies would be more inclined to negotiate on the weaker ones.

Weinberg thought this strategy made economic sense, but that Garruto did not understand that this was a community with strong bonds. They wanted someone who would fight just as hard for the weakest among them.

The Q&A ended, and Bostick asked the lawyers to stay so people could talk with them. At least a dozen people lined up in front of Weinberg. He glanced over at Garruto and Farrell. They sat alone, and soon left. Neither would reappear in the New Jersey hemophilia litigation.

IN PHILADELPHIA, David Shrager was still thinking over the case. He and Spivey were interested but did not seem willing to pull the trigger. They set up a meeting with Weinberg in December 1992, at their law offices.

By then, Weinberg had reached out to several potential experts but was not having much success. Many had already agreed to testify for the industry.

There was the family physician from California who claimed to be a qualified expert on everything related to his cases, but he had no real expertise in blood coagulation, protein biochemistry, or AIDS. Weinberg decided not to work with him. Then he talked to a leading expert in hematology and blood coagulation therapy, but the man was getting older and decided he wasn't interested in consulting. Next was a prominent New Jersey physician and scientist who knew all about viruses and seemed perfectly suited to discuss risk and duty. They spent a couple of hours talking, but he would not agree to help. He had ongoing relationships with the companies.

At least he was getting his meeting with Shrager and Spivey, on a Saturday morning in December. Weinberg's youngest, Mike, was a couple of months old; brothers Arnie and Jake were nearly four and five. It was hard for Weinberg to get away on weekends so he left for Philadelphia early, before they got up, stopping at a Dunkin' Donuts for a large regular, skim milk and no sugar. He was in a Saab 9000 Turbo, a fast sedan with a manual transmission that he loved to drive hard. Bruce Springsteen was on the cassette player. It was a cloudy morning, not too cold, and Weinberg put the windows down on Route 1 South, turning Bruce up high.

He felt a sense of beginning. If there was a way of working with Shrager and Spivey, he intended to find it.

The offices of Shrager McDaid Loftus Flum & Spivey were in a sleek, high-rise building in Center City Philadelphia. Weinberg parked in the basement garage and took the elevator up. The receptionist led him to Shrager's corner office, where he and Spivey were waiting. Shrager wore dress slacks, expensive leather shoes, and a dress shirt unbuttoned at the collar. Spivey was bigger than Weinberg remembered from Washington, with the build of a football nose guard, and was far more casual—jeans, Docksiders, and a polo shirt.

"Come in, Eric," said Shrager, pointing to the breakfast spread on the credenza. "Have something to eat."

"Great," Weinberg replied, and picked up a bagel and cream cheese. They sat at a table in comfortable leather chairs. The coffee was good.

"So we've looked over everything you sent us," Shrager said. "You've done some really good work here. You know we represented several hemophilia families from Canada against Armour, so we have more than a passing familiarity with the issues involved in these cases. Wayne and I have been thinking about what you said in Washington. Frankly, we are undecided about whether to jump in. If we do, we would be all in, and would be very interested in working with you. Have I summed it up correctly, Wayne?"

"Yes, I think so," Spivey said.

"How do you think the New Jersey Supreme Court will rule on a manufacturer's duty to protect against an unknown risk? Wayne and I think that's the soft spot in your theory," Shrager said.

"The risk is not defined as a particular virus," Weinberg replied. "When scientists were trying to limit the spread of hepatitis by screening out diseased blood donors, they knew they were dealing with known but also unknown viruses. The question, I think, is whether the product defect was known or knowable. The defect was the failure to sterilize. There was a safer alternative design. I think that takes us past the motion to dismiss."

"And the safer alternative design was Behringwerke?"

"Yes, in part," Weinberg said. "It was albumin, too. In fact, the safer alternative designs were the designs they eventually developed and sold."

Spivey, who Weinberg knew was more critical than Shrager, wanted to know about experts, and asked if he had one who would testify that the products could and should have been virally inactivated before HIV came along.

"Not yet," Weinberg admitted. "But I've identified a guy who might be key: Dr. Edward Shanbrom. He invented clotting-factor concentrates. He holds more patents for clotting factor than anyone alive. He worked at Hyland and developed the first product there in the 1960s."

Michael Rosenberg, the hemophilia activist from Northern California, had told Weinberg about Dr. Shanbrom. He was an important historical figure. Rosenberg had warned Weinberg that Shanbrom was a hard guy to figure in terms of his loyalties: he was an industry man but might be willing to tell the truth. Weinberg had not yet decided how to approach him, but he had Shanbrom's address in Orange County, California.

"I haven't talked to Shanbrom yet, but I intend to," Weinberg said. "Also, I've made plans to visit with scientists from Behringwerke next month in Germany. We might find an expert there as well."

Shrager stepped in then.

"We don't see these cases as individual lawsuits," he said. "There are just too many people who would have claims, and to litigate them one by one would be impractical, and wouldn't help them get compensation soon enough. You're dealing with a very sick group of clients, Eric, and the way to help them is to file a class action complaint, and try to get a class certified. Parallel to that, we would file an application to the U.S. Judicial Panel on Multidistrict Litigation for assignment."

"Explain that to me, please," Weinberg said. He had only a superficial understanding of the MDL process.

The strategy would be to file two pleadings. One would ask the judicial panel to determine that the hemophilia litigation had the characteristics that would justify consolidation of all cases, for discovery purposes, to a single federal judge. If the application was granted, then all cases filed in federal court, or filed in state court and removed to federal court by the defendants, would be transferred to this judge. The judge would appoint a number of lawyers to litigate the case. The plaintiff firms would form a steering committee.

"It would be our intention to be appointed as lead counsel," Shrager said, "meaning we would manage the overall litigation and make recommendations, in the event of a settlement, about the allocation of fees."

"Are fees paid on cases?" Weinberg asked.

"Yes, but since the steering committee does all of the work, lawyers representing clients have to pay a percentage of their fees to a fund managed by the committee. In a large case, that fund can be substantial. That's where the lead counsel has great latitude."

Weinberg understood. Shrager intended to be lead counsel and if Weinberg made the right deal, he would be on the steering committee and would get fees from the fund.

"Now, separate and apart from the MDL, and once it's assigned, we would file a federal class-action complaint," Shrager said. "As I said, it would be on a parallel track; typically, the signatories to the complaint are the steering committee members. The strategy is to gear toward a class trial, which puts tremendous pressure on the defendants. We try the case, or we negotiate a settlement."

Weinberg had not been expecting this. It was an approach that was completely new to him. He needed time to think about it.

"Interesting," he said. "But what about the clients whose cases are filed?"

"They go into the MDL," Shrager said.

"Are individual cases actually tried?"

"If the MDL judge decides to, he or she can send the cases back to their home courts for trial," Shrager explained. "In the case of your clients, the cases would be transferred from New Jersey to the MDL court, and when the cases have been worked up, they could be sent back to New Jersey for trial. Of course, if there is a class-action trial, the chance that individual cases would also be set for trial is pretty remote."

This was a problem for Weinberg. Andrea Johnson had retained him to try her case; so had Ron Niederman, Sallie Weiss, and many others. It was confusing, and he was not sure he could reconcile Shrager's approach with his. On the other hand, it was clear that these guys knew what they were doing, and that he needed their help.

"This has been productive," Weinberg said. "I want to let it settle in."

Shrager was gracious. He and Spivey were interested in continuing the discussion, he assured Weinberg. They agreed to meet again soon.

8

All for Business

Weinberg had been vetted by the Hemophilia Association of New Jersey and hired by nearly twenty hemophilia families, and he was becoming known by activists as a lawyer with some credibility, or at least a lawyer worthy of the benefit of the doubt. But the community's distrust of lawyers and others was entirely justified. They felt they also had been deceived by the government, the companies, their physicians, and the National Hemophilia Foundation.

When it came to the safety of clotting-factor concentrates, the not-for-profit NHF, headquartered in New York City, had taken some controversial positions that seemed blatantly influenced by industry ties. Formed in 1948 to advance the interests of the nation's hemophiliacs, the NHF had nurtured its relationships with the blood-product manufacturers— companies that by the early 1980s were supplying nearly 23 percent of NHF's funding, according to the organization's financial records.

Starting two days before the Centers for Disease Control's July 1982 public announcement that AIDS was killing hemophiliacs, the NHF began issuing the first of its patient alerts, medical bulletins, and newsletters that played down the risk of HIV. The first alert, sent to NHF chapters and hemophilia treatment centers nationwide, said the risk was "minimal" and that the CDC "is not advising a change in treatment regimen at this time."[1]

A year later, the summer 1983 issue of *Hemophilia Newsnotes*, the NHF's annual meeting preview, included an article on page 2, highlighted in a box, that began with the headline, "NHF Urges Clotting Factor Use Be Maintained." The NHF was concerned, the article said, that reported reductions in clotting-factor sales meant that people weren't using as much product. This was "an inappropriate response" and hemophiliacs should "maintain the use of clotting factor." It quoted the NHF medical codirector, Dr. Louis Aledort, as saying that "the risks of not treating exceed the risk of contracting AIDS," and reminding everyone that uncontrolled bleeding was their leading cause of death and serious orthopedic complications.[2]

In another article from the same issue, the NHF announced that the Food and Drug Administration had recently approved the sale of the first heat-treated Factor VIII, but the article seemed to downplay it for use in patients who already had been "heavily exposed" to unheated products. It did recommend the heated product, produced by Hyland, for infants and others who "have had relatively little exposure to concentrates," a clear indication that the NHF understood it was too late to protect older users.[3]

It was a dilemma. By this point, some doctors, but not many, were telling their patients to revert to cryoprecipitate.

Ultimately, the NHF would be added as a class-action defendant, not just because of its view of the science but because of its decisions on legal issues as well. A key document was a resolution adopted by the NHF board of directors in October 1985 in which the group—with wording suggested in part by Duncan Barr, the national counsel for Bayer and its Cutter division—opposed a potential class action filed in California, in a case called *Gannon v. Cutter*. The resolution said the class action "would not be in the best interests of persons with hemophilia." Barr was invited to speak at an NHF meeting, but the lawyer for plaintiff Kathleen Gannon, widow of a dead hemophiliac, was not. She lost her case.[4]

Later in the 1980s, when people with hemophilia began to die from AIDS, two former NHF medical directors and some doctors who served on its medical advisory committee testified against patients who sued the drug companies. When the NHF was asked its position on lawsuits against the drug manufacturers, its then-president wrote that he considered the companies to be "constituents" and "family members."

The anger of the hemophilia community was also directed at prominent hematologists who, like the NHF, had seemed to develop too-cozy ties to the manufacturers. It was not unusual for doctors who served on the foundation's medical advisory committee to be paid by the companies for conducting clinical trials, or as consultants or speakers. Several of those doctors became expert witnesses for the industry, testifying against their patients. Their defense of the companies was based upon two primary arguments. First, most severe hemophiliacs were probably infected long before anyone knew about HIV. Second, at that point, it made more sense to keep using the concentrates.

To the activists, a letter written by Duncan Barr to an opposing lawyer was particularly galling: he warned that if the case was litigated, he intended to call Dr. Aledort, the plaintiff's own doctor, to testify on behalf of Bayer. The hemophiliac's lawsuit was dropped.

There was more. In December 1982, Dr. Aledort counseled an FDA advisory panel against requiring the companies to use virus-killing processes in clotting products, according to a transcript of the meeting. Dr. Aledort argued that this could drive prices higher than hemophiliacs could afford, because heat killed a lot of clotting proteins, meaning more plasma had to be used to produce the same amount of medicine. That point also was made in the NHF's summer 1983 issue of *Hemophilia Newsnotes*.[5]

"I would just like to get one clarification from Dr. Aledort, and see if I really heard what I thought I heard," said an FDA doctor, Robert Gerety, at the meeting. "'You would rather leave the viruses in the product that is administered by parents . . . than to attempt to remove the viruses that we know we can remove?'"

"Well, I am glad that I don't have to give you a yes or a no, like on the witness stand," Dr. Aledort replied. "I will give you a qualified answer. Yes, I would leave it the way it is, until you could tell me that making it better is really better."

"Well, I thought that is what we did," Dr. Gerety said.

"No, you didn't," Dr. Aledort retorted.

The FDA panel met again in July 1983, after the companies had begun screening donors to try to weed out those at high risk of carrying HIV. Should the panel recommend recalls of older products made from unscreened plasma? An industry official told them that up to 30 percent of the clotting products on the market at that time were made from blood donated before the screening program began. This time, Dr. Aledort told the panel that the NHF board wanted the government to order recalls, but his personal view was that "this is not the time." The AIDS risk, he said, was "not clearly established," and there was "great concern about the continued supply" of medicine, according to the meeting transcript. So the advisory panel did not recommend a recall, and the FDA went along with it.

Three months after the meeting, Dr. Aledort was gone as the NHF's medical codirector.

At this point, Weinberg's focus was not so much on what had been said or done in 1982 and 1983 as it was on the earlier history of factor concentrates. In January 1993, he contacted a scientist at the National Institutes of Health, Dr. Edward Tabor, who had written a couple of chapters in a textbook called *Viral Hepatitis* and had also authored an important article published in the *Annals of Internal Medicine* in 1977 titled "Transmission of Non-A, Non-B Hepatitis." Dr. Tabor said he had done quite of bit of work on viral inactivation and that he had favored heating plasma products. He seemed perfect as a possible expert for the case. He asked Weinberg to write a letter so he could get NIH approval to speak to the lawyer further. So Weinberg had high hopes.

A few weeks later, Dr. Tabor called to say that NIH had declined the request.

In the hunt for experts, Weinberg realized that Michael Rosenberg was right: it was essential that he go to Germany. Rosenberg had authored a defining manifesto of activism, titled "Causes and Effects of the Hemophilia/AIDS Epidemic," in which he had laid out his accusations against industry and the NHF. He also had sent Weinberg some correspondence that he and others had had with a German physician and professor at the University of Heidelberg, Dr. Klaus Schimpf, who was a leading hemophilia doctor in Germany and director of the World Hemophilia Federation's International Hemophilia Information Clearinghouse. Rosenberg also sent memos of conversations he had had with representatives of Behringwerke, which had developed the world's first heated clotting-factor concentrate. The Behringwerke technology was based on the process developed by Dr. Cohn in the 1940s.

Weinberg wrote to Dr. Schimpf, seeking a meeting, and to Behringwerke AG in Marburg, Germany, where the company is headquartered, asking for information about its viral inactivation process. To his great surprise,

Weinberg received courteous replies from both. Dr. Schimpf was willing to meet, and Behringwerke said that its processes were proprietary, but if he had further detailed questions, he could submit them. Weinberg then called Dr. Schimpf, who seemed willing to introduce him to key Behringwerke scientists.

Weinberg also wrote to Dr. Norbert Heimburger, a retired German physician and colleague of Dr. Schimpf, who had been director of research for Behringwerke. It was Dr. Heimburger's research, begun in 1977, that led to the company's virally inactivated clotting factor. He didn't reply, so Weinberg called him. Dr. Heimburger said he had regrets about what had happened in the hemophilia community. The fact that he had developed a process that would have prevented the tragedy of AIDS, but that was not used until it was too late, was a failure he would always regret. He agreed to answer more specific questions after Weinberg's meeting with Dr. Schimpf.

In January 1993, Weinberg took leave of his wife and three sons. Waiting to board his flight at Newark Airport, he took out his journal and wrote: "Many questions. Doubts. Concerns. Complications. Something here. Something real, dangerously real, real life, what happens, what the confluence of industry and passive government can do, can bring—the decisions dropped on us that end up, when they go wrong, killing thousands of people, unnecessarily, and all for the sake of profit. All for business."

In the spirit of adventure, he rented a BMW at the airport in Frankfurt. Somehow, though his knowledge of German was practically zero, he found his way to the Autobahn. He pushed the Bimmer to 100 miles an hour, but most drivers were passing him, so he pushed to 130 miles an hour, holding the steering wheel as hard as he could, making his way to the beautiful university town of Heidelberg, deciphering German signs until he arrived at the Der Europaische Hof Hotel Europa.

The hotel, which had served as a headquarters for the U.S. Army after World War II, was elegant and comfortable. Weinberg relaxed in his room, then took a long walk to the Neckar River and around the Old Town, which had escaped Allied bombing. He stopped at a pub, had a dinner of schnitzel and unbelievably good beer, then returned to his room to watch *The Simpsons* dubbed in German, until he fell asleep.

The following day, he found his way to the campus of the University of Heidelberg. Dr. Schimpf had said he would wait outside his office for him. It was a good January day, with some sun, and not terribly cold. Weinberg walked through a quad and saw an older man, tall with thin, graying hair and a firm posture, standing across the way. He walked toward Weinberg so that they met halfway, each man's hand extended to the other as they approached.

"Mr. Weinberg, I presume," he said with a slight smile.

"Dr. Schimpf, it's a pleasure to meet you, sir."

He smiled more broadly. "I assumed you to be much older."

"It's my voice," Weinberg replied.

"Perhaps, but I think more your grasp of the issues," Dr. Schimpf said. "Come, we can walk to my office and be comfortable." He took Weinberg's elbow, and they entered the university building.

Dr. Schimpf's office was comfortable, in a square, modern building. It was neat, uncluttered, the office of a man who was mostly retired. Dr. Schimpf invited Weinberg to sit. He had an air of heaviness about him, as if he was carrying a weight that had been bearing down on him for a very long time, and which he was ready to lift—perhaps by talking to this young Jewish American lawyer. As they spoke, Weinberg got the impression that, like Dr. Heimburger, he harbored some concern, perhaps even guilt, about what had happened to the community of patients to which he had committed his professional life.

"You are aware that an investigation into the effects of factor are underway here in Germany?" Dr. Schimpf asked.

"I am not aware," Weinberg said.

"Questions have been asked about the extensive use of clotting factor, particularly at the Bonn Center," he replied.

"Forgive me, doctor. I have been working hard to learn but there is so much to know. Please explain."

"Of course," Dr. Schimpf said. "It is a complicated and broad story. Let me say that I had concerns for some time before the HIV epidemic about the risks associated with factor. Germany was the most lucrative market in the world for factor-concentrate products. The major hemophilia treatment center here is in Bonn. Patients were heavily dosed with this product. On average, perhaps three to five times as much factor was prescribed to an average patient here than in the United States."

"Why was that?"

Dr. Schimpf paused a moment. "It was a lucrative arrangement for all concerned," he said.

"Which product?"

"I believe it was primarily the Cutter product. This was a contentious issue among the physicians caring for people with hemophilia in Germany. We did not all agree."

"Was it priced the same here as in the United States?" Weinberg asked.

"In fact, the price of factor was higher in Germany."

"So this was a significant market for the fractionators," Weinberg said.

"Oh, yes indeed," Dr. Schimpf replied. "They made more profit in Germany than in any other country in the world."

"You published an article in the *New England Journal of Medicine* in 1989, reporting on the effectiveness of pasteurization, or heating," Weinberg noted. "It said that pasteurized factor concentrates do not contain infectious HIV."[6]

"It was, and remains, an excellent product," Dr. Schimpf agreed.

"What was the impetus for the research at Behringwerke that led to the pasteurized product?"

Dr. Schimpf smiled. "The impetus, frankly, was Dr. Heimburger," he said. "He had the idea that concentrates could be made hepatitis-safe. Of course, there was a business reason as well: Dr. Heimburger was a Behringwerke employee and wanted the company to do well. The first company to perfect a process would realize a significant marketing advantage. Behringwerke is a large company, but not on the scale of Bayer or Baxter."

"How did Dr. Heimburger proceed?"

"Behring had developed a purified product," he said. "You understand the difference between purification and inactivation of viruses?"

"I think so," Weinberg replied. "Purification is removal of contaminants, inactivation is actually killing the viruses?"

"Very good," Dr. Schimpf said. He spoke quietly, directly, with a kindness ingrained from treating patients with compassion for many years. Weinberg liked him very much.

"A critically important part of the Behringwerke product was that they engaged in a purification step first," he continued. "This was somewhat controversial within the company, because purification results in a loss of about 15 percent of the starting material."

"An economic consideration?"

"Very much so," Dr. Schimpf agreed, "particularly since Behringwerke had to purchase raw plasma from the Americans."

"And from there?"

"The decision was made to follow the methods used to sterilize albumin," he said.

"Were there concerns in the medical community about using the heated product?" Weinberg asked.

"Some, yes, but not significant," the doctor said. "We recognized there was a possibility the clotting factor could be altered by heating. But the data convinced me and others that we should prescribe heated factor. Physicians in Germany in general were pleased to have it, and were comfortable with it, given the history of safety and efficacy of albumin. Of course, supply was an issue."

"Was that a function of the manufacturing process, or the availability of raw plasma?" Weinberg asked.

"Both," Dr. Schimpf replied. "Heating destroyed a good amount of the starting material."

"And you did not prescribe heated concentrate to patients who had been using unheated products?"

The physician paused. "This is my regret," he said, "that I continued those patients on unheated product, rather than switch them to cryoprecipitate. We simply did not have enough heated product and I, and others, believed that the risk of death from bleeding was greater than the risk of death from AIDS."

"Yes, you wrote in 1983 that reports of AIDS in the press were exaggerated, and that bleeding remained the main risk to the lives of hemophilia patients."

"I believed this. I was wrong," he said. "But I also wrote that measures had been taken to eliminate the risk of hepatitis infection, and that the hepatitis-safe products had been available since 1981. I also felt that widespread therapy with heated factor concentrates was desirable, since the treatment that inactivated the hepatitis viruses would presumably also inactivate HIV."

Before arriving in Germany, Weinberg had some understanding of what Behringwerke had done. One of the lawyers he had gotten to know during his research was Debra Thomas, a partner of a prominent Chicago trial lawyer named Leonard Ring. Weinberg had talked to Thomas twice just before leaving for Germany. She said that Ring was interested in the viral-inactivation theory, too, and through his international contacts had retained a former Behringwerke scientist named Heiner Trobisch to testify in a case Ring was preparing for trial. Dr. Trobisch was not directly involved in the research that led to the first heated product, though.

Weinberg told Dr. Schimpf that he needed more details about the Behringwerke process. Dr. Schimpf could not answer some of his questions but said Dr. Heimburger could. He picked up his telephone and dialed Dr. Heimburger. Dr. Schimpf finished the call and turned back to the lawyer.

"Dr. Heimburger will accept some written questions from you," he said. "He is willing to return to his offices at Behringwerke to get the answers from his files."

"Thank you, Dr. Schimpf. I would like to compensate you for your time."

"It is not necessary. I am pleased to help."

Weinberg took his leave and returned to the Europa, where he spent a couple of hours drafting questions for Dr. Heimburger. Then he took another walk, up to an ancient castle on a hill overlooking Heidelberg and the Neckar River valley. He had made progress. The fact that Germany was the most lucrative market in the world, with physicians using much larger doses than in the United States, and that Germany had been the first country to administer heat-treated hemophilia medicines was, he thought, significant new information.

He was eager to continue on his journey.

The next day, Weinberg drove to Frankfurt and checked into a Hilton hotel that could have been anywhere for its lack of distinctiveness and charm. Frankfurt was a modern city, and the downtown reminded him of Atlanta. He was going to meet with Jack Bechhofer, a German lawyer with hemophilia. He had agreed to share his insights and to assist Weinberg, if necessary, in dealing with German-speaking scientists.

Bechhofer's offices were modest and functional. His Jewish family had fled the country during World War II and had returned after the war. He was slight and walked with a pronounced limp, reminding Weinberg physically and in his wry manner of Joe Salgado.

Bechhofer represented hemophiliacs in Germany, where a government inquiry into the HIV epidemic was just beginning. Weinberg had edited his questions for Dr. Heimburger, and together they refined them. Then Bechhofer translated them into German. They mailed the letter and went to dinner. Bechhofer drove them to an Apfelweinstube (apple wine pub), an institution in Frankfurt, in an old building that had the feel of hundreds of years of history. It was fitted with long, heavy tables, which customers shared. They sat with a young family, ate wiener schnitzel and salads, and drank several stoneware pitchers full of apfelwein, a sweet and tasty beverage that went down easily. Bechhofer returned Weinberg to his hotel after midnight.

Weinberg slept fitfully and was awakened early in the morning by the ringing of the bedside telephone. He found it with some difficulty.

"Hello," he managed.

"Mr. Weinberg, this is Dr. Heimburger. I do hope I have not wakened you."

Weinberg sat up immediately and took a quick, deep breath to clear his head.

"Uh, no, it's fine. I'm glad you called," he said.

"Are you certain?"

"Truth be told, Dr. Heimburger, a friend took me out for apfelwein last night, and I think I drank a bit more than I should."

Dr. Heimburger laughed deeply and promised that his head would soon clear, that drinking the wine of the apple was an acquired skill, and that he hoped Weinberg had enjoyed his evening out. Weinberg agreed that he had.

The doctor said he had received Weinberg's letter with the questions Bechhofer had translated, and that he would go to Behringwerke to retrieve some technical data to help him with the answers. Though Weinberg was smarting from his apple wine hangover, he was elated.

Later in the morning, Weinberg met again with Jack Bechhofer, who took him on a tour of the Rhine valley. They stopped in a couple of villages and got back in the late afternoon. The next morning, Weinberg caught a train to Amsterdam. He had permission from Diane to spend a few days as a tourist. Amsterdam was an artistic and architectural wonder. He found the very best rijsttafel (Indonesian-style spiced rice) restaurant in the city and had an indulgent meal there, then toured the Rembrandt House Museum and walked along the canals, marveling at the simple beauty of what had been created there. He stopped in a pub and glanced at a group of attractive young women at a table nearby, laughing as he scribbled in his journal. He visited the Anne Frank House, feeling a connectedness to his family and his religion. Each evening, when Weinberg went back to his hotel, he wrote careful notes about his meetings in Germany, and what he would do upon his return to New Jersey.

It was time to go home. Weinberg flew to London. At Gatwick Airport, waiting for his flight to Newark, he wrote more in his journal. He was feeling triumphant. A trail he had been following had led him to a German university town. That he was an American Jew on German soil, finding the evidence to tell the story he now believed in so firmly, was exciting. He was hunting for truth, and in the belief that he had found it, expressed himself with what now seems to be sincere, yet naïve, exuberance: "The first fucking American lawyer to meet Dr. Schimpf, to have discourse with Dr. Heimburger. If nothing else, I am doing it differently than all who have come before. And since all who have come before have lost, perhaps it is I who have the best understanding of how to do it right. How to win. That, for God's sake, for Joe's sake, for Clyde and Andrea, their beautiful tormented child, for all of them—that is the point."

AROUND THE TIME that Weinberg was in Germany, a Florida jury decided against Armour Pharmaceuticals and awarded two million dollars to the parents of a boy with hemophilia who had died of AIDS in 1992. One he was back in the United States, Weinberg called the family's lawyer, Jere Fishback, to congratulate him, and to tell him about what he was doing. Fishback told Weinberg he had been able to establish that the child, Jason Christopher, had been infected with HIV sometime between January 1983 and May 1985, a late infection window. Fishback had argued that Armour had failed to warn Jason's doctor about the risk of HIV transmission, and that the duty to warn began at the end of 1982. The jury agreed and awarded each parent one million dollars. The two lawyers agreed to keep in touch.

But Weinberg was most anxious to share the news of his trip with the people who needed it most. He called Elena Bostick, Joe Salgado, Michael Rosenberg, Andrea Johnson, and other clients.

The information gave hope to Andrea Johnson. She was ill and trying to make it to tomorrow every day. The progress Weinberg had made meant they were winning small battles, moving into territories not yet explored, and finding what might be treasures.

Bostick was just as excited, but her perspective was different; she was as close to the hemophilia-HIV community as anyone could be without suffering from the condition herself. Bostick was their rock, their safe harbor, their mother hen. She lived her job.

From Michael Rosenberg and Joe Salgado, two men he looked to repeatedly, the reactions were grounded in intellect and faith. Michael Rosenberg knew he was dying; his brother and four close friends already were dead from AIDS. His anger was so deep Weinberg could feel it through the phone. Rosenberg would have gone to Germany if he had been physically able. Salgado had faith in God, completely and openly. He took great comfort in God's plan for him and was slow to blame or anger. So when Weinberg told him about Germany, he listened quietly, asking a question here or there.

In late January 2003, Weinberg took the Metroliner to Washington, D.C., and caught a subway from Union Station to the campus of George Washington University Medical School to meet with Dr. David Aronson, who had a laboratory and research position there. Dr. Aronson had worked at the old NIH Division of Biologics Standards, the regulatory body formerly responsible for blood plasma products, from the mid-1960s until 1972, when the office moved to the FDA. He had retired from government service in 1985 and two months later was on retainer to Cutter. Dr. Aronson had been the government's point man for clotting-factor products, assigned the primary regulatory role for industry. Now he was an expert witness for the companies.

Dr. Aronson was an important historical figure in the story of factor products, though he was essentially a midlevel bureaucrat when he retired. Together with a scientist named Robert Gerety from the National Heart, Lung, and Blood Institute (NHLBI), Dr. Aronson had organized the 1976 meeting that Weinberg had previously decided was critical to the case, the one that resulted in the report titled *Unsolved Therapeutic Problems in Hemophilia*. Many of the world's leading infectious-disease experts had attended, and the conference materials included cutting-edge scientific articles they had authored about clotting factor, hepatitis, and hemophilia.

Weinberg had read the conference publication repeatedly. His photocopy of it was so marked up that he had to make another one. The report in many respects supported his theory of the case. But to Weinberg, the most interesting part concerned a previously unknown virus, which they called non-A, non-B hepatitis, which was being transmitted to hemophilia patients. Later, non-A, non-B hepatitis would come to be known as hepatitis C.

For purposes of his theory, this report was clear, incontrovertible evidence that new viruses could erupt in blood products, making such occurrences foreseeable. It meant that government and industry both had recognized long ago that something had to be done to clean up clotting drugs.

Weinberg was interested in what Dr. Aronson knew, as the chief regulator during the 1970s, about the emerging viral risks, and what if anything the government had told the manufacturers to do about them. Dr. Aronson would have known what was being discussed by government and industry. He had published several articles and had organized and made presentations at several scientific meetings over the years.

Weinberg also wanted to find out what he knew about the Behringwerke research, and when. The company's research was in the public domain by 1979, six years before Dr. Aronson retired from the government.

Dr. Aronson was receptive when Weinberg called, and agreed to meet.

Walking across the George Washington University campus, Weinberg felt confident. In Germany, he had learned things no other lawyer knew. The way he was framing his case was new, and the industry attorneys did not understand it nearly as well, so he doubted they would have prepared Dr. Aronson for the kinds of questions he intended to ask.

Weinberg knocked on the partially opened office door, and Dr. Aronson appeared. He invited the lawyer inside.

Weinberg took in the surroundings. It was a modest office, somewhat haphazardly decorated. He thanked Dr. Aronson for agreeing to meet with him and began his questions. He had many. In particular, he asked about the report on unsolved problems in hemophilia.

Slowly, Dr. Aronson's manner changed from open and friendly to more cautious and guarded. Weinberg switched to questions about another article, but it was too late. The doctor was looking at his watch. Weinberg saw it was time to leave.

But he had what he wanted. If there was a good reason to explain why it had taken so long to cleanse clotting drugs, Dr. Aronson would have given it to him. Weinberg felt he hadn't.

But the government had done little to assist Dr. Aronson. His FDA laboratory had been minimally funded and, to Weinberg, hardly capable of fulfilling its mission to guard the public health.

Weinberg took the subway back to Union Station to catch the Amtrak train home, writing up his notes along the way.

9

Somewhere Here, I Have
the Documents

After his interviews with Drs. Aronson and Schimpf, Weinberg knew he had to find an expert to say that a process to kill viruses could have been commercially available in 1980 if not earlier. He had been thinking about how to pursue the lead Michael Rosenberg had given him about Edward Shanbrom, who had been the medical director at Baxter-Hyland, and the leader of the research team that developed the first commercial clotting-factor concentrate in the 1960s. As far as Rosenberg knew, Dr. Shanbrom had never been interviewed by lawyers from either side.

"Dr. Shanbrom could be an important witness in your case," Rosenberg urged. "He agrees, at least based on what he has said, that viral inactivation of clotting-factor concentrates was feasible before HIV entered the blood supply."

"What do you think my approach should be?" Weinberg asked. "You've told me his loyalties aren't clear. So he's a guy who knows a lot but might not say it, right?"

"Write to him," Rosenberg replied. "Just keep in mind that he is a very smart guy whose motivations might be complicated."

Through a patent search firm, Weinberg found that Dr. Shanbrom had at least twenty patents. His name was on as many patents for hemophilia clotting factor, or related products, as anyone else in the world. He was the real deal, a true expert. Several of his early patents were licensed to Baxter, but Dr. Shanbrom had left the company in the mid-1970s, and his patents from that time forward were held by him personally.

What was most interesting was that Dr. Shanbrom was a pioneer in clotting-drug cleansing. In 1980, he had submitted a patent application for a method using detergents, not heat, to kill viruses. The use of detergent was intuitive—in everyday household use, detergent had been used for decades to kill germs. Dr. Shanbrom's method was also commercially viable: the New York Blood Center, one of the largest not-for-profit manufacturers of clotting drugs, had licensed it in 1988, and the medicines manufactured using his technology had proven to be virus-free.

But would he talk to Weinberg?

There was considerable risk that even if Dr. Shanbrom was willing to criticize the industry, he would be attacked. Weinberg could almost hear the questions from the other side: Dr. Shanbrom, if it was so easy, why didn't you insist that the work be done? Did you ever notify your employer,

FIGURE 9.1. California physician and researcher Dr. Edward Shanbrom led in the development of the first Factor VIII concentrates while working for Hyland in the late 1960s. After leaving the company, he invented a highly effective method of using detergents to cleanse viruses from blood products. The rights to his process were purchased by the New York Blood Center in 1988.

Credit: University of California, Irvine.

write a memo to the file, or publish your opinions? Did you file for any patents, or intellectual property protection, for the technology you now say was "available" in the relevant time period? If so, Weinberg would need those documents.

He and Rosenberg discussed it.

"Why would a pharmaceutical company resist doing research that might lead to a competitive marketing advantage?" Weinberg asked.

"Dr. Schimpf told you there were concerns in Germany," Rosenberg reminded him, "when Behringwerke was moving forward with its inactivation program, about the effects of heat on the products, whether heat might stimulate other proteins or components of the plasma that might be harmful, and whether the products could be made on a large scale."

"Yes, but they were breaking into a market dominated by others," Weinberg replied. "Bayer and Baxter had been at it far longer."

"Well, if you had a license to produce a product and you were making profits from it, would you go to the regulators and say, make us do more work on this product before you let us sell any more of it?"

Rosenberg's point was well taken. The big four producers were all making good money. Government regulators seemed to have given them a pass on hepatitis, calling it an unavoidable risk. If the companies told the FDA they wanted to inactivate viruses, the regulators might require them to spend the time and money nailing it down. So why raise a red flag and potentially ruin a good thing?

A couple of days later, Weinberg got a call from Ron Grayzel, from the Levinson Axelrod firm. He had settled a significant asbestos case and had persuaded the firm's management committee to take another look at the hemophilia case.

Weinberg was anxious to get an agreement in place. He had not heard back from David Shrager or Wayne Spivey since their meeting two months earlier. And the telephone calls from potential hemophilia clients were pouring in, sometimes more than one a day. Weinberg told Grayzel that he was traveling to California in a few days. Grayzel wanted to meet before that. Suddenly, it seemed, he was anxious to make a deal.

Weinberg needed the help. His costs were substantial. Every minute he spent on the hemophilia litigation took away time from other cases or business development. He still had money in the bank from the swimming-pool case, and other cases that were settling, but as he was closing them out, he was replacing them with more hemophilia cases. The adage about keeping eggs in different baskets is a wise one, but he was moving toward a single basket.

So in February 1993, Weinberg set out to meet with Grayzel and one of his partners, David Wheaton, at their offices in Edison. Grayzel came into the lobby, shook hands warmly, and led Weinberg to Wheaton's office. Wheaton was one of the managing officers of the firm, and Weinberg knew him from being around the Middlesex County Courthouse. He had a reputation as a capable lawyer and nice guy. He was a sailor, and his office was decorated with boating paraphernalia. The lawyers sat down and Weinberg starting talking about the case, beginning from scratch for Wheaton.

As he was talking, Richard Levinson, the senior partner, stopped in to say hello. So their interest was real. Grayzel asked Weinberg how many clients he had; at that point it was about thirty and they were still calling. They talked about Weinberg's theory of the case. He described his trip to Germany and what he had learned from Dr. Schimpf, who he hoped might be an expert in the case. But Weinberg said he really wanted to talk to another scientist, this one from California, whom he had identified as the man largely responsible for inventing clotting-factor concentrates. He had worked for Hyland in the 1960s and also had developed virus-killing methods still in use. Weinberg said a source had told him that this scientist was willing to talk and would agree that such methods had been feasible before HIV entered the blood supply. But would he agree to serve as an expert? Weinberg didn't know but said he was about to go to California to talk to him. He promised Wheaton and Grayzel that he would call them when he returned.

Weinberg had to get Dr. Shanbrom to cooperate. Keeping in mind what Rosenberg had said, he carefully drafted a letter to the doctor. He explained who he was representing, and that his research so far indicated that it had been technically feasible to inactivate viruses before the HIV epidemic. He said he had read of Dr. Shanbrom's work, and that he had been told by Dr. Thomas Drees, a former president of Alpha Therapeutic Corporation, that the industry hadn't been interested in licensing his method. He also told him of his conversation with Dr. Aronson.

Weinberg said he was coming soon to Pasadena, near Dr. Shanbrom's home. Would he agree to a meeting then?

Weinberg already had two meetings scheduled for this California trip. One was with Dr. Drees, who had been publicly critical of his former company, one of the big four. The other was with Dr. Donald Francis, the fiery former Centers for Disease Control scientist who had been outspoken in sounding the alarm about hemophiliacs and others dying from HIV. As described in Randy Shilts's book *And the Band Played On*, Dr. Francis pounded on the table with his fist during a January 1983 meeting of government, industry, and blood-bank officials, many of whom were in denial about HIV in the nation's blood supply. "How many people have to die?" he shouted. "How many deaths do you need? Give us the threshold of death that you need in order to believe that this is happening, and we'll meet at that time and we can start doing something."[1]

The week before his flight to San Francisco, Weinberg was taking a deposition of a defense expert witness in a case he was preparing for trial. The client's husband had been killed when an electrical cabinet powering an industrial furnace had overheated and exploded, blowing open the metal doors and striking him. In the midst of the deposition, at about 10:45 A.M., Weinberg's secretary called him on the intercom.

"Dr. Shanbrom just called and left a message for you. I thought you would want to know."

Weinberg turned to the witness and his lawyer.

"I've got to return a phone call right now," he said. "I'm sorry to interrupt but let's take a short break, please."

They agreed, and Weinberg went into his office to dial the number that Dr. Shanbrom had left.

"Hello?"

"Hello, this is Eric Weinberg, returning your call."

"Yes, Mr. Weinberg. I received your letter. I take it you are interested in my work on virus inactivation in factor concentrates?"

"I am. The families I represent have asked me to investigate whether their HIV infections were avoidable. Once I learned that the timing of the epidemic was, for the most part, prior to 1983, it appeared to me that their recourse was to establish that the fractionators failed to adequately research and develop clean clotting factor. I've been chasing that theory for some time. It led me to you."

"I know something about that, of course," said Dr. Shanbrom. "I developed a process to inactivate viruses and offered it to the fractionators many years ago. They were not interested and I ended up selling it to the New York Blood Center, where it is still being used."

"When did you develop it?"

"I started thinking about the problem before I left Hyland. I filed an application for a patent in 1980."

"For the detergent process?"

"That is correct."

"The detergent process kills hepatitis and HIV?"

"Indeed it does," Dr. Shanbrom said. "The New York Blood Center tried to patent the same process but their application was turned down. They were aware of my work that proved detergents do work. They contacted me and we worked out a deal to license my patent. It was adversarial at first, but we became friends. If you want to find their method in the literature, you can search Horowitz or Prince."

"I will."

"I have been wondering when a lawyer for the plaintiffs would contact me. Everything you wrote in your letter is correct. Hepatitis B was a medical problem that required a solution, but many of the patients had developed antibodies after infections before using the concentrates. It was when antibody-positive hemophiliacs developed new-onset hepatitis symptoms that I realized we had another problem. Of course, AIDS was not known then."

"But foreseeable," Weinberg added.

"I understand your theory, and it has merit."

"Dr. Shanbrom, I've stepped out of a deposition to speak with you and I am being rude to counsel and the witness, but I would very much like to continue this conversation with you. I'm planning on being in California next week. Would it be possible to meet with you while I am there?"

"Yes, I think so. Why don't you call me back in a couple of days? I have to speak with counsel. I have the greatest sympathy for your clients."

"I'll call you on February 27, if that is okay? I'll be in California then," Weinberg said.

"That will be fine."

"May I compensate you for your time?"

"I'm not interested in taking money from you," Dr. Shanbrom said. "By the way, how old are you?"

"I'm thirty-seven."

"Hmm. You're young."

Weinberg returned to his deposition, elated. Later, when he had time to think, he had the feeling, as Rosenberg had predicted, that Dr. Shanbrom was going to be complicated. He had mentioned, for example, that he needed to talk to a lawyer. Yet he had confirmed Weinberg's theory. He was as expert as anyone in the world, and agreed that everything Weinberg wrote to him was true.

WEINBERG MET in San Francisco with Dr. Francis on February 26, 1993. Dr. Francis had already testified in cases for plaintiffs and was a hero in the hemophilia community. He agreed to testify in Weinberg's cases, too. He was a "warnings" expert, who would say that there was reasonable evidence by the middle of 1982 that the new disease was likely blood borne, based upon its similarities to hepatitis B. He had been frustrated in his role as an infectious disease epidemiologist at the CDC. He thought someone in a position of responsibility would listen when he publicly demanded that steps to be taken to improve the safety of the blood supply. Yet he did not anticipate the resistance of the blood bankers and industry. He knew, and would say, that an opportunity to warn hemophiliacs and others was missed. He could not help, however, on the question of safer design of clotting factor concentrates. Whether the products could have been cleansed sooner, and how, was outside his area of expertise.

Weinberg called Dr. Shanbrom again the day after meeting with Dr. Francis.

"Are you in California?" he asked.

"Yes, San Francisco," Weinberg replied. "I'm flying to Los Angeles on Monday. I'm meeting with Tom Drees in the morning and then I plan to come see you."

"Drees can say what they were doing at Alpha. His chief scientist used to work for me."

"Did they consider using your methods?"

"They do calculations to say it's not a problem, so they don't need to change. I spent years talking to them. I was also talking to the New York Blood Center. They had published on some methods that didn't work. But my son was killed in 1986, seven years ago, and for a long time after that, I wasn't really able to focus on anything."

"I'm sorry," Weinberg said.

"Thank you. By the way, I discussed your letter with an attorney from Baxter."

"Who is the attorney?" Weinberg asked.

"It's not important. He told me to tell you the truth."

"That's good. I'll see you in a couple of days."

"I think your premise is a correct one," Dr. Shanbrom added. "For a long time, nothing was done. I feel responsible for that."

Weinberg's meeting with Dr. Drees was on the morning of March 1. He agreed with the lawyer's theory, saying that viral inactivation of clotting products was not a priority for his company in the 1970s because the industry, doctors, and patients were not so concerned about hepatitis. Dr. Drees had general knowledge about Alpha's viral inactivation project, but not enough to be meaningful to the case. He seemed earnest and knowledgeable, but Weinberg didn't want an expert who couldn't hold up to cross-examination. He thanked Dr. Drees for meeting with him. By the time he got home, Weinberg had a bill from him for one thousand dollars for their one-hour session.

Weinberg drove south from Los Angeles to Orange County, for the meeting with Dr. Shanbrom. On the way, he picked up the Sunday *Los Angeles Times*. On the first page of the Orange County news section was an article about Helen Shanbrom, wife of Dr. Edward Shanbrom, who had become an activist for truck safety after their youngest son, David, had been killed when his car was hit by a truck on a California highway. The article reported a steep decline in highway fatalities involving trucks in the five years since Mrs. Shanbrom had become an advocate for trucking safety. She, too, had made a difference.

Weinberg arrived at the Shanbroms' home in Santa Ana in the afternoon. The house was perched on a large hill with an expansive view of the valley below. He pulled into the driveway and Dr. Shanbrom came out to meet him. He was fit and trim, handsome, in his sixties, with gray hair and mustache, and carried himself with assurance. He greeted Weinberg cordially.

"Come inside," he said. "You can meet my wife, and then we'll talk."

Their home was modern, with an open floor plan and wide windows. Light streamed into the living room, illuminating the paintings on the walls and a collection of sculptures. Mrs. Shanbrom greeted Weinberg and asked if he would like coffee, which he accepted. Dr. Shanbrom excused himself for a moment—he had a call to take—and his wife and Weinberg sat in the airy kitchen and chatted. Dr. Shanbrom returned a few minutes later.

"I'm sorry—I had to take that call," Dr. Shanbrom said as he strode back into the room. "Let me show you my office and laboratory."

Weinberg followed him downstairs for a tour. Then they went outside, to sit in the sun on a patio overlooking the valley.

"So, why don't you ask me a question and I'll answer it, and we'll see where the discussion takes us?" Dr. Shanbrom said.

"Let's start at the beginning," Weinberg said. "How did you get involved in developing blood products?"

"I was recruited by the president of Hyland Laboratories sometime in the early 1960s. I was practicing medicine here, and Hyland was here, and they were looking for a medical director. I had an interest in inventing things, I guess, so he wanted me. And I joined. Soon after, I was sent up to Stanford, to meet Judy Pool. You know who she was? She discovered cryoprecipitate, and Hyland was in the plasma-fraction business. We made albumin, intramuscular gamma globulin, and other products."

"Was the albumin heat treated to remove viruses?" Weinberg asked.

"For hepatitis, yes. In water baths," Dr. Shanbrom replied.

"Heated in liquid state with stabilizers to protect the protein?"

"Correct," Dr. Shanbrom said. "At Hyland, we had a doctor named Murray Thelin, who was himself a hemophiliac, and Fred Marquardt, the president, brought me in to work with Murray, to find a way to commercially manufacture a product. We were successful in developing the first lyophilized product in 1968 or so, for the treatment of hemophilia A. We called it Factor VIII, for the protein missing in hemophilia A. Unfortunately, Murray had died by that time, of a heart attack."

"Was the product heat treated?"

"No," said Dr. Shanbrom. "The prevailing belief at the time was that hemophiliacs were exposed to hepatitis already. There wasn't a compelling need to kill hepatitis in clotting factor because it was in cryoprecipitate and they were infected anyway. That's what we thought at the time."

"Did things change?"

"Yes, at least from my point of view. I was the medical director, so my focus was on more than sales. We were giving the product to patients locally, in Los Angeles, and we saw that patients who already had antibodies to hepatitis B were getting acutely sick again. How could this be? Then we began to see that the workers in the plasma-fractionation plants were getting sick, too. Many of them also had antibodies to hepatitis B."

"This was years before scientists posited a new hepatitis virus," Weinberg noted.

"Yes, we were probably the first to realize that there was a different hepatitis that was so prevalent in the pools of plasma being mixed in the vats that it became airborne in plasma mists. So I came to the medical conclusion, based on the evidence we had at the time, that these products had the potential to transmit another kind of virus, one we did not know about yet, and that they were dangerous, because the virus was concentrated in the plasma pools."

"You came to this conclusion when you were medical director at Hyland?"

"I did."

Weinberg knew this was important. It meant that the company had knowledge of a previously unknown virus in its products in the early days of production and marketing.

"What did you do?" Weinberg asked.

Dr. Shanbrom then said something that he would say again and again, over the next four years, as Weinberg tried to persuade him to produce the evidence.

"Somewhere here, I have the documents," he said.

"What documents?"

"I expressed my concerns in writing," Dr. Shanbrom said. "This would have been around 1970 or so. One of the problems with these companies is they don't look into the future. The executives have short-term vision. They're more concerned with how they look to the board of directors. It's about now, not tomorrow. I had begun to look more closely at the sources of plasma Hyland was using to manufacture the clotting factor, and it concerned me."

"Why?"

"We were getting human plasma from some dubious places," Dr. Shanbrom replied. "The plasma center in Los Angeles was smack in the middle of Skid Row, the worst neighborhood in the city, and we were paying alcoholics and drug addicts for plasma. As bad as the city centers were, the prison centers were even worse. We had a huge plasma center at Angola Penitentiary in Louisiana. You should investigate it. Hepatitis was rampant there. It was a farm, and the prisoners fertilized the crops with human waste that came from infected prisoners. Everyone in the prison was infected, and we bought plasma from Angola and used it to manufacture clotting factor. I raised this issue, but the executives weren't interested in my concerns."

"So what happened?"

"I was removed as medical director, and given a consulting position with the company," Dr. Shanbrom replied. "They sent me to Illinois to consult for Baxter. It was really a deprogramming mission. I was let go by Baxter in 1972 and started to do my own research here."

"Did you communicate with the regulators at the Division of Biologics Standards?" Weinberg asked. "Because from what I've seen, there was concern about hepatitis at DBS, expressed to Baxter, and Baxter sort of minimized the risks. In fact, when Baxter applied for its Factor IX license, there was a decision not to mention hepatitis at all, because the company thought FDA would become preoccupied with the problem once Baxter ran it up the flagpole."

"No, I was out of that loop," said Dr. Shanbrom. "So when I left, I worked on different aspects of clotting-factor production. The idea was to have a purified, clean product, and that was my focus. I have some patents on that, which I licensed to industry."

"When did you start to think about viral inactivation?"

"I was working for Merck in the mid-1970s, say around 1974 or '75, on vaccines. I read the scientific literature regarding the production of

killed- and attenuated-virus vaccines. I learned about the use of detergents to kill viruses in the production of vaccines and had the idea that
the same approach could be used with clotting-factor products. That's
when it started."

"And you applied for a patent for inactivating virus in clotting factor
using detergent in October of 1980, right?"

"Seems so," he said.

"Did you do any work for the fractionators on the detergent
process?"

"I approached all of them," Dr. Shanbrom said. "They were not
interested."

"When?"

"I don't recall. I'm sure it's in my documents."

"Would it be possible for me to look at your documents,
Dr. Shanbrom?"

"Perhaps," he said, "but not today. I have to find them."

10

More Lawyers, More Experts

Weinberg's interviews in California were almost done. He had one more to go, with an old friend and client. His journal entry for March 2, 1993: "Again, after two-plus years, at Wilma's on Balboa. I'll see Patrick in a while. Time to get my ducks in a row. Really tough; pitfalls at every turn. Francis will help, but is he the saint he seemed to be? Or is Shanbrom—and will he be the one? And how do I turn him around?"

March 2 broke as a brilliantly cool and sunny California winter day. Weinberg drove over the bridge from his hotel to Wilma's on Balboa Island for breakfast. His friend and client, Patrick, the airline pilot rendered quadriplegic in the swimming-pool accident, was living with his mother at the family home near Newport. Weinberg finished breakfast and drove to Patrick's home, a tract house in a development. It was good to see him; it had been nearly two years since the trial. He was in good spirits, happy to see Weinberg, and assured him that he was doing okay. But it was sobering to see him, a guy he had known before his injury, a pilot, a vibrant young man, now reduced to being an invalid completely dependent on others to survive.

Patrick's mother and brother were there, and they spent a couple of hours talking and looking at family pictures. Pat was the eldest of three brothers, and from the time Weinberg had first met him, he had been strong for his family. But with Weinberg, one on one, he would let his guard down. He knew he was in a bad way. He was anxious about the things people who cannot care for themselves are anxious about—catheters, skin breakdown—but was most concerned with burdening his family. After dinner Weinberg left him, his mind imprinted with the image of those frail and useless hands that once worked the controls of jet airplanes.

Weinberg flew home from John Wayne International Airport in Orange County. On the plane, he closed his eyes and thought about his sons. Mickey D was nearly five months old. He missed him and his brothers terribly. The older brothers, Diane told her husband, took seriously their obligation to help out while their father was away. Jake would be six in April, and Arnie was four and a half. The more time Weinberg spent on the road, the less he spent with them. The same was true of the courthouse. Money was always a concern, and neither Weinberg nor his wife had fully understood how long this litigation would take. But Diane, who was staying home full time even as she received multiple calls from recruiters, remained fully on board. She believed in him and the case, and he took her faith in both seriously.

So Weinberg felt invigorated. He had been trained as a prosecutor, and she as a microbiologist. Both liked to work a case, to read, to research, to uncover. He also did not like the patronizing attitudes of the industry's big-firm lawyers, whose condescension he believed was by design. By belittling his case, they could throw him off stride. They weren't sure exactly what Weinberg was up to, so were determined to make him doubt himself. But he had the feeling, flying high on the plane, that he would win.

Besides, he had found an excellent expert in his own backyard. Dr. Donald T. Dubin was a professor of molecular genetics and microbiology at the University of Medicine and Dentistry of New Jersey–Robert Wood Johnson Medical School, and director of the medical school's viral culture and HIV facility. He also was a member of the scientific advisory board of AmFAR, the American Foundation for AIDS Research. He was a distinguished physician and academic, educated at Harvard and Columbia, and had published and presented his research extensively.

By examining their medical records, Dr. Dubin could tell Weinberg the likely dates when many of his clients were infected with HIV, since the hospital had done these tests as a matter of routine. Johnson, Niederman, and Weiss, for example, were among the Robert Wood Johnson patients whose blood samples were frozen at the hospital. This information was crucial, in no small part because Judge Pisano had ordered Weinberg to find it, then hand it over to the industry lawyers immediately.

Weinberg met with Dr. Dubin in his office at the Waksman Institute of Microbiology in Piscataway, across from the Rutgers Golf Course. He was in his early seventies, somewhat short, a bit round, and very pleasant and friendly, with a quick smile. His office was filled with books, papers, pictures, and boxes. He invited the lawyer to sit on a small leather couch, and sat across from him. Together, they reviewed the information that Weinberg needed.

Weinberg followed up by sending Dr. Dubin more information about his clients. Among them were three wives who had been inadvertently infected by their HIV-positive husbands.

In March 1993, a case management conference and motion hearing was scheduled before Magistrate Judge Pisano in the Newark Federal Courthouse. At the previous conference, the judge had been rather testy in ordering Weinberg to expedite the handing over of information. He had produced some information, but the defendants were not satisfied and had filed applications for sanctions and dismissal of the complaints. Weinberg filed responses, and now had the experts he needed to move forward.

The company lawyers were huddling, as usual, in the hallway outside the courtroom. They greeted Weinberg courteously and he responded, then went inside to set up his files on the table nearest the jury box—always where the plaintiff sits. Everyone was ready. Judge Pisano entered and took his seat up on the bench.

"Good morning, counsel," he said.

The lawyers responded in chorus. "Good morning, Your Honor."

"When we were last here, on January 11, I considered adjourning today's conference. However, as I've given more thought to the matter, I think these sixty-day conferences can help us focus this litigation. We are behind, and so I intend today to establish an expedited schedule for discovery. Let me hear from defense counsel first."

Ed Matthews spoke first, for Cutter. He was an experienced and respected defense attorney.

"Thank you, your Honor. I'm still not sure what the plaintiffs' theories are in this case. I'm not sure the product liability theory is grounded in the facts or the law. For example, we still need to establish a date of seroconversion for each of the plaintiffs. This is a very important part of the case and we've been asking for eighteen months, and have not been responded to."

"It is not my intention to make the defendants wait any longer," said Judge Pisano. "Ms. Sharko, what else?"

Susan Sharko was local counsel for Armour. She pointed out that Weinberg had promised to produce all product identification evidence within forty-five days of the previous conference, but she was still waiting. Nor had Weinberg handed over the suggested dates of seroconversion of his clients. She asked the judge to permit the defense lawyers to file motions for dismissal, unless Weinberg could produce what he had promised, and award monetary sanctions against the plaintiffs if he didn't follow through.

"Thank you," said the judge. "Mr. Weinberg?"

"Your Honor, I assure the Court and counsel that I have been working diligently to provide the information requested. I understand the Court's concerns about moving this case forward and providing the defendants with the information they seek. As the Court is aware, the theory of liability I have articulated is novel. As to the immediate issues, I wish to advise the Court that I have retained an expert, Dr. Donald Dubin, who is currently a professor of molecular genetics and microbiology at the Waksman Institute, certainly a person with world-class credentials, who will be prepared to offer opinions as to dates of seroconversion of the plaintiffs within very short order. Furthermore, I make a proffer to the Court that I have identified potential witnesses who will lend credence to the notion that development of virally safe products was feasible long before HIV entered the blood supply. I have met with scientists and physicians in Europe and in the United States who have confirmed to me that the basic premise of the plaintiffs' cases has merit. For example, the evidence of a new, previously unknown virus transmitted in concentrates first arose in the early 1970s, when the fractionators recognized what was then called non-A non-B hepatitis, now known as hepatitis C. There were methods of inactivation, including heat and detergents, yet the defendants took little if any action to develop them to clean up the concentrates.

"I understand that this process has taken longer than the Court and counsel have liked, and for that matter longer than I have liked," Weinberg continued. "But I would ask the Court to keep in mind that the issues in these cases are critically important not only for these three families, but for thousands more. Literally every person with hemophilia who was infected with HIV could have a basis to proceed against an entire industry that failed to protect them from harm. Given the complexity of the issues and the magnitude of the litigation, I would ask the Court to deny the defendants' motions and permit these matters to proceed."

"Thank you," said Judge Pisano. He had a different tone than Weinberg had heard before. "While there are some arguments under Rule II, I don't know that you can be blamed, Mr. Weinberg. I believe there is some prejudice, and there has been some fumbling, but you have raised meaningful issues to the Court, and I am inclined to let you proceed. However, you will be compelled to put up or shut up. So, you will file amended complaints in these matters within fourteen days, and you will state the causes of action upon which we shall proceed. Take out any surplusage. Put in the meat of the cases.

"Within sixty days, Mr. Weinberg, you will produce to the defendants evidence of the seroconversion dates of each of the three plaintiffs or their decedents. You will also produce all of the evidence you have of product identification—that is the brands of clotting-factor concentrate used by the plaintiffs prior to seroconversion. The parties will prepare a database of product usage, and it will be agreed upon, so the issue of what product was used and when it was used will not be in dispute.

"For the record," Judge Pisano added, "I am denying the defendants' applications without prejudice. There needs to be more direction in this litigation, counsel. I expect to see it. That is all. Thank you."

Weinberg was pleased. The judge was getting it. And he could sense growing concern on the other side.

In late March, Weinberg finally settled a case he had been preparing for trial. The client, James, had been working on a construction site in North Plainfield, laying storm drainage pipe in a thirty-foot-deep trench. The owners of the property and their contractor were supposed to ensure that the worksite was safe. However, the drainage system was inadequate, and the trench was not properly shored or braced. It also had water in it. As a result, it was dangerously unstable. While James was working at the bottom of the trench one morning in November 1989, the upper sections of the trench collapsed, and he was buried alive.

Although he survived, James suffered extensive injuries, including spinal and rib fractures, and chest injuries resulting in permanent respiratory problems. The defendants had argued they were not responsible for the condition of the worksite. A week before trial, the defendants offered $700,000 to James, who agreed to accept it, and Weinberg prepared the paperwork. His fee was $185,000, an especially substantial amount in 1993. Yet, once again, he was closing out a good case and replacing it with another hemophilia-HIV claim. Even more eggs were in one basket now, but he felt there was nothing he could do about it.

He wrote again to Dr. Shanbrom, telling him that he had let Judge Pisano know about some of the information the doctor had given him on his early interactions with industry—and that the judge was impressed enough to change his view on Weinberg's arguments.

Again, he asked Dr. Shanbrom to provide the documents he had mentioned during their meeting. He also asked if Dr. Shanbrom would be willing to consult with Dr. Dubin.

Meanwhile, the lawyers he had been working with informally on the hemophilia litigation were beginning to interact with one another, forming a group. They decided to meet in Dallas on April 13. The meeting was hosted by Charles Siegel, a partner in a Dallas law firm that represented a group of Costa Rican hemophiliacs who were infected with HIV via clotting drugs in 1985, when industry couldn't sell unheated products in the United States anymore.

The lawsuit alleged that Cutter had sold the unheated clotting drugs, made from plasma that had not been subjected to screening tests, in Costa Rica at a time when heat-treated products and screening tests were available or about to be available. The Costa Ricans had been advised of none of this, according to the lawsuit.

In addition to Weinberg, others at the Dallas meeting included Charles "Chuck" Kozak, a retired marine, who had been fighting with the fractionators for several years and was fiercely dedicated to the case. Jan Adams, from St. Louis, was a former paralegal who, after raising her children, had finished college and law school. She had family members with hemophilia and had persuaded her boss, a well-regarded trial lawyer named Jim Halloran, to become involved in the litigation. Also attending was a contingent of lawyers from Florida who had been involved in these cases since the 1980s, including Bob Parks, who had represented the Ray brothers and had opened his files to Weinberg. Judy Kavanaugh, who had been cocounsel with Parks in the Ray case, was there as well. So was Debra Thomas, who worked in Chicago for Leonard Ring, one of the country's great trial lawyers.

David Shrager and Wayne Spivey did not come to the meeting. They were still trying to decide whether to get involved.

Jere Fishback joined by telephone and walked everyone through his case involving Jason Christopher, who had died from AIDS complications in 1992. A jury had awarded the Christopher family more than two million dollars in damages against Armour, but the company was appealing.

Fishback had used incriminating internal documents to convince the jury that the company should have warned physicians about the risks of HIV by December 1982. Born in 1981, Jason, who had suffered from moderate hemophilia, had used no clotting factor before July 1982, and a relatively minimal amount prior to July 1983. Jason's pediatrician had testified that he would not have prescribed clotting factor to Jason if he had known about the risk. The jury had agreed with the argument that, under federal law, the company had a "duty to warn" by the end of 1982. Fishback agreed that a different strategy would be required to win for patients who were infected in 1982 or earlier.

Charles Siegel played a videotape that summarized his Costa Rican cases. The companies were defending themselves by suggesting that his clients could have been HIV-positive before 1985. They didn't want to directly address the facts: they had sold HIV-tainted products in Costa Rica and several other countries after the FDA had belatedly asked—not ordered—them to halt sales in the United States.

But the trickiest question, the lawyers agreed, was what expert could testify that killing viruses in these products was possible earlier.

Trial lawyers tend to have strong egos and beliefs and are not easily persuaded to give up on ideas they think will work. Still, they wanted to explore how their views might dovetail into a single, winning theory. So there was unanimous agreement to meet again, and to continue sharing information.

Weinberg returned to New Jersey with another to-do list. For starters, he would have to search the medical literature to find every reference, from the 1960s forward, of the need to cleanse clotting drugs. Who from the medical community had publicly called upon the fractionators to do this?

"I told him you had been here to see me. He wanted to know what I told you," Dr. Shanbrom said. "So I told him. Then he wanted to know what I was going to do. I told him I was going to tell anyone who asked me what I knew."

"Did he ask about your work on inactivation of viruses in clotting-factor concentrates?"

"Not much," Dr. Shanbrom replied. "But there were other lawyers. I'm working on a method to inactivate hepatitis A, and the companies are interested. There was recently an outbreak of hepatitis A in blood products in Germany. We are negotiating, and some, what I will call implied threats, have been made in the context of the negotiations."

"What kind of threats?"

"Implied," Dr. Shanbrom repeated. "That my cooperation with you is problematic, I suppose."

Weinberg questioned Dr. Shanbrom closely. How many other lawyers? Who were they? Besides Limbacher, there were three more. Dr. Shanbrom said he couldn't remember the names of two of them. But the third was Duncan Barr, the national counsel for Cutter. Barr was formidable, a highly effective advocate who had dominated the litigation and provided key witnesses such as Drs. Aledort, Aronson, and Margaret Hilgartner, a prominent treating physician.

According to Dr. Shanbrom, Barr had remarked that he had been litigating hemophilia HIV cases for nearly a decade and had never heard of Dr. Shanbrom until recently.

"How do you think he learned about you?" Weinberg asked.

"He probably found out from someone at Baxter," Shanbrom replied. "I am in touch with Baxter people frequently. I'm continuing to work on improvements to the products. I mentioned to you my research on iodine treatments."

Dr. Shanbrom liked to dodge. Weinberg had not asked him to keep their meeting confidential, and he doubted that the doctor would have agreed to that.

Two days later, he called Weinberg again.

"Do you know this lawyer in Hawaii who has named me as an expert witness?"

"What?"

"The industry lawyers are suggesting to me that they will not approve any contracts to license my new methods of sterilization because some plaintiff's lawyer in Hawaii submitted my name as an expert witness," Dr. Shanbrom said. "Do you know about this?"

"No," Weinberg said. "But I'll find out." He figured it must be Chuck Kozak.

"I'm not going to voluntarily testify for anyone," Dr. Shanbrom said. "You can subpoena me and I'll tell the truth to anyone who asks. I don't like being threatened by anyone. If they think they can blackball me, they're wrong."

"I'll work on it," Weinberg promised.

"You should obtain an intermediary, an expert I can talk to. I can give him information about my work and the industry response."

"OK. I think Dr. Dubin would be perfect for that role," Weinberg said.

Dr. Shanbrom also told Weinberg about two former Baxter employees who might be willing to talk to him. One was a technician who had worked on clotting-factor concentrates. The other had worked in plasma procurement.

When they had talked in his home months earlier, Weinberg had known that Dr. Shanbrom would be a challenge. He thought, though, that the man wanted to help, and that he had forged a connection with him. Now, Weinberg was getting another dose of reality.

In retrospect, Weinberg thought that perhaps he should have pushed harder that day to get those elusive documents and a sworn statement, or forget about them and move on. Instead, he closed the conversation and hoped that in time, Dr. Shanbrom would state on the record what he had said privately.

IN LATE APRIL, Debra Thomas called Weinberg to say that she and Leonard Ring wanted to meet with him. Could he come to Chicago? Weinberg was honored to be summoned by Ring. On May 21, he flew to Chicago and took a cab to their office. Thomas met him in the lobby and brought him to see Ring. He sat at his desk in a large corner office, and stood to greet Weinberg.

Ring represented the estate of Stephen Poole, a hemophiliac who had died of HIV-related illness in 1987, leaving his widow, Peggy Gruca, and two young children. Ring was preparing the Poole case for trial in late 1993.

"Debra tells me you might have access to an important witness," Ring said.

"Yes, Dr. Shanbrom," Weinberg said. "I met him at his home a few months ago. I hope he can help us. But it's not simple with him."

Ring chuckled softly. "It never is."

Ring said he had another possible witness: Heiner Trobisch, a former Behringwerke scientist.

"We were pleased to have retained him, but presenting his testimony, as you say, will not be simple," Ring said.

"Are you trying to prove to the jury that the product was defective?" Weinberg asked.

"Negligent failure to sterilize it," Ring replied. "Trobisch is a good man but we are at risk with only his testimony. He will give ground we can't afford to give, I'm afraid. How can we find out whether Shanbrom will testify, and if he will, what he will say?"

"When I met with him, he told me he had documents that proved he had offered his methods to industry," Weinberg said. "The patents are a bit late for our purposes, but he claims to have had dialogue with industry before the patents were filed. I asked him for the documents, and he said he would get to them in time."

"Indeed. Here is lunch. Debra has to be in court this afternoon so unfortunately won't be able to join us."

Ring and Weinberg sat at his conference table, forty floors above Lake Michigan and the busy streets below. They talked for an hour about their practices, families, and interests. Ring said he was the only senior partner, with twenty junior partners, but none had a vote. When he wanted to have a "partners' meeting," he would get into his chauffeured car alone, have the driver cruise around town, talk to himself for half an hour, and then take the only vote that counted.

Weinberg told Ring he would reach out again to Dr. Shanbrom and do his best to persuade him to produce his documents, and testify in Ring's trial.

When he returned to New Jersey, he went through his interview notes about Dr. Shanbrom. He decided to call the two former Baxter employees that the doctor had recommended: the technician who supposedly would verify Dr. Shanbrom's efforts to develop a cleaner concentrate, and the plasma procurement expert who he said would confirm his concerns over paid donors.

Weinberg started with the technician, who agreed to speak with him. He didn't know exactly what to ask the man since Dr. Shanbrom hadn't given him much direction. So he began with the development of clotting-factor concentrates. Hadn't the technology to inactivate viruses existed at the time these products were developed, and wasn't it true that the industry did not research or develop these methods soon enough?

The technician replied that he wasn't so sure. For example, research-ers had, in fact, experimented with viral inactivation as far back as the 1940s, when they tried UV radiation in albumin. It did not kill hepatitis. The same issue would have applied to factor concentrates.

Weinberg switched to Dr. Shanbrom's solvent-detergent method. Was it true, as Dr. Shanbrom had insisted, that the companies weren't interested until it was too late?

The technician sighed. You have to consider Ed's sense of timing, and the number of projects he worked on simultaneously, he said. Dr. Shanbrom had a tendency to spread himself very broadly, making it hard for companies to justify buying in to all of his ideas.

And it wasn't as if the research leaders didn't care about the hepatitis problem, he added. They very much did. He noted that Dr. Murray Thelin, who helped develop the concentrates at Hyland in the 1960s, suffered from severe hemophilia. He was the company's first hemophilia patient, testing the product on himself.[2] Researchers at other companies also suf-fered from hemophilia, or had family members who did. They had every reason, personal and professional, to want the products to be safe.

Dr. Shanbrom, the technician said, sometimes proposed ideas with little evidence to back them up. Not all of them panned out.

This was not how Weinberg had anticipated the conversation would go.

Surely, he pressed, the industry did not consider it a priority to clean up the products before HIV.

The technician disagreed. It didn't make sense for any company to kill its customers, he said. But it wasn't just a question of timing—there was cost to consider as well. If the manufacturing costs were exorbitantly high, would society be able to pay for it?

The conversation was disconcerting to Weinberg. He thought the technician would confirm what Dr. Shanbrom had said. Instead, although the man acknowledged and complimented Dr. Shanbrom's creativity, he painted a picture of an eccentric and somewhat scattershot inventor. Dr. Shanbrom's credentials were impeccable, but his choice of this technician as a reference gave Weinberg serious pause.

Next, he contacted the second man, Charles Smiley. He was a fascinating guy. He had been on the scene at the outset of the U.S. blood-banking industry, right after World War II. Smiley told Weinberg that he had helped open a blood bank in Nashville in 1945. He returned to California to attend the University of California at Berkeley. In 1950, he was offered a job running the not-for-profit community blood bank in Oakland. He was responsible for all aspects of its operation, became involved in blood-banking organizations, and came to know Dr. Judith Pool.

In 1964, the same year Dr. Pool discovered cryoprecipitate, the president of Hyland Therapeutics, Fred Marquardt, offered Smiley a job. Hyland operated one plasma donor center, in downtown Los Angeles. At the time, Hyland was getting most of its plasma from unpaid donors at community blood centers, Smiley said. Marquardt wanted to expand the operation, and Smiley built up the procurement system by opening plasmapheresis centers where donors would be paid cash. By the time Smiley retired in 1984, there were 450 licensed plasmapheresis centers in the world. Hyland owned 36 of them and also bought plasma from a large number of contractors. Plasma procurement thus became a big business, because human plasma was an incredibly valuable commodity.

Weinberg asked Smiley whether, in terms of product safety, there were differences between the not-for-profit and for-profit plasma centers.

"We did all of the testing and screening of viruses known to be effective at the time. We had MDs in all of our centers," he said. "I delivered raw material to Hyland, and then I had no more to do with it."

"Did you have concerns that the paid donors might be more likely to transmit infectious diseases? Was it a concern when a new hepatitis virus was theoretically in the blood that other safety issues could arise?"

Smiley paused. "If there was something we felt had a potential risk, if there was anything we knew would interfere with a good product, we'd deal with it," he replied. "You're asking me if we were clairvoyant. We had no suspicion about other agents. In 1982, when HIV was found, we learned that it was coming from homosexuals, drug addicts sharing hypodermic needles, and Haitians."

"But before that, was there concern about the risks of hepatitis with concentrate infusion?" Weinberg asked.

"I have very deep, ingrained principles," Smiley said. "I did the best I could, the best I knew. You don't get a second chance when you're dealing with people's health and safety."

"So was there an effort to clean the concentrates before HIV?" Weinberg pressed.

"Do you have a jack in your car?"

"Yes."

"You'd be mad as hell if you got a car without a jack. You hope you never have to use it, but you want to protect yourself before you need protection. The product was brought to the door as safe as I could do it. But safety has to be part of the next step, too."

"Did Dr. Shanbrom push to kill the viruses before HIV?"

"Ed was a very conscientious person," Smiley said. "He would not like to drive without a jack, either. He developed an improved product. I don't recall exactly when. Does that answer your question?"

"It does."

"I worked in laboratories for years," Smiley added. "I was a licensed clinical lab technologist. It was how I paid for my education. I understood and knew what could happen if something wasn't done right in a blood transfusion. A lot depended on my anticipating what could go wrong. My job was to deliver the safest blood."

"How about the concentrates?"

He paused again. "There came a time," he said, "and I can't recall when, when we realized the smaller the pool, the less the risk. It was in 1983, I think, when the community blood banks went back to single-donor products because we all thought there was less risk. I cared about the hemophiliacs, too—I worked with the Hemophilia Foundation in Oakland and in Los Angeles."

"I understand," Weinberg said. "I appreciate the time."

Smiley, like the technician, was a mixed bag. He did not verify what Dr. Shanbrom had said. Weinberg still did not have a clear picture of what Dr. Shanbrom would say under oath, whether he could help the case, or whether the doctor was playing him. If Weinberg was going to help get the evidence that Leonard Ring needed for his trial, he still had a long way to go.

11

A Meeting with Roger

The 1993 baseball season was well underway. The Yankees were looking pretty good so far, although their pitching was suspect. But with guys like All-Stars Don "The Hit Man" Mattingly, Paul O'Neill, and Bernie Williams in the starting lineup, they were a threat at bat and on the field. You could never count them out, certainly not this early.

In late May, a nine-year-boy named Roger Holt came to Weinberg's office with his grandmother, Dee Crooker, a registered nurse, who had custody of Roger. He was gangly and puppyish and wore a Mets baseball cap. He was born in 1983 and not diagnosed with hemophilia until late 1984, when heat-treated clotting products were already on the market. But he had been given underheated medicine that contained live AIDS virus.

"I've heard you are helping people," Crooker said. "I wanted to see if you might be able to help us."

Weinberg had spoken to her by telephone already, and knew something about Roger's situation. He was HIV-positive and frequently ill. His T-cell ratios, a calculation based on the number of white blood cells crucial to the immune system, were poor. This meant he was becoming more and more susceptible to infection. His prognosis was grim.

Weinberg's three boys were a little younger than Roger. Jake was six. Weinberg was his T-ball coach and was proud of his son's natural baseball swing. Arnie was four and an authority on bugs of all sorts. Mike was almost a year old, chubby with long blond curls. Now, here was Roger, an innocent kid infected with a deadly virus, accompanied by his grandmother, her life devoted to keeping him alive.

"I think I can help," Weinberg said. "There are no guarantees. This will be hard."

"We're not here for miracles," Crooker said. "We need someone on our side."

Roger was looking at the pictures of Weinberg's boys.

"That's Jake," Weinberg said. "He's a baseball player."

Roger smiled but didn't say anything. Weinberg looked at Crooker and saw her eyes filling with tears.

"Dee, would it be OK if Roger and I just sat together here and got to know each other a little? You know, just us guys?"

She managed a weak smile. "That would be nice," she said.

"Michelle can make you a cup of coffee," Weinberg said.

Crooker thanked him and told Roger she was going outside for some air and that he should sit with Weinberg for a while. Roger watched her leave and then looked again at Jake's photo.

"How old is he?"

"Six," Weinberg said. "How old are you?"

"Nine."

"Wow. You're big for nine, aren't you?"

"I don't know. I guess so," Roger said with a shrug.

"Do you play baseball?"

"Yes."

"What position do you play?"

"Usually first base," Roger said. "Sometimes I pitch. I missed some games when I was in the hospital."

"Has that happened a lot?"

"Yeah, pretty much," said Roger. "It's 'cause I'm sick."

"I know. That must be no fun at all."

"It's only sometimes. How old is he?" Roger was pointing to a picture of Arnie.

"He's four, almost five," Weinberg replied. "I have three sons. Mike is the third. He's only ten months old."

"I wish I had a baby brother."

"I'll bet you would be a great brother."

"Yeah," Roger said.

"So I guess you're a Mets fan?" Weinberg asked.

"How did you know?"

"I can figure things out. Some guys just look like Mets fans. Actually, I looked at your baseball cap. It says Mets, so I guessed."

Roger smiled broadly. "You're a good guesser."

"I'm a Yankees fan," Weinberg said. "But I like the Mets, too."

They talked a while longer, about baseball and school. Roger was a bright and engaging child. He seemed to enjoy being with Weinberg, knowing he was a father of three boys, knowing he liked baseball. He didn't even mind being teased about the Mets. Yet there was an aura of sadness around him. Roger knew more about life and death than Weinberg did, and they both knew it. Weinberg could not fathom what it meant to be nine and realize you were dying.

Weinberg brought Crooker back into the conference room and asked Roger to sit in the waiting room.

"Does he know he has HIV?" Weinberg asked.

"He knows he's sick," Crooker replied. "I haven't explained it to him, but I haven't hidden it from him, either. He's a very smart boy. I think he's figured it out."

"How does he handle it?"

"He's a boy," Crooker said. "He doesn't let it bother him, usually. I don't baby him. He's had a life's share of heartache already. It's just one more burden for him to bear."

"What's the prognosis? Has he stabilized?"

"It's not good, Mr. Weinberg. I have to face reality, too. His counts are low. He's had a number of infections and other issues. We just keep hoping, you know? That they will find something for him."

"I hope so too," Weinberg replied. "Do you have Roger's infusion records?"

"Here are all the records I have right now," Crooker said, and she put a six-inch stack of paperwork on the conference table. "If you need more, I can get them."

Weinberg took the records. Another client, another file, another horrible tragedy. This one was harder than most.

ON MAY 26, he got a call from Judy Kavanaugh, a lawyer who, along with her husband, Bill Earl, was representing hemophilia clients in Florida. They were members of the group that had met in Dallas.

"Eric, things are moving very fast," she said. "I know you're focused on the case but you also need to keep your eye on what else is happening."

"I know," Weinberg said.

"There is the litigation, and there is the politics of the litigation," she stressed. "You're working too hard not to be on top of both."

"What's going on, Judy?"

"We've entered into an agreement with Levin Middlebrooks," she said. "They are the best mass tort firm in Florida, probably in the country. Fred Levin is on this, along with Mike Papantonio, who is becoming the leader of the firm. Bill and I felt we needed their experience and resources, and Bob Parks agreed."

"I think it's a good move," Weinberg said. He knew exactly what she meant about needing more resources from a larger outfit.

"I've told Mike about your work and he wants to come up to New Jersey and visit with you," Kavanaugh said.

"Of course. Any time."

"We've spent a lot of time thinking this through, Eric. We're convinced we need an MDL. We've told David Shrager that we are moving on this. He's still thinking about what he wants to do, but we aren't willing to wait. We're filing a petition for MDL assignment."

She was referring to Multidistrict Litigation, the same thing that Shrager had proposed. Federal rules provided for consolidation of multiple similar cases pending in federal courts around the country into a single case and assigned to a single judge. A panel of senior federal judges was assigned to hear MDL applications, and both plaintiffs and defendants could avail themselves of the procedure. Once a party, or parties, applied for MDL handling, the panel would schedule an oral argument. The panel met in different cities.

"Where do you think the case should be assigned, if the panel decides it's appropriate for an MDL?" Weinberg asked.

"We would probably ask for Florida, although Houston and Chicago are possibilities," Kavanaugh said. "We've gotten some pretty good rulings on statute-of-limitations issues in the Florida Supreme Court, and we just got a reversal of a summary judgment order on a case."

"What's your thinking about a cause of action?"

"Mike wants to discuss this with you," she replied. "The viral-inactivation theory would cover every infected hemophiliac, so we would plead that as a global theory of liability. We think it will be difficult to win failure-to-warn cases where the seroconversions were early. For our clients who were infected late, though, we think failure to warn is a viable theory, in conjunction, perhaps, with the viral-inactivation claim."

"I like the strategy," Weinberg said. "What can I do?"

"Just what you're doing," she replied. "We're exploring other theories of liability, such as the way the companies marketed their products. How did they advertise this stuff to the medical community? We've got to research the literature."

"It would be helpful to show that the manufacturing processes were similar," Weinberg said.

"We're asking for laboratory notebooks," she agreed. "We want to get discovery from patent cases, where the fractionators sued each other for infringement. Donohue from FDA said Cutter was using the Behringwerke process—we want discovery on that. I've subpoenaed documents from the National Hemophilia Foundation. Industry helped fund them, as you know. There is a rumor that the companies are going to offer one hundred thousand dollars per hemophiliac to settle."

"Is that for real?"

"Probably not," Kavanaugh said. "But we'll see. I'll keep you posted. What are you doing with your cases?"

"Fighting them in Newark," he said. "I'm close to making a deal of my own with a bigger firm. I talked to David Shrager, but he hasn't gotten back to me, either. I'm going to talk to him next week, but I think I'm going in another direction."

"I hope he makes a decision soon," Kavanaugh said. "No matter what you do, we'll work together."

"Yes. Thanks, Judy," Weinberg said.

It was good to know he had a friend, since he seemed to be losing some. For example, he had not heard back from Dr. Heimburger, the retired director of research for Behringwerke, since his trip to Germany, even though he had written to him twice.

Finally, a letter arrived in early June. Dr. Heimburger said he assumed that Weinberg was acting on behalf of a party in a lawsuit pending in the United States. He did not want to be involved at all. The man who six months earlier had told Weinberg how much he regretted what had happened to the hemophilia community, how he had felt partially responsible, and had laughed so genuinely about Weinberg's apfelwein hangover, was now saying he would not answer any questions. He hoped that the lawyer would understand his position.

Weinberg dialed his number, and the doctor picked up the phone.

"Dr. Heimburger, this is Eric Weinberg calling from the United States."

"Mr. Weinberg, there is nothing to discuss."

"I'm sorry to bother you, but I really thought you would at least answer my questions."

"It is not possible," he said. "I cannot say anything further. I must hang up the telephone. I am sorry, Mr. Weinberg."

That was all. Weinberg guessed what had happened. Behringwerke had business relationships with one or more of the fractionators he was suing—Cutter, as Judy Kavanaugh had mentioned, and perhaps others. Dr. Heimburger had told Weinberg in January that he would have to go back to Behringwerke's offices, since he was now retired, in order to check his old files before answering the questions. Executives there must not have looked kindly upon their former director of research helping an American lawyer. When they had spoken in January, his voice had been kind, his laugh hearty and real. No more.

Several days later, Weinberg spoke at length by phone to David Shrager and Wayne Spivey. He told them about Dr. Heimburger. They suggested that Weinberg let Dr. Heimburger know that Horst Schwinn, his former colleague, was working for the defense.

They talked about the New York Blood Center process, licensed from Dr. Shanbrom. They talked about case issues: where to file, what benefit would follow from an MDL petition. Yet, at the end of the call, they still did not tell Weinberg whether they were in.

Pressure was mounting on him. Grayzel was ready to pull the trigger, so Weinberg felt he had to move forward. He cut the deal with Grayzel to cocounsel the cases with his firm, Levinson Axelrod. Weinberg would bring in about seventy clients, with more to come. Grayzel's firm would provide the financial backing he needed to litigate the cases. Weinberg and Grayzel would both be actively involved in representing the clients. Weinberg felt it was a good situation and was relieved that the decision had been made. Shrager would simply have to understand his position.

WHILE MUCH of the legal activity in the hemophilia-HIV case was centered in the United States, the epidemic and the backlash that resulted were certainly not restricted to one nation. Far from it: there were thousands of infected hemophiliacs around the world, basically anywhere the clotting concentrates had been sold. In addition to the victims and subsequent investigations in Canada, Germany, Costa Rica, the United Kingdom, Australia, and Japan that Weinberg already knew about, there were many more. Among the other nations that conducted civil and in some cases criminal proceedings were Ireland, Italy, Portugal, Switzerland, France, and Iran.

Iraq, under dictator Saddam Hussein, had one of the more shocking responses to the tainted-blood episode that affected his citizens. He imprisoned a number of HIV-infected hemophiliacs, then forced them to sign a pledge "vowing not to work, marry, attend school, use public swimming pools or barbershops, visit a doctor's office or tell anyone about their condition." If they violated the pledge, they faced the death penalty. Eventually, the Iraqi hemophiliacs banded together and filed lawsuits, too.[1]

In France, where about 4,000 people, including 1,250 hemophiliacs, had contracted the AIDS virus, there was considerable public outrage, and in 1992, three former government health officials were found guilty on charges related to distributing tainted blood. Two of the three received hefty fines and prison terms, and the third got a suspended sentence. But, as is often the case when powerful people are involved, higher-level cabinet ministers escaped prosecution at that point, even though one of them, a former deputy health minister, testified that he and other government officials had known that the country's supply of factor concentrates was tainted more than four months before they were ordered withdrawn.[2]

That outcome changed as more information began to be revealed. In 1992, a government report concluded that plasma collected at French prisons had accounted for 25 percent of all the nation's contaminated blood products. A prison in Réunion, a French island in the Indian Ocean, was still collecting blood as late as 1991.[3] *Libération*, a French newspaper, revealed additional incriminating documents in 1994. Each new development created more big headlines. Finally, in 1999, three high-level officials, including a former prime minister and two former cabinet members, were tried on charges including criminal negligence, manslaughter, and involuntary injury. Two were acquitted ,and the third was found guilty but received no sentence. The court ruled that the proceedings had taken so many years that they had deprived him of the right to be presumed innocent. After the verdict, Edmond Herve, the former health minister who was convicted, told reporters that the court "didn't have the courage to find me fully innocent. Nor did it have the courage to convict me, really."[4]

In Great Britain, where 4,670 hemophiliacs were infected with HIV, hepatitis C, or both, House of Lords member Peter Archer conducted a two-year investigation and concluded there had been a "horrific human tragedy" but blamed no individuals or companies. He did note that, when it came to the American companies, "it is difficult to avoid the conclusion that commercial interests took precedence over public-health concerns."[5]

Lord Archer's report was issued in 2009, a week after British health officials announced that the deadly human form of "mad cow disease," more properly known as variant Creutzfeldt-Jakob disease, had been identified for the first time in a dead hemophiliac. Officials stressed that this was not the cause of death but acknowledged that eleven years earlier, the victim had received UK-sourced and produced clotting medicine that later was found to include the plasma of a donor with v-CJD.[6]

As of this writing, the most recent investigation was concluded in March 2015 in Scotland, nine years after the Scottish Parliament first called for a public inquiry. Led by Lord Penrose, a retired judge, it resulted in a report of 1,811 pages with a single-sentence recommendation: that the government take "all reasonable steps" to offer hepatitis C testing to anyone in Scotland who had a blood transfusion before September 1991.[7] On behalf of the government, Britain's then prime minister David Cameron apologized publicly to all the victims.[8]

In Japan, about half the country's four thousand hemophiliacs were infected, according to the Tokyo Hemophilia Fraternal Organization.

Lawsuits in Japan asserted that Baxter, Cutter, and Green Cross Corporation, Alpha's Japanese parent, imported untreated clotting products from the United States after they were considered unacceptable by Americans. Green Cross and another Japanese firm also made products from American blood plasma, the suits stated.

Two separate lawsuits, in Tokyo and Osaka, had been filed in Japan. Weinberg met with lawyers from there, introduced by Masami Kobayashi, a Japanese woman who was living in San Francisco. He spent a couple of hours talking to the Japanese lawyers, and they agreed to help each other. They would send him patents, written in Japanese, and he would send them documents and articles.

When it came to Green Cross, there was a particularly ghastly historical element: The company was founded by doctors who had worked in Japan's notorious Unit 731, which in World War II conducted horrific germ-warfare, vivisection, and other experiments on civilians and prisoners of war held in China. Instead of going to prison, they and others from the unit were permitted to use what they had learned there to build successful companies and careers.[9]

Spurred by hemophilia activists like the Committee of Ten Thousand, pressure was mounting in the United States as well for a government investigation. Michael Rosenberg was among the most vocal in demanding scrutiny of the FDA and the industry. In response, in mid-1993, a bipartisan group including Senator Robert Graham, a Democrat of Florida, Senator Ted Kennedy, a Democrat of Massachusetts, and Representative Porter Goss, a Republican of Florida, persuaded Donna Shalala, then secretary of Health and Human Services, to commission a study of the events that had led to the epidemic. By this time, it was understood to affect not some small number but the majority of Americans with severe hemophilia—thousands of people, mostly young men and boys, and some spouses who had unwittingly been infected because their men had been told not to worry, just keep taking your medicine. Shalala referred the investigation to the Institute of Medicine (IOM), part of the National Academy of Sciences. An IOM committee was formed, made up of investigators with no prior ties to industry or to the hemophilia community. Their charge was not to ascribe blame, but to review the history and recommend policy changes to improve the safety of blood and blood products.

The IOM announcement was met with skepticism in the hemophilia community. Activists wanted a full-fledged congressional investigation, but it appeared that they were being placated with one of those toothless, blue-ribbon inquiries that never resulted in any meaningful action.

Shortly after the IOM commission was empaneled, Weinberg received a call from its director, Lauren Leveton. Someone had given her his name. He urged her to look at the issue of whether the industry had moved quickly enough to kill the viruses in clotting-factor concentrates. He was trying to keep an open mind about whether this group would do anything useful.

In July, Weinberg prepared to appear again before Magistrate Judge Pisano at the federal courthouse in Newark to argue against a defense motion for what is known as a protective order, in which the defense sought to limit his access to corporate documents. He had asked for the documents the previous month, and now the defendants were accusing him of demanding materials that went way beyond not only what the court permitted but what he had said he would ask for.

Weinberg thought his requests were well focused. He wanted documents that would detail what led to the research on cleaner factor concentrates. What were the economic considerations? What did the companies see as the evidence of risk—for example, did they consider the fact that some of their own employees were becoming infected with hepatitis on the factory floor? Weinberg wanted to see patents for factor concentrates, documents related to plasma collection from commercial and other sources, communications with physicians and others regarding product safety, and communications with the National Hemophilia Foundation. His requests totaled nine full pages of single-spaced topics, twenty-four in all, with a few subtopics just to keep things clear.

Weinberg spread out the defense objections on his conference table, read them several times, and began to formulate a response. He actually was encouraged by the tenor of their motion, as he had obviously struck another nerve. This was fun.

His brief in opposition was thirteen pages, double-spaced, and argued that the documents were relevant to the defendants' duty to investigate inactivation of live viruses. It was very relevant as well, he wrote, that the plaintiffs should know the extent to which the companies purchased plasma from paid donors at high risk of transmitting blood-borne diseases. He wanted to know why the fractionators were able to heat-treat their products in 1983 but not in 1979, given that the technology had been developed decades earlier and the companies were using it for other plasma products. He wrote:

> Defendants also persist in refusing to litigate the claims that the Court has said are to be litigated in these cases. There is no 'meandering' in this discovery. It is specific, focused, and relevant to the failure of these defendants to manufacture a safe product. Defendants' persistent refusal to live in the present tense of this litigation—to face the fact that plaintiffs accuse them of designing a product that could have, but did not, prevent HIV infection—should not preclude plaintiffs from seeking and obtaining discovery relevant to the failure to manufacture a safe product by 1978, or 1980, or whenever any person with hemophilia infused clotting factor that infected him with HIV.

What's more, Weinberg advised the court that the discovery at issue was likely to have far broader relevance than just to the three cases before it. He announced that he intended to file another thirty-three cases, and a class action complaint in New Jersey. And he noted that an MDL had been filed in federal court in Florida by Judy Kavanaugh, Bob Parks, and Levin Middlebrooks.

If Weinberg thought that Judge Pisano was going to be impressed at this outpouring of detail, he was wrong. Instead, the judge agreed with the companies that the information Weinberg sought was overly broad and burdensome, and that each company had defenses and positions that were unique. Judge Pisano granted their motion for the protective order but without prejudice, meaning that he might change his mind if he received more information. Then he ordered Weinberg to submit information about exactly which clotting products had been used by Clyde Johnson, Ron Niederman, and Marty Weiss.

But in what Weinberg considered a minor but important victory, the judge permitted him to draft a proposed set of uniform questions and document requests. In sum, his cases had survived another challenge.

The next day—July 27, two months after his initial meeting with Dee Crooker and her grandson, Roger—Weinberg spoke to a group of hemophilia families in New York City at the invitation of Denise Maloney, the assistant director of the Hemophilia Association of New York (HANY). Maloney was the widow of James Leroux, a hemophiliac, and was friendly with Elena Bostick and others in New Jersey. Maloney wanted Weinberg to meet the families. She was very helpful, although he learned that others in HANY were more reluctant to get involved in a lawsuit. They were close to prominent hemophilia physicians in New York who had agreed to testify for the industry.

About fifty families came to the HANY meeting. Weinberg had come to expect the reaction that he received; many were stunned into silence, but a few came forward, asking if they could contact him later.

At the end of July, Weinberg flew to San Francisco for the annual convention of the Association of Trial Lawyers of America (ATLA). A year earlier, when he had gone to the ATLA convention in Washington, D.C., he had asked why nobody was pursuing the viral inactivation theory. Now, a year later, he was invited to make a presentation.

Ron Grayzel and Weinberg had arranged to fly Dr. David Van Thiel— the gastroenterologist from Oklahoma who in 1978 had called upon the fractionators to clean up the viruses in clotting factor—to San Francisco to meet with them. They talked with him for an hour. He was fully on board to testify that hemophiliacs exposed to clotting factor were known to suffer from non-A non-B hepatitis long before HIV entered the blood supply, and that the fractionators had a clear duty to treat their products to eliminate both known and foreseeable viruses. He would be an impressive expert witness.

A few days later, the AIDS Litigation group met. Grayzel and his partner Richard Levinson were there to hear Weinberg's talk and also to network. The meeting was well attended; more than one hundred trial lawyers and staff were there. The MDL filing in Florida had stoked interest in the hemophilia-HIV cases.

Weinberg spent fifteen minutes laying out the essentials. Levinson told him it was the best presentation of a new case he had ever heard in a seminar. Jan Adams, the lawyer from St. Louis, was there, carefully taking notes. Wayne Spivey, David Shrager, and Leonard Ring all offered compliments. Grayzel said he was proud to be working with him. Later that day, he and Weinberg walked for a couple of hours through the streets of San Francisco, down to the harbor, talking about the litigation, their families, and life.

The next morning, Leonard Ring and David Shrager called a meeting. At last, Shrager had decided to fully commit to the hemophilia litigation, as well as the viral-inactivation theory.

But first, he took Weinberg aside to say he had been surprised to hear that he was not going to team up with the Shrager firm. Weinberg reminded Shrager that he had come to him first but was facing tremendous pressure from his cases, not to mention Magistrate Pisano. Weinberg said he had taken Shrager's indecision as a sign that he needed to pursue other opportunities. Shrager was gracious, but Weinberg sensed some anger beneath the surface.

Shrager and Ring agreed to colead a group that would file a federal class action premised upon the viral-inactivation theory. Fred Levin and Mike Papantonio had filed their MDL petition in Florida, and there were intense discussions among them, Ring, and Shrager about how best to proceed. Should they keep the filing in Florida or pull it in favor of a different venue?

Weinberg didn't really care where they filed. He was thrilled.

There also were rumors at the meeting that some other well-known lawyers were seriously interested in jumping into the case. The news drove Shrager to run even harder at closing the deal with Ring and Levin. Now that he was committed, Shrager was determined not to let this litigation get away from him. He was accustomed to being the big gun, and he was good at it.

Before leaving for San Francisco, Weinberg had talked again to Dr. Shanbrom and had suggested that they meet while he was in California. The doctor had agreed, suggesting his vacation home on Catalina Island during the first week of August.

Once and for all, Weinberg intended to pin down Dr. Shanbrom, to get the documents he said he had. He wanted him to repeat, on the record, that there was early knowledge in the industry that new viruses, or previously unrecognized ones, would likely show up in blood. He wanted him to repeat, on the record, that there had been opportunity and feasibility to cleanse clotting drugs before HIV entered the blood supply.

After the ATLA meeting, Weinberg caught a flight to Los Angeles, rented a car, and drove to Long Beach to catch the Catalina Island ferry. He had heard that Jan Adams was heading south to try to meet with Dr. Shanbrom, too. He had noticed that she had left the ATLA meeting a day early.

When he arrived at the ferry dock in Long Beach, Weinberg called Dr. Shanbrom. He answered, and he was aggravated.

"She showed up at my home with a video operator in tow. On top of that, she was late," Dr. Shanbrom said.

"Who?"

"The woman lawyer," Dr. Shanbrom replied. "She called me from San Francisco and asked for a meeting. I told her I was leaving on vacation and she said she would leave a day early to get here, and when she did she wanted to videotape me."

"Dr. Shanbrom, I apologize. Please understand that I didn't know her plans," Weinberg said. "I'm about to leave on the ferry and would still like to see you."

"I'm sorry, but I'm too upset to meet with you," he replied. "I'm on vacation now. I need to relax with my family."

"I already paid for my ticket," Weinberg pleaded. "I'll call you when I get there."

"Do as you like," Dr. Shanbrom said, and hung up.

Weinberg decided to continue to Catalina. He had made the plans, the hotel was booked and nonrefundable, and he thought there was a slight chance that Dr. Shanbrom would relent and meet with him. The ride to Catalina took about an hour. Once on the island, he got a map, and his modest hotel room was within walking distance of the ferry terminal, on a hill overlooking the harbor town of Avalon. Weinberg checked in and got some dinner. He decided to wait until morning to call Dr. Shanbrom, to give him a chance to calm down.

Weinberg rang him the next morning. Dr. Shanbrom still refused to meet with him, but they talked on the phone for about half an hour. He said he had tried to get the industry to focus on detergents to inactivate viruses in pooled plasma. When, Weinberg asked. In the late 1970s and early 1980s, Dr. Shanbrom replied. He tried to get a Japanese company interested, but they wanted to heat the products instead. He did get Merieux, a French company, to do some research, and they did much of the work concerning detergents, he said. Ultimately, the process was patented, and industry integrated it into manufacturing. Dr. Shanbrom said the New York Blood Center, a reputable, not-for-profit manufacturer of clotting-factor concentrates, used his process, and paid him for it. It worked very well, he added.

By the end of their conversation, Dr. Shanbrom had softened his tone a little. He suggested that Weinberg prepare a subpoena and said he would appear for a deposition and tell all he knew about viral inactivation. Weinberg promised to call Dr. Shanbrom's attorney to make the arrangements as soon as he got back to New Jersey.

He felt he had averted disaster. The case was still on track.

Weinberg put his swim trunks in a bag and walked down to the Avalon harbor. He trekked to a secluded spot on the coastline the hotel manager had recommended. He rented a mask, snorkel, and fins and spent a couple of hours in the cool, clear Pacific, checking out the fish and plant life just a hundred yards from shore. In those beautiful waters, in as peaceful a setting as one could wish for, the case was still on his mind. He was immersed.

12

An Act of Man

It was the dog days of August, and the 1993 baseball season was peaking. The Mets, going in the other direction, were sinking toward what would be a last-place finish in the National League East. Weinberg thought of Roger, the ever-faithful fan, his Mets cap set crooked on his head.

Two new clients, Bud Herbert and his hemophilic son, Dave, came to see Weinberg that month. It was another emotional meeting.

Bud was powerfully built, silver-haired, and clearly comfortable as the big dog in the room. He was a prominent real estate broker from Putnam County, New York, among the nation's wealthiest counties, and a major Republican fund-raiser. He counted George Pataki, who was about to be elected governor of New York, and Al D'Amato, then a U.S. senator, among his friends.

And now, he was firmly on the warpath on behalf of his child. Bud said he'd had an epiphany as he listened to Weinberg at the Hemophilia Association of New York meeting. Bud and Dave had been shocked and, together with Bud's wife, Carole, were ready to sue.

Dave was a very mild hemophiliac, likely infected in 1984, at the age of fourteen, during a knee surgery, when he was infused with clotting factor for only the second time in his life. He had been given unheated product that carried no HIV warning, even though by that time, the manufacturer had a license to make a heated version. Dave's doctor, an old country pediatrician, had felt sure it was safe. By 1984, with all that was known about HIV and blood, what reputable company would continue to sell the older medicine, and what responsible government regulators would sit silent and let it happen?

Bud was no stranger to the courthouse, but his experience was in commercial real estate litigation. He also hewed to the Republican line about the need for tort reform to prevent frivolous lawsuits by get-rich-quick schemers. Personal injury litigation was anathema to him. But love for his son trumped politics.

Weinberg cautioned that the industry would surely raise New York's statute of limitations as a defense. Dave had turned eighteen in 1988, and if the courts decided he knew he was HIV-positive then, it was possible that he had missed his chance to sue. But Weinberg was already thinking about how to overcome such a defense: lobbying state legislatures to open temporary "windows" in their statutes to allow HIV-infected hemophiliacs to sue despite the passage of time. Bud was enthusiastic. He had the political experience and connections to help change New York's law. Now Weinberg had a powerful new ally.

Later, following up on Dr. Shanbrom's suggestion, Weinberg called the doctor's personal attorney, who said lawyers for Cutter had visited Dr. Shanbrom recently and had let it be known that his participation on behalf of hemophilia plaintiffs would effectively end any interest the companies might have in his ongoing research. In effect, Dr. Shanbrom would be blackballed. The lawyer said his client would, nonetheless, respond to a subpoena to testify—and yes, would bring his documents.

Weinberg briefed Elena Bostick about the developments in the case, including the near miss with Dr. Shanbrom. He also called Joe Salgado, his sounding board. Salgado laughed about Weinberg's desperate ferry ride to see Dr. Shanbrom. Weinberg laughed with him. Salgado knew that absurdity was sometimes the nature of the world. He was highly amused at the picture of Weinberg having carefully nurtured a relationship with Dr. Shanbrom, and of another lawyer running from the San Francisco conference down to Orange County to beat the crowd in general, and Weinberg in particular. As he often did, Salgado put things into perspective. They agreed to meet for lunch.

Weinberg knew Salgado was a key adviser to Bostick, but the two men had never openly discussed the fact that Salgado had hemophilia and HIV. So when they sat down to eat at a Chinese restaurant in Somerset, halfway between their offices, Weinberg sensed what was coming—a conversation long avoided.

"When I sent Andrea to you, I figured you would tell her there was nothing that could be done," Salgado said. "I knew there had been a dozen trials and the fractionators had won every case. But she wanted to talk to a lawyer. I figured you would listen to her and do your homework and tell her the case would be difficult if not impossible. I thought you would be nice to her and let her down easy.

"And now, Eric, you've screwed everything up for me," Salgado said. "I always believed that having hemophilia was pretty much like the companies said, an act of God. In my life, I've been able to sustain myself in the worst of times through prayer, and I never let it defeat me. When I was diagnosed with hepatitis, I knew it was God's will. When they told me I was HIV-positive, I believed that my faith would get me through it.

"Then you started digging, and every time you told me what you had found, it shook me more deeply. I never let on to you what kind of impact you were making on me. And now, I don't think being infected with HIV was an act of God at all. I think it was an act of man.

"I can handle whatever comes. I will fight HIV, the same way I've fought hemophilia and hepatitis. But I have a wife and two children and if I'm gone, they need to be taken care of. I want you to represent me, Eric."

Weinberg replied that he would be honored.

They finished lunch and drove their separate ways. In the distance, as Weinberg left the parking lot, he could see the house his parents bought in 1962, where he was raised. He thought about his father and regretted that he could not hear his voice again.

A few days later, Judy Kavanaugh called Weinberg again with an update from Florida. She was very upbeat. The relationship with the bigger law firm was working out well. After so many years of working alone with her husband on the hemophilia cases, now the litigation was taking shape as a mass tort, with a committee of experienced and successful litigators in charge. These were heavy hitters with deep resources. Kavanaugh said she also liked the fact that the group included lawyers like the two of them, who had dedicated themselves to putting the case together.

Shrager called next and he, too, was enthusiastic. He and Spivey were going hard after the procedural and scientific issues. He felt strongly that

the National Hemophilia Foundation should be a defendant in the litigation, saying that the NHF had misled its constituency, had made medical
recommendations that were both misplaced and wrong, and was too
beholden to industry. He faxed Weinberg and the other lawyers an NHF
publication dated July 16, 1993, in which the foundation tried to dissuade
its members from joining or supporting a class action or even individual
lawsuits against the companies.

Shrager cautioned that a major issue for Weinberg was whether there
was an inconsistency between representing individual clients and the class.

"Damages per capita may be less than what individuals could be
entitled to," he said. "So the question is, would lawyers who represent
clients opt out the so-called good cases, leaving lesser cases in the class?"

Weinberg understood. He was pretty sure he had more individual
cases than anyone else in the group. If there was to be a deal, would he
undercut it by telling his clients to keep fighting rather than settle? Or
would he participate in a class settlement?

Weinberg reported these developments to Grayzel, who was convinced that they should seek a class action in New Jersey. They drafted a
complaint that included a plasma-collection company called Sera-Tec
Biologicals, which had its corporate headquarters in North Brunswick,
New Jersey, not far from Weinberg's office. He knew Sera-Tec well: when
he attended Rutgers as an undergraduate student, several of his fraternity
brothers would go to the Sera-Tec plasma center on New Street in
New Brunswick and sell their plasma for ten dollars, a hot dog, and a soft
drink. By including Sera-Tec, which sold frozen plasma to one or more of
the fractionators, as a defendant, they could maintain jurisdiction in
Middlesex County. Their case was assigned to Judge Jud Hamlin, before
whom Weinberg had tried the swimming pool case in 1991.

Grayzel was hopeful that Judge Hamlin would certify a class and asked
Weinberg to impress upon the Hemophilia Association of New Jersey the
logic and benefit of pursuing it, both for their local clients and as a way to
further the national litigation. Weinberg liked Grayzel's passion, and his
reasoning made sense to him. He met with the HANJ board of directors
and asked for, and got, its support.

Not everything was proceeding so smoothly. Dr. Shanbrom's lawyer
called to say that his client had reversed course. He would not produce

documents after all, saying that he simply didn't have the time to go through his boxes of old records. The lawyer also advised Weinberg to narrow his subpoena, because both Dr. Shanbrom and federal judges in California would resist anything they deemed too broad. Grayzel and Weinberg agreed that Weinberg would continue to work on Dr. Shanbrom, but either way, their case was moving forward. Judge Hamlin had scheduled a case management conference for early September. The New Jersey litigation was off and running.

By the end of September, Shrager and other lawyers had devised a class action fee agreement for those participating in the case. The decision was made to file on Leonard Ring's turf, the Northern District of Illinois, in Chicago. Shrager and Ring would be proposed as co-lead counsel. The Florida group was withdrawing its MDL petition and was on board with this strategy.

Weinberg was asked which of his clients he would agree to put forward as a class plaintiff. The screening process required that such a client have an ironclad case regarding the statute of limitations, with solid product identification and later seroconversion preferable. Weinberg agreed to speak to Dee Crooker about being a class plaintiff on behalf of Roger.

At this point, discussions had begun with at least two companies, Armour and Baxter, about a potential national settlement. As Shrager had feared, this made Weinberg very nervous, because such a deal almost certainly would mean less money than what he might get for his clients—if he won—if he tried his best cases individually. The opt-out issue was something he'd have to think about, and hard.

First, though, Weinberg had a somewhat more personal issue to deal with: a letter from Baxter lawyer Bob Limbacher accusing him of violating legal ethics rules by making contact with "two former high level Baxter employees," Dr. Shanbrom and the technician. Limbacher's letter asked him to "refrain from any further contact with any former Baxter employees." If he continued to "engage in such conduct," Limbacher wrote, "we will have no choice but to bring this matter to the Court's attention." Counsel for the other three fractionators were copied.

Weinberg liked Limbacher and chalked the letter up to him doing his job, but now he needed his own lawyer. He was confident that he had violated no ethics rules; neither Dr. Shanbrom nor the technician had been at a high enough level to be part of what the courts called the "control group"—that is, they hadn't made executive decisions that bound the company's acts. Furthermore, Baxter had fired Dr. Shanbrom. Still, Weinberg wanted to be sure, particularly since he hoped to keep talking to the scientist.

So Weinberg and Grayzel consulted Ray Trombadore, a Somerville lawyer considered one of the leading practitioners of ethics law in New Jersey. He reviewed the history and said that no, Weinberg had done nothing unethical, and gave them an opinion letter for their files. Weinberg continued to speak with Dr. Shanbrom. He never heard from Limbacher or Baxter about the issue again.

The federal class action was filed in Chicago on September 30, 1993, with Jonathan Wadleigh, the cofounder and first president of the Committee of Ten Thousand, as the lead plaintiff. The defendants were Rhone-Poulenc Rorer Inc. and its Armour Pharmaceutical subsidiary; Miles Inc. and its Cutter Biological division; Baxter Healthcare Corporation and its Hyland Therapeutics division; Alpha Therapeutic Corporation; and the National Hemophilia Foundation.

The Multidistrict Litigation petition came soon after and was assigned to the MDL panel for argument in November in Miami. Weinberg was included as class counsel, and Dee Crooker, as Roger's representative, was one of the class plaintiffs. The case was assigned to Judge John F. Grady, who was presiding over an individual lawsuit filed by Stephen and Peggy Poole, with Debra Thomas and Leonard Ring as their lawyers. According to their complaint, Stephen Poole was a hemophiliac who from 1975 until his AIDS-related death in 1987 used clotting medicines manufactured and sold by the four companies. Thomas and Ring were arguing that they had failed to perform screening tests and heat-treating and had failed to warn Stephen Poole of the risks.

At an October meeting of the lawyers involved in the class action, Ring gave a report on the progress of the Poole case. He expected it to go to the jury at the end of November. It would be an important test case since they were using the same arguments as they would in the MDL.

The next meeting was set for November in Miami, where the MDL panel would consider whether to grant the MDL designation. The lawyers needed to firm up the proposed membership of their Steering Committee, and they scheduled a day-long session at Judy Kavanaugh's offices.

Weinberg expected a substantive discussion of trial strategy but left disappointed. Most of the day was spent on the politics of the organization they had just formed, particularly with respect to how fees would be paid and shared. Among other things, Shrager was looking at a plan to require each lawyer to put fifty thousand dollars into a litigation fund.

Shrager also was leading the talks between the plaintiffs' team and company lawyers, and Weinberg had no clue what was being discussed. He had brought the case and his clients to Shrager, yet he was not in the inner circle when it came to the settlement discussions.

Perhaps the highlight of the Miami meeting was Leonard Ring's update at dinner on the progress of the Poole case. He felt it was going exceptionally well. "The jury is with us," he told his colleagues.

Later, in his journal, Weinberg wrote: "Uh-oh. Sounds too good to be true."

This was not the day Weinberg had hoped for, and he was worried because his cash flow continued to be tight and expenses constant. With few exceptions, what had gone away were the kinds of cases that sustain a law practice—smaller cases that can be developed, litigated, and settled within a year or two. They required visibility and marketing, but the hemophilia litigation was moving in so many different directions, it was becoming impossible for him to do much else.

Weinberg decided to skip the MDL hearing. As a lone practitioner, he wasn't used to working this way. For him, this case had too many lawyers, too many issues, and too much political wrangling. Before he left, he wrote more in his journal: "A sense that this trip was not necessary, productive. A sense I want, still, to do things my way. A sense this class action, like others, has as its main goal the production of big fees for the lawyers. Time to work on my game plan."

The following week, the jury in the Poole case made its decision. It ruled in favor of the companies on every issue, including Weinberg's theory of viral inactivation. The former Behringwerke scientist mentioned by Ring when Weinberg saw him in Chicago had testified for the plaintiffs, saying the products could have been cleansed much earlier, but as Ring had feared, he was ineffective.

The verdict was a deep disappointment to Weinberg and the other plaintiffs' lawyers, especially given Ring's optimism. Leonard Ring was one of the best trial lawyers in the country. As with any trial, though, there was much to be learned from it.

Weinberg took some time to enjoy the holidays with his family, then flew to Syracuse to attend the Rutgers-Syracuse football game with his college roommate. When he got back, he put together an outline for himself. He summarized the case, the theories of liability, the new experts and evidence at his disposal that Ring did not have or use, the defendants' strengths, how his cases should be classified and prioritized for trial, and, finally, three pages of notes on what should be done next.

There were some bright spots to the Poole case. Judge Grady, in an error later determined by an appeals court to be grounds for reversal and new trial, had permitted the defendants to tell the jury that the plaintiffs could have sued the Food and Drug Administration, which was not true. And Baxter had presented a witness who had testified that Hyland's plasma donors were a completely wholesome bunch, not mentioning others such as the prison inmates. So there was another opening to be exploited.

In December, the MDL panel granted the plaintiffs' petition and assigned the litigation to Judge Grady. Shrager called for a meeting of the class action counsel to review the Poole trial, formalize the proposed Steering Committee, and set a course.

By that time, another heavy hitter, Alan Laufman, had joined the team. He was a lawyer and physician, a graduate of the University of Pennsylvania, Harvard Law School, and the University of Texas Southwestern Medical School. He and Weinberg created a timeline of events to help support the argument that clotting-factor concentrates could have been made safer before HIV. Weinberg had been chasing that theory for more than two years and was grateful. He felt reassured to be working with such a knowledgeable colleague in building that part of the case. Laufman had ideas about how they might combat the FDA defense the companies had successfully mounted in the Poole trial. And he raised another point: Who first came up with the notion that clotting products like Factor VIII and IX could *not* be cleansed of viruses? If it was industry, then perhaps it was a negligent standard.

Weinberg talked frankly with Laufman about his discomfort with what had happened in Miami, and where things were headed. Weinberg was unsure whether the federal class was a good fit for him. He could litigate his cases in New Jersey, in state court, with a local team and a good number of cases, and avoid the politics and fee issues.

Weinberg just wanted to get his cases to trial. His clients were sick and dying, and needed the money. He continued to spend enormous amounts of time with them, chasing down medical and scientific articles, and interviewing potential experts and witnesses.

Among them, still, was Dr. Shanbrom, but after his attorney said he didn't want to look through his documents, Weinberg and Grayzel became increasingly concerned about using him as a witness. The companies might pull out their own documents and undercut what Dr. Shanbrom had to say. But Weinberg knew the industry lawyers viewed Dr. Shanbrom as a potentially huge problem. The way to keep him in line, they apparently had concluded, was to play on his fears about losing his corporate research funding.

Dr. Shanbrom was a thinker and an inventor who pursued multiple ideas at once, some of which were impractical and others that would lead to improved products, and thus were of great value. But in conversations with Weinberg toward the end of 1993, he was all over the map. One day, he would insist that it was so well known, as far back as the 1960s, that detergents would destroy viruses that one had to ask why the blood-product companies waited so long to implement these processes. In the next conversation, he would express his concern about Weinberg's role in the litigation and advise him to cut the best deal he could and get out. He also mentioned that he had a new contract with one of the defendants.

In short, Dr. Shanbrom was exhausting him. Yet Weinberg felt they had to keep talking. He only wanted to deliver him, and the critically important opinions he had expressed, in the litigation.

At year's end, the Baxter attorneys visited Shrager and Spivey to discuss a Baxter-only settlement in the range of one hundred million dollars, a number that might seem huge but had to be divided among the lawyers and thousands of clients, most of them with annual treatment costs well into six figures. Shrager quickly informed the Steering Committee and was not dismissive of the numbers, especially after the loss in the Poole case. Had the plaintiffs won, there would be hope for a relatively early and more sizable settlement. But the Poole case confirmed that such cases were defensible, and settlement figures should thus be lower.

Weinberg shared the details with Elena Bostick and Joe Salgado. There were many other interested parties to consider besides the Hemophilia Association of New Jersey: by this time, activist groups including the Hemophilia Federation of America, the Committee of Ten Thousand, the Hemophilia/HIV Peer Association, and others were banding together to better represent the interests of the community. Coincidentally, a meeting of the Hemophilia Federation had been scheduled for January 1994 in Newark, New Jersey. Shrager decided he must attend, so he could explain the strategy for the proposed deal.

ACTIVIST MICHAEL ROSENBERG, to whom Weinberg and so many others owed so much, died on New Year's Day, 1994. He followed his brother, who had died of AIDS in 1991. Weinberg heard from one of his Japanese contacts that Rosenberg had exhausted himself in October at the annual meeting of the National Hemophilia Foundation, held in Indianapolis. There, in a moment of anger and frustration, Rosenberg reportedly had confronted NHF president Glenn Pierce, himself a person with hemophilia, grabbed Pierce's tie and yanked it hard. Afterward, Rosenberg was said to be deeply upset and left to recuperate in his hotel room, unwilling to speak with anyone.

In the early 1990s, when most in the hemophilia community were still stunned, silent, or confused, Rosenberg had organized the Hemophilia/ HIV Peer Association. In May 1992, he had authored his manifesto, "Causes and Effects of the Hemophilia/AIDS Epidemic," a rallying cry in which he blamed industry, government, doctors, and the National Hemophilia Foundation for the genocide afflicting hemophiliacs. He was instrumental in sparking the activist movement, and he was right on all counts. Weinberg had considered Rosenberg a mentor and hero, and his death the loss of a colleague.

Despite Rosenberg's death, or perhaps because of it, the Hemophilia Federation did not cancel its upcoming Newark meeting. After all, they already had lost so many people. It was becoming a horribly routine part of their lives.

As researchers from the Centers for Disease Control and Prevention would later report, the median age at death for a hemophiliac in the United States was only forty in 1968. Then, with the introduction of clotting concentrates, that figure increased dramatically, to a high of fifty-five years in 1979–1982. At that point, with the AIDS epidemic exploding, longevity began to plunge. From 1987 to 1990, the median age of death was down to 40.5 years. All the gains were lost. Tainted blood was taking a horrible toll.[1] It was estimated that HIV-infected hemophiliacs were dying at the rate of one per day.

Shrager called Weinberg the day before the Hemophilia Federation meeting to discuss what he would say there. Shrager understood that he needed the support of the community both in general and for whatever settlement might be proposed. His plan was to hold a couple of smaller, informal meetings and then speak to the larger audience on the morning of January 8.

Shrager laid it out for Weinberg: Baxter would be the first to do a deal, and Armour likely would follow. But the companies wanted to know exactly how many cases they were dealing with, and were worried about the more damaging ones—those involving people who could prove they were infected after AIDS was known to be blood-borne and heat-treated products were available.

Shrager suggested what he called "benchmark figures" for certain kinds of cases: Post-1985 infections, $2 million; post-1983 infections, $500,000; pre-1983 infections, $100,000. Overlaying these potential values were case-specific issues, like statutes of limitation and cases in which a specific company's products could be blamed. Overall, Shrager told him, he was confident they could get about $500 million.

Weinberg had a proprietary feeling about the litigation and was beginning to realize that he might be too vested in it. He believed very deeply that the industry was guilty of negligence and worse. Yet Shrager was right when he said the cases would be extremely difficult. Several experienced lawyers had declined to become involved, and those who did saw it as perhaps the hardest case they had ever handled.

So, while a deal made sense, Weinberg was not at all sure the community would accept it. They were being asked to reduce their suffering, and dying, to a mathematical formula that factored in no consequences for the other side other than cash, and the industry had plenty of that. They couldn't demand that the companies be driven out of business because, even now, hemophiliacs and many others relied on them and their products. To cripple the fractionators would be to hurt themselves even more.

But the incident between Michael Rosenberg and Glenn Pierce in Indianapolis had energized the activists, who would be there in Newark. The lawyers needed to understand the group's position—that its members had suffered serious wrongs at the hands of individuals and institutions they had trusted. They also needed to understand the hemophilia community's nascent resentment against at least some of the lawyers, who were starting to be seen as opportunists seeking fat fees.

Weinberg urged Shrager to go slowly. Discussion of settlement might be okay, but had to be done with care.

Weinberg arrived in Newark that morning. It had snowed heavily in New Jersey the day before, but the roads were cleared and he got there in time for breakfast with Shrager, Bostick, Salgado, and others.

The people who arrived to hear Shrager's presentation were infected with HIV and hepatitis, or loved people who were. They had lost spouses, parents, and children—in some cases, more than one. They were enraged and wanted justice. They had little patience for what they saw as excuses about the difficulty of their cases.

To Weinberg, Shrager seemed to badly misread his audience. Rather than centering on the people he represented, he went right to the numbers. He drew what looked like a pizza on a whiteboard and described how it would be sliced, based on dates of infection and product identification. The audience didn't buy it; fairly or not, he seemed far too interested in the lawyers' piece of the pie.

As Shrager left, he told Weinberg he was pleased with his presentation and felt he had connected well. Weinberg returned to the conference, where he heard otherwise. Several of his clients, Dee Crooker among them, asked for reassurance that the lawyers would fight for them and not sell them short. Later, he reported to Ron Grayzel that he thought the airing of the details was useful, but the day was unsettling. Weinberg and Grayzel had better win the New Jersey motion for class certification.

Spivey and Laufman both called Weinberg, who concluded that they, too, must have heard some negative feedback about the meeting and wanted to hear what Weinberg had to say about it. He also learned that he was not the only lawyer who was having second thoughts; at least one other had not yet committed to the Steering Committee strategy, even though Ring and Shrager had offered to pay his fifty thousand dollar assessment. Apparently, too, there were major differences of opinion about how the fees would be divided. Some firms were pressing for equal shares for everyone; Shrager, Weinberg, and others strongly disagreed.

On February 3, 1994, Leonard Ring died suddenly and unexpectedly at the age of seventy. After a long and distinguished career, his last trial was the Poole case. Shrager was now the sole lead counsel in the hemophilia litigation.

Ring's death was the first of two blows to Weinberg that day. Unbeknownst to him, another lawyer involved in the hemophilia litigation had scheduled Dr. David Van Thiel—the surgeon and chief of transplantation medicine at the Oklahoma Transplantation Institute who was one of the experts Weinberg had identified and cultivated—for a deposition.

Dr. Van Thiel, like Dr. Shanbrom, was a potentially vital witness. His research in the 1970s had led him and his colleagues to call for a major effort to inactivate viruses in clotting factor in an article published in the *New England Journal of Medicine*, one of the foremost medical journals in the world. But when Weinberg read the transcript of Dr. Van Thiel's deposition, his stomach turned. It was a disaster. Dr. Van Thiel did not know the subjects for which he was being offered as an expert, rendering him useless.

This was something completely outside of Weinberg's experience. It was difficult to find good experts in these cases. Dr. Van Thiel could speak from his professional experience about the increased risk of liver failure associated with hepatitis-tainted clotting concentrates. He could express opinions about the foreseeability of liver damage going back to the time the products were first licensed, which would support the viral inactivation theory. He knew there was more to worry about than just hepatitis B—that new, previously unknown viruses were swimming around in those huge, gleaming vats of human plasma. He could have addressed a pretty wide range of subjects. But now he was compromised.

Weinberg had a long talk with Grayzel, and they agreed they must demand more control if they were to continue in the national litigation. They wrote a list of conditions to give to Shrager. Among other things, they both wanted seats on the Steering Committee, an active role in further negotiations, and a better deal on the fees.

Shrager, though, was pressing Weinberg to commit to the Steering Committee's guidelines. He said most of the lawyers had already agreed to them. They discussed the concerns of Weinberg and Grayzel, in particular the fact that the Steering Committee wanted half of the fees they earned from what by then were 114 clients in New Jersey and New York. It seemed almost ridiculous to Weinberg that he and Grayzel would be asked to pay such an enormous share. As far as Weinberg knew, the only other lawyers that had nearly as many clients was the Florida group, which represented about 60 people.

Shrager said he would think about it and get back to him.

Weinberg had not heard back from Shrager by February 16, the day of the next Steering Committee meeting, to be held in Atlanta, but had already decided he couldn't work within the structure that had been proposed. He didn't attend the meeting. He and Grayzel instead focused on their own clients. They also talked about working on legislation to extend the statute of limitations in New Jersey, since this was a key point in the industry's favor.

Both Alan Laufman and Judy Kavanaugh called Weinberg the day after Atlanta. Each asked why he hadn't been there, and what his intentions were. Weinberg replied that he needed more time.

In Chicago, Judge Grady held a case management conference. Weinberg didn't attend, but an army of other formidable lawyers did. Shrager did most of the talking for the plaintiffs' side, and Duncan Barr, from San Francisco, represented Miles and its Cutter unit.

Judge Grady raised the subject of the Steering Committee, as he would have to formally appoint the members. Earlier, Shrager had devised a list of eleven names, including Weinberg's, but now another group of lawyers had emerged, and they had their own agenda and their own list. They would have to be accommodated.

Judge Grady appointed Shrager as lead counsel, and between them, they agreed that Shrager's list would have to be pared down to include some from the other group. Weinberg ordered a transcript of the hearing and saw that his name had not been mentioned. He felt certain that he was being cut. After all of his work, the MDL would go ahead, with or without him.

Weinberg had to balance the opportunity to stay in the group against the opportunity to stay out and focus on his own clients. He had a couple of non-hemophilia cases still to try but otherwise, new business was not coming in.

And another Weinberg baby was on the way.

13

The Trouble with Torts

Tort: n. from French for "wrong," a civil wrong or wrongful act, whether intentional or accidental, from which injury occurs to another.

—Law.com

The tort reform movement, long a contentious political issue in the United States, aims to sharply reduce the numbers of civil lawsuits. As described by John T. Nockleby and Shannon Curreri in a 2005 law review article:

> In the 1970s insurance companies, tobacco interests, and large industry launched a political campaign attacking the American civil justice system. Unlike previous reform efforts that sought to change rules of law through case-by-case adjudication in the courts, the self-styled tort "reform" movement pursued a much grander vision: transforming the cultural understanding of civil litigation, and especially personal injury lawsuits, by attacking the system itself. . . . Before the tort reform movement galvanized conservative politicians in the 1970s and 1980s, most nonlawyers had no idea what a "tort" was. By the 1990s, however, the Republican Vice President of the United States could give speeches proclaiming that the tort system was broken, and that his party was prepared to fix it.[1]

Across the country, the reformers persuaded state after state to enact tort-reform measures, including limits on the types of civil cases that could be filed and caps on monetary damages (and thus, legal fees). In the early and mid-1990s, as the hemophilia cases were coming to trial, this movement was gaining momentum. The hemophilia advocates and their lawyers had to push back, and hard.

New Jersey's activists were in the vanguard. Ron Grayzel became a leader and advocate, helping to form a coalition of citizen interest groups to do battle in Trenton against the tort reformers. He asked Elena Bostick and the Hemophilia Association of New Jersey to join the coalition, and they agreed.

It was a natural fit, and a savvy move by Grayzel. HANJ was a strong organization, and no group had a greater interest in preserving its members' rights to sue. Grayzel and Weinberg enlisted them in a push to create an exception, or window, to the state's statute of limitations—one that would briefly allow people with hemophilia and HIV to sue the drug companies even though the statute clock had run out.

In March 1994, the coalition held a dinner in New Brunswick, featuring Ralph Nader as the keynote speaker. Grayzel was master of ceremonies. Weinberg and his wife, Diane, sat a table with Bostick, Salgado, and others. The atmosphere was charged; for this audience, tort reform was an effort to portray their life-and-death struggles as frivolous and greedy.

The coalition represented the frontline troops, and Grayzel was their leader. He strode to the podium and began to address the buzzing crowd. They were with him from the start, cheering when he identified himself as HANJ's lawyer.

Grayzel exhorted them to fight. He was as animated as Weinberg had ever seen him. Then he introduced Nader, the champion of the underdogs, and the crowd roared even louder. Grayzel had become the face of the hemophilia litigation in New Jersey, and Weinberg realized that he had to accept that. Particularly now, he needed a big firm alongside him, because his relationship with Shrager continued to deteriorate.

Shrager was writing him letters that began with sentences like, "We now have the written commitment of every committee member to the guidelines, except for yourself." With some discomfort, the two of them agreed to meet for dinner.

On the way, Weinberg met with the security director at Nordstrom's department store in the Freehold Raceway Mall. He had been representing Nordstrom's Menlo Park store for a year, prosecuting shoplifting cases. It was an easy payday with a great client, and the files were typically thin and manageable. Then Weinberg drove south to meet Shrager at a small

Chinese restaurant in a strip mall. Weinberg got there early and started with tea and fried noodles.

Shrager arrived and they ordered food. He asked how Weinberg's wife was feeling; she was a month away from having the couple's fourth child. The small talk dispensed with, they switched to business. Shrager updated Weinberg on the settlement talks with Baxter and Armour. He'd told the companies that the number to settle was one billion dollars. Shrager said the court would approve one hundred million dollars in legal fees, five million for each lawyer on the Steering Committee, and the rest divvied up.

Weinberg was not persuaded. Shrager became angry, and then blunt: Weinberg needed to let go, suspend efforts involving the New Jersey class action motion, and let him run the show. If he refused, Shrager would file an "intervention," advising the court in New Jersey that a separate class action was not in the best interests of the community. He was confident that the court would listen to him, and that Weinberg would lose control of his cases. His fees would be entirely subject to Shrager's decision making.

It was a highly unpleasant meeting, which nonetheless, oddly, ended on a cordial note as Shrager again wished Weinberg the best for his family. It was carrot-stick-carrot.

In mid-March, Acting New Jersey Chief Justice Robert L. Clifford assigned all New Jersey hemophilia-HIV cases to Judge Douglas K. Wolfson in New Brunswick. Weinberg knew him well: when he was a freshman pledge to the Alpha Epsilon Pi fraternity at Rutgers, Wolfson was a senior, and Weinberg had to go to his apartment to get his signature. Weinberg disclosed his relationship with Wolfson to the fractionators' lawyer; he disclosed to Weinberg that a close relative of Wolfson worked for one of their clients. Weinberg and Grayzel considered it a wash and raised no objection to Judge Wolfson's appointment. They were surprised, though, that the cases were not assigned to Judge Hamlin.

A lengthy fax arrived from Shrager. He demanded that Weinberg and Grayzel tell him immediately whether they were in or out of the class action in Chicago. The two of them could not work "both sides of the street." Shrager warned that "these cases will end up being processed and managed in a global fashion," and that the key question was "who will be the attorneys who will commit in support of the global effort and participate in the fees which are earned." He concluded by saying, "Whatever you or I need to do, the important point is we will remain buddies."[2]

That night, Weinberg made notes in his journal. His two older boys were staying with their aunt. Mike, his youngest, was asleep in his crib, unaware that soon it would belong to a new sibling. Diane was asleep upstairs. It had been a week of stunning intensity, Weinberg wrote.

Then Grayzel called. He had spoken to Shrager and was itching for a fight. So was Weinberg.

Alan Laufman called just before midnight to try to broker a peace, but minds were made up.

Shrager faxed another letter to Weinberg and Grayzel. His tone was fairly neutral but the message was pointed. They would be deleted as class counsel, and Dee Crooker, Roger Holt's guardian, would be deleted as a class plaintiff. Shrager also drafted a recommendation to the court in which Weinberg was withdrawn from consideration for the Steering Committee "by mutual consent."[3]

At the end of March, Weinberg attended a meeting of Hemophilia Federation activists in New Brunswick. Ron Niederman, among others, was there for HANJ, and Corey Dubin and Jonathan Wadleigh represented the Committee of Ten Thousand.

Founded in 1989, COTT was rapidly evolving into one of the most influential and persuasive national voices for the hemophilia community. Indeed, it was amazing how so many of these activists—in an era before social media—had managed to find one another and organize so effectively, even though they lived hundreds, sometimes thousands, of miles apart, and many already were quite ill.

Dubin, a long-haired, mustached radio and print journalist from Goleta, California, was among the first patients to receive Factor VIII after it was developed, and when news of a mysterious virus in blood products began circulating, he started demanding more information. He was accused of being too angry. Wadleigh, of Brookline, Massachusetts, bespectacled and bookish-looking, had a career in computers and software. Like Dubin, he had overcome severe hemophilia and its many debilitating side effects to become a husband and successful professional. Wadleigh's activism had begun when he was in high school in Virginia; then, his causes were civil rights and ending the Vietnam War. In the mid-1960s, before factor concentrates were invented and could help protect him from bleeding episodes away from home, he nonetheless helped organize and participated in a number of public protests, getting arrested twice. Then, in the early 1980s, he learned from his physician that yes, there might be some problem with his medicine. For Wadleigh, this notification came at a group meeting in an auditorium where the doctor, one of the best hemophilia specialists in the country, told his patients that, even though they were HIV-positive, they had little to fear. This was a shock since Wadleigh didn't even realize he'd been tested. Not to worry, he said he was reassured: for the most part, only people with other risk factors, like being gay or IV-drug abusers, would come down with AIDS. This became known as "the immunity theory," and hemophiliacs and their physicians alike clung desperately to it.

Weinberg, stung by the back-and-forth fight with Shrager, advised the activists to form their own steering committee to better keep tabs on their lawyers, and the activists liked that idea. The new group, called the Community Advisory Committee, would become an influential force in the litigation and negotiations with industry.

Shrager and Weinberg continued their tense conversations via memos. Weinberg said it was inaccurate to tell the court that he had withdrawn by mutual consent. He said the discussion of fee division and assessments was premature and accused Shrager of taking inappropriate unilateral action, including the threats to intervene in New Jersey, holding talks with the defendants without fully informing the clients, and deleting Weinberg's name as class counsel. These were, after all, his clients, and they had hired him, not Shrager. Weinberg even called for Shrager to step down as lead counsel and offered himself as his replacement.

Shrager responded with an offer to compromise on the fees and the New Jersey cases. "You were the lawyer most responsible for persuading me to commit to this global effort," he wrote. "You cannot know how happy I would be to put this business behind us."

They both wanted to settle this fight. Other lawyers, as well as activist leaders including Wadleigh, wanted a resolution as well.

Weinberg needed another perspective and turned to Joe Salgado, whose advice was simple and logical: if you need the resources that Shrager would bring to the table, then find a way to compromise. Weinberg talked to his wife and she agreed.

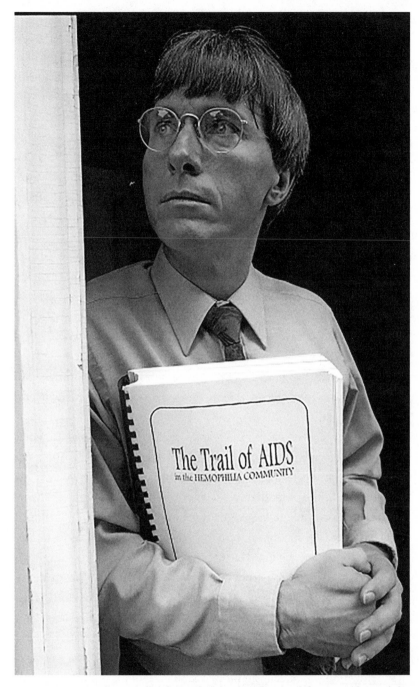

FIGURE 13.1. Jonathan Wadleigh, one of the founders and first president of the Committee of Ten Thousand, a hemophilia activist group, holds a COTT booklet containing government, corporate, and National Hemophilia Foundation documents that trace some of the history of the HIV epidemic in blood-product users. Wadleigh, who was the lead plaintiff in what advocates hoped would be a class-action lawsuit against the industry, died in 2008.

Credit: Tom Herde/The Boston Globe/Getty Images.

He went home, grabbed a leash, and walked Spike down to Donaldson Park, then along the path beside the Raritan River. The park was nearly empty, and he let Spike run off the leash. Yes, he had to make peace with Shrager. The fighting had become a distraction and there was too much at stake.

Weinberg went home and called Shrager. They settled their differences. Weinberg packed his bag and drove to Philadelphia to spend the next day, Saturday, working with Shrager, Wayne Spivey, Alan Laufman, and Jere Fishback. It was time to concentrate solely on the case.

ON TUESDAY, April 19, 1994, at about three in the morning, Weinberg's fourth son, Noah Vincent, was born. His brothers Jake, who had just turned seven, and Arnie, who was five, were excited. Mike was eighteen months old, so only vaguely aware of what was going on. Diane was fine and home with the new baby in two days. The bris and party would be the following week. Once again, Weinberg counted his blessings.

His joy over his new son did not lessen even when, three days after Noah was born, Judge Hamlin denied the motion to certify the New Jersey class.

The judge shot down Weinberg and Grayzel on every issue. He noted that the chief justice had already assigned management of the case— whether as a class action or consolidated litigation—to Judge Wolfson, but said he thought the proposed class of approximately five hundred infected individuals could be managed in a consolidated fashion. The judge acknowledged that his initial thinking was to approve at least a limited class, but ultimately, he decided that the products of the four companies were not enough alike to permit a single trial based on product defect.

Grayzel came to Weinberg's house with the opinion in hand. He talked to Diane while Mike played in the backyard and Noah slept peacefully in his stroller. The ruling did not change her mind, and later, after Grayzel left, she urged her husband not to give up. Yes, it was true that the scope of the litigation was already far beyond anything they had anticipated, but so what? Keep at it, she insisted.

Shrager was relatively gracious. After all, while the ruling concerned him as a precedent, it further consolidated his power. Weinberg was relieved that he had made peace with Shrager before the decision was released. The embarrassment would have been far worse if he had had to go to Shrager with his tail between his legs.

Now, each and every case would have to be painstakingly prepared for trial. There also needed to be some political action. Bostick enlisted New Jersey State Senator John Lynch, a member of HANJ's board of directors. Lynch was the state senate's former president, a former mayor of New Brunswick, and perhaps the most powerful politician in the state at that time. He agreed to lead the fight, against what undoubtedly would be heavy industry opposition, for legislation to open a one-year window in the state's statute of limitations. If the effort succeeded, this would override the normal two-year time frame in which people could sue, starting with the date they knew they were injured. This was important because, just like Jonathan Wadleigh, many hemophiliacs had been told by their physicians that they would not get AIDS, even though they were HIV-positive. They also had been told that the companies could have done nothing to prevent what happened. There was plenty of denial to go around.

Shrager, meanwhile, was trying to make good on his efforts to get Weinberg and Grayzel added to the Steering Committee, but Judge Grady said no. The committee was large enough, he said. They could be appointed if someone else dropped out. Shrager promised that he would try again, but in the meantime wrote to the other lawyers and told them that Weinberg and Grayzel were "to be treated fully as members of the Committee."[4]

Despite Judge Hamlin's rejection of the New Jersey class and the verdict in the Poole case, Baxter and Armour still wanted to settle, and preliminary talks continued through May 1994. The companies saw benefits to a settlement in terms of their ongoing business relationships with the hemophilia community: They would be perceived as the good guys, the ones who were willing to acknowledge responsibility and pay. Together, they had about 30 percent of the market during the HIV infection years, and some good PR could help them cut into Bayer's dominant share of the clotting-factor market. Plus, this was a way to finally end their legal exposure.

Shrager now felt that individual cases had little chance of success. Besides the setbacks with the Poole case, and in New Jersey, an effort to certify a class in Idaho also had failed. Shrager was pessimistic about the prospects for Judge Grady to certify a class and saw a settlement as an opportunity that would be lost forever once the judge denied the motion.

On June 1, the Steering Committee met in Chicago and designated an executive committee to reach a settlement with Baxter and Armour. The committee included Weinberg, Shrager, Philadelphia litigator Dianne Nast, and others.

Weinberg, still flying around the country in search of more documents, missed a connecting flight and ended up in New Orleans. At 6:39 A.M., he woke up and wrote in his journal about a dream he'd just had: He was in his office, chatting with twenty or so other lawyers, when one of them leaped from his chair and said, "Yeah, but what about the FDA defense?" Another lawyer turned on the radio and all the lawyers, including Shrager, got up and started dancing. They formed a conga line. But Weinberg wasn't interested in dancing. He got up from the table to discover that he was wearing only gym shorts. He left to put on a suit.

The executive committee began meeting with the lawyers for Baxter and Armour in Philadelphia on June 15. Also present were activists Jonathan Wadleigh and Ron Niederman. The Baxter and Armour attorneys talked about the companies' plasma-collection practices, admitting to using some prison plasma but denying risky practices. They said they had implemented state-of-the-art testing as soon as it was available. They described their insurance reserves and denied that viral-inactivation methods could have been implemented in time to prevent HIV.

Overall, their position seemed to suggest, as before, that they were talking about a total settlement in the range of $100 million to $150 million—which, depending on the number of claimants, would translate into perhaps $25,000 to $35,000 per claimant, with everyone getting the same amount no matter the relative strength of their cases.

The executive committee had a much more ambitious deal in mind: assuming as many as eight thousand victims, a settlement with all four companies should be $2 billion, or $250,000 per person, but given the admitted difficulties in the litigation, they would accept half that amount. Based on their market share, Baxter and Armour's combined share—discounted for their willingness to do an early deal—would be in the range of $200 million. Wadleigh and Niederman reluctantly agreed, conditioned in part upon their lawyers' willingness to aggressively pursue the case against Bayer and its Cutter Laboratories unit.

By early July, the framework of the deal was in place, but the numbers were further whittled down. Together, Armour and Baxter would pay between $140 million and $160 million. A memorandum of understanding was drafted.

Everyone on the plaintiffs' side thought it was too low, but that it probably was the best they could do. The Steering Committee voted in favor of the offer and Wadleigh, Niederman, and the Hemophilia Federation agreed to recommend it.

The next step was to get the blessing of Judge Grady, at a hearing set for August 5.

In the days leading up to the hearing, Shrager, Wadleigh, and others talked to a number of media outlets, including the *Wall Street Journal*, the *New York Times*, the *Philadelphia Inquirer*, and CBS News. The *Journal* quoted Wadleigh as saying that the settlement would be "a real milestone. If not an admission of guilt, it is at least an acknowledgement of culpability." Shrager noted in the article that many of the individual lawsuits had serious weaknesses. Wadleigh told the *Philadelphia Inquirer*: "Today, our community can begin to taste victory."[5]

The day before the hearing, Alpha's lawyer contacted Shrager to say his company also was ready to bargain.

Judge Grady, however, had other ideas. On the day of the hearing, held in his vast courtroom in the glass and steel Everett M. Dirksen U.S. Courthouse in downtown Chicago, he seemed puzzled, even annoyed.

In terms of the proposed settlement, "the suitability of it is not self-evident in light of what we all know about the extent of the injuries and damages claimed by the class members . . . we're talking here about medical conditions that are about as serious as anyone can be afflicted with," Judge Grady said.

Shrager, who had just finished outlining the deal, appeared somewhat startled but said he understood the judge wanted "just to stoke the discussion." He explained that this was a partial settlement, being proposed only because the individual cases were so difficult to win.

"To what extent, Mr. Shrager, does the question of whether the court will grant class certification here impact the fairness of this settlement?" the judge asked.

Shrager paused only briefly.

"If a class were certified, I could not stand up and look you in the face and say that this settlement was fair," Shrager replied. "It's as simple as that. . . . If it had been certified, I would have resigned before I would have recommended this settlement."[6]

Judge Grady said the deal had "utterly surprised" him, and that he had "considerable misgivings" about it. He told everyone to go to lunch and think things over. For both sides, the tension was rising.

After lunch, everything changed. Judge Grady announced that he would file his opinion on the class certification toward the end of the next week. Exasperated, Shrager pressed him for more details.

"If everyone would like to hear what I am going to rule, I'll tell you," the judge responded.

"I'd strongly encourage it," Shrager urged.

Judge Grady then announced his decision. He would certify the class for the negligence claim. Other issues, such as compensatory and punitive damages, and the likely cause of each plaintiff's injury, would be decided separately because of individual facts affecting each case.

In other words, the primary class issue would be possible negligence in light of the defendants' failure to manufacture virus-free products. It was the very theory that Weinberg had fixed upon so long ago, after his first visit with Andrea Johnson and her daughter.

In his written opinion, issued twelve days later, Judge Grady wrote, "The defendants have cited no case law from any state pertinent to the question of whether a defendant has a duty to guard against unknown but allegedly foreseeable risks. The court believes the general rule would be that there is such a duty. The question is not whether the particular risk is known, but whether it is of a kind that was foreseeable to the defendant."[7]

Now, the landscape of the litigation had changed. Weinberg felt vindicated, but he didn't have the luxury of letting that linger too long. The trial would be scheduled for October 1995, meaning he and the other lawyers had a very busy year ahead. The Steering Committee, invigorated by Judge Grady's opinion, immediately began to plan discovery and litigation strategies. Everyone's cases would be accelerated, with thousands of victims or their survivors perhaps getting their day in court after all.

The class certification also likely would mean more plaintiffs. An AIDS diagnosis was something that many victims did not want to reveal even to their own friends and family, much less in public court documents. But a class action would allow a measure of anonymity for those who might not otherwise come forward.

It was new territory for the companies as well. Certification upped their risk, so if they still had hope of a settlement, they might have to sweeten their offer. They also had to contend with a community that, emboldened by Judge Grady's order, was getting more organized and speaking out in increasingly public venues.

14

I Murdered My Child,
But Not Alone

If hemophilia-HIV families and activists feared that the year-long investigation by the federal government's Institute of Medicine (IOM) would be mere bureaucratic window dressing, the IOM took full opportunity to remedy that situation on September 12, 1994. From all over the United States and Canada, dozens of hemophiliacs and their loved ones showed up that day for an emotional, public IOM hearing at a nondescript auditorium in Washington, D.C., to describe what had happened to them. At times, their testimony was almost too much to bear.

One by one, they took to the microphones to speak to IOM's Committee to Study HIV Transmission Through Blood Products. The speakers trembled and wept. They shouted and pounded their fists. They waved photos of dead family members, thrusting them toward the committee so each person would be forced to take a closer look.

They all wanted to know: How could the U.S. government have allowed this to happen?

Some, like Petra Jason of Miami, described the horror of sticking needles into the veins of their little boys, only to find out later that the medicine they were injecting was contaminated with deadly viruses.

"I murdered my child," testified Jason, her voice trembling. Her only son, Bradley, died in January 1992, just after his first semester at Tulane University, where he had earned four A's and two B's. "But, members of this commission, I did not do this alone."

Jason had learned of her son's condition after a hysterical phone call from her ex-husband on November 2, 1983. He had just been notified that a donor whose plasma was used in Bradley's medicine was believed to have AIDS. Did she have any unused bottles from Lot Number NC8477? Jason had rushed to her kitchen junk drawer, where she kept the box tops from the medicine Bradley had already used. There, she had found a box top stamped NC8477. Then, five more just like it.

The fourteen IOM committee members, most from prestigious medical and law schools including Harvard, Dartmouth, Yale, Georgetown University, and two campuses of the University of California, had been tasked with reviewing decisions made between 1982 through 1986. They were to hold hearings and conduct interviews with a wide range of experts, including federal health officials, blood bankers, industry consultants, hemophilia activists, physicians, and researchers. The September 12 meeting was a chance for what the committee termed "interested parties" to speak; fifty-nine such parties gave oral testimony and another fifty submitted written statements.

Ultimately, the panel was supposed to determine if there had been adequate safeguards and warning systems, and then come up with recommendations. This mandate did not go nearly far enough to satisfy those who were demanding a full congressional investigation, as well as criminal charges at the federal and state levels.

As mothers, fathers, wives, husbands, and children told their stories, tears flowed through the audience, even among some of the normally cynical journalists covering the event and, somewhat more discreetly, among some IOM panelists.

Witnesses recounted how they and their loved ones were urged to use clotting medicines even for non-life-threatening bleeding episodes. Protestant minister Dana Kuhn, a mild hemophiliac from Virginia, said that in 1983, after breaking his foot, he was given the only dose of clotting concentrate he had ever used, as a precautionary measure. It was contaminated with hepatitis and HIV, which he unwittingly passed on to his wife. She died from AIDS-related complications four years later, leaving him to raise their two young children.

Others described how they had been assured that the chance of a hemophiliac contracting AIDS was one in a million. Authorities had used

FIGURE 14.1. Dana Kuhn, a mild hemophiliac who was administered a clotting drug only once in his life, speaks at a rally in Washington, D.C., in support of the Ricky Ray Act. A former Presbyterian minister, Kuhn contracted hepatitis and HIV from the drug and then unwittingly infected his wife, who died of AIDS complications, leaving him to raise their two small children.

Credit: Dana Kuhn.

that figure repeatedly until it was almost a mantra. Even after people tested positive for HIV, they were told that they wouldn't get sick, because only promiscuous gay men would get AIDS.

When hemophiliacs did become ill, many lost friends, homes, jobs, and health insurance. Marriages dissolved. Wives and children sometimes were infected. Other couples made the painful decision not to have more children or any children at all. Savings were exhausted and bankruptcies were filed. And for many, it was too late to sue, as their state statutes of limitation had expired.

Several witnesses cited internal corporate documents that were being made public as a result of the litigation—documents that showed at least some manufacturers seemed well aware of the dangers but sounded more worried about profit margins and market share.

"I am outraged," testified Lisa Smith, an Illinois mother whose husband died the month before the hearing. "I know beyond a shadow of a doubt . . . that my husband died needlessly."

Donna Cialone, of Florida, described how first her father and then her mother succumbed to AIDS. Doctors told her this was "an unavoidable tragedy," she testified.

Another woman, Joyce Lawson, of Tennessee, showed a photo of her husband when he was healthy, then another of him lying in bed, emaciated, just before he had died the previous week.

Other witnesses reminded the committee that the scandal wasn't restricted to North America. Hemophiliacs from all over the world were affected.

Etsuko Kawada, a Japanese woman whose eighteen-year-old son contracted HIV after using clotting factor, said she and her family had been forced to go into hiding. Speaking in halting English, she told the committee: "Anger wells up in my heart, thinking I have to clarify the cause and responsibility of my son's suffering."

Jonathan Wadleigh also testified, and accused government, industry, and the National Hemophilia Foundation of "a conspiracy to downgrade these grave dangers." He said he hadn't realized that being HIV-positive meant he'd eventually get AIDS until his brother, Robin, died in 1986. Robin was among the first hemophiliacs to succumb. It devastated Jonathan.

"This slow death our families endure, this genocide," he said, "we now know could have been entirely prevented."

IN NEW JERSEY, Grayzel and HANJ were lobbying hard to introduce the legislation that would open a one-year window allowing hemophiliacs to sue the companies despite the statute of limitations. They succeeded in late September, when Senator John Lynch, the Democratic minority leader, and Senator John Matheussen, a Republican, introduced a bill in the state senate. A similar bill was introduced in the state assembly by cosponsors Assemblywoman Barbara Wright and Assembly Speaker Garabed "Chuck" Haytaian, both Republicans. It was the first such proposed hemophilia legislation in the nation.

But the industry, buttressed by the fact that so many pharmaceutical companies had large operations in New Jersey and thus wielded great political influence, fought just as hard from the other side. At hearings in Trenton, industry lobbyists insisted that the companies had aggressively pursued methods to cleanse their products. They brought in their own political heavyweights such as John Sheridan, who had been cochair of New Jersey governor Christine Todd Whitman's transition team. Other lobbyists, such as the American Blood Resources Association, opposed the bill on several grounds. They said that if it passed it would make hemophiliacs a privileged group and would run contrary to the state's goal of tort reform. They warned that this would increase the costs of health care in New Jersey by opening up doctors and hospitals to lawsuits. The bill was amended to exclude suits against doctors and hospitals.

Because Weinberg and Grayzel had some New York clients, they initiated a similar effort there. Weinberg started by sending a copy of the New Jersey bill to the legislative chair of the New York Trial Lawyers Association. In contrast to HANJ, though, the leadership of the Hemophilia Association of New York was not as helpful.

But Weinberg's client Bud Herbert, the influential New York businessman whose son with mild hemophilia had been infected with HIV, used his political connections to get a bill introduced in Albany. Denise Maloney, the assistant director of HANY, rallied families in support.

Weinberg helped fund the New York effort by hiring lobbyists and public relations firms, and writing the bill. He donated money to Republican candidates and the party, and had his photo taken with U.S. Senator Al D'Amato at a fund-raiser.

The litigation, though, still took most of Weinberg's time. Since the hemophilia AIDS epidemic was global, the lawyers were searching anew for experts from Europe. In England, they found Dr. Arie Zuckerman, a renowned hepatitis researcher, author, and clinician; Dr. Richard Tedder, a virologist; and Dr. Peter Jones, a hematologist. The lawyers went to London in October to meet them, and all three pledged their support.

In particular, Dr. Jones, director of a hemophilia treatment center in Newcastle-upon-Tyne, felt very strongly about the issue. In June 1980, in a letter published in the *British Medical Journal*, he had expressed concerns about imported Factor VIII products made with the plasma of paid donors, especially those from developing nations. He listed several places that he said had plasma operations, including Nicaragua, Belize, Brazil, Colombia, Haiti, Korea, Lesotho, Mexico, Panama, the Philippines, Puerto Rico, Thailand, and Taiwan. "That this practice can be excused by arguing that

the purchase of plasma increases the standard of living of the donors concerned is fallacious, because it hinders the World Health Organisation's
policy of encouraging the development of self-sufficiency in these countries," he wrote.[1]

In July 1985, Dr. Jones wrote to the manufacturers to further express
his concerns about their plasma-collection and -processing methods, in
light of the HIV outbreak in hemophiliacs. He received a reply a month
later from Armour's Dr. Michael Rodell, the vice president of regulatory
and technical affairs, who said the company shared his concerns about
AIDS, and noted that its Factor VIII medicine, Factorate, was now heat-
treated. He also assured Dr. Jones that Armour "has never utilized plasma
collected outside the continental United States in the production of clotting factor concentrates, nor do we intend to in the future." Nor, he said,
did Armour use plasma from U.S. cities designated by the CDC as "high
risk AIDS areas."[2]

In February 1986, Dr. Jones announced at a Newcastle medical conference that there was evidence that some hemophiliacs had contracted HIV
from heated Factorate. He was censured by his chief medical officer for
even suggesting this. In March, Armour executives in England wrote to
Dr. Jones and issued what they called a defense statement. They insisted
that live AIDS virus "has never been isolated from heat-treated Factorate"
and that their scientists believed the company's heating process "likely"
eliminated any living virus.[3]

Seven months later, Armour relinquished its licenses to sell Factorate
in Britain after two hemophilic children who had used the medicine tested
positive for HIV. But in a meeting with British regulators, Armour officials
still insisted there were no laboratory data to suggest the heating process
was ineffective, according to a corporate memo summarizing the meeting.
"On the contrary, three studies have indicated that the Armour process
inactivates virus in excess of" the theoretical maximum, the memo
stated.[4]

Armour officials also met with the FDA, which concluded there was
insufficient evidence to remove Factorate from the U.S. market. It
remained there for another fourteen months, until news that six patients
in Vancouver, five of them children, had tested positive for HIV after
using it.

The lawyers also met with British journalist Michael Gillard, who in the 1970s had sold his plasma to multiple U.S. collection centers despite using false identification, and then reported on it. Gillard produced four boxes of materials rich with information about plasma-collection practices in those years; Weinberg made copies of everything and had them shipped home.

Returning to the United States, Weinberg went back to searching through government archives. He discovered the Federal Records Center in Suitland, Maryland, where he met with historians for the FDA and the Public Health Service. Every federal agency sent their records to this massive facility. Still, he couldn't find everything he wanted, and came to realize the Catch-22 of bureaucracies having employees with starkly competing interests: the historians, who wanted to preserve every document, and the record managers, whose job it was to destroy them.

As a result of Judge Grady's memorandum certifying the class, however, there were waves upon waves of document boxes—eventually, thousands of boxes—arriving from the defendants. The Steering Committee members hunkered down to read through this mass of material. Something important could be in any of those boxes, hiding in plain sight.

In late 1994, some of those documents were crucial in preparing the lawyers for a key pretrial deposition, offering dramatic evidence of the dependence of the National Hemophilia Foundation upon the companies. The fractionators were regular contributors; at the peak in 1982, they accounted for 22.8 percent of the NHF annual budget, the documents showed.[5] It should have been no surprise, then, that the NHF tended to listen to industry lawyers when they advised the foundation not to oppose them in lawsuits.

Donald S. Goldman, a New Jersey lawyer and Superior Court judge who was the NHF's former president and board chairman, testified in a deposition that the manufacturers sometimes threatened to withhold their financial support if the foundation took positions they opposed. He cited the example of Baxter, which he said once dropped its support of an NHF nursing program after the foundation criticized one of the company's marketing plans.

A letter written by Goldman in 1986 also stated that the NHF was reluctant to get involved in any litigation as it was "sort of between family members (i.e. between one of our constituents, the fractionators, against others of our constituents, those with hemophilia)."[6]

Describing the companies as "family" and "constituents" seemed to Weinberg as an odd and dangerous point of view. Yet this apparently was the nature of the relationship.

Goldman also testified that when the NHF tried to force a cleanup of potentially tainted products, it got little support from the FDA. "The FDA made it absolutely clear to those of us involved in NHF that it neither had the capacity, the legal authority nor the willingness to attempt to recall product under those circumstances, and that unless the NHF could obtain a voluntary withdrawal of those products, there was nothing the FDA could or would do," he said.[7]

He offered an insider's view of the frightening and confusing period in which hemophiliacs first began to suffer from AIDS symptoms. Goldman, a severe hemophiliac, testified that Factor VIII medicines had so improved his life that even though he believed as early as December 1982 that HIV was transmissible through blood products, it was "an irrelevancy" to him. He described what it was like to grow up without clotting concentrates: He had missed 100 out of 180 school days as a high school senior, and had to be taken by stretcher to his National Merit Scholarship qualifying test. In his first year of college, he got around in a wheelchair or golf cart. Then, because of clotting concentrates, he said, he was able to go to law school, have a career and family, "and participate in life the way I was able to participate in it."

Tragically, there was hope early in the epidemic, when so little was known about the virus, that perhaps, once exposed and HIV-positive, people with hemophilia might be immune, he said.

Still, Goldman said that he and most of the foundation's leadership had disagreed with the foundation's co-medical director, Dr. Louis Aledort, who had told him in early 1983 that it was pointless to take any clotting drugs off the market, because it was likely that they were all tainted. He noted that he and Dr. Aledort had a long-running feud.

Weinberg was struck by the way in which the NHF had surrendered when it got no support from the FDA. True, the agency had been ineffective when it came to product safety. Perhaps, he thought to himself, if the NHF had known about the source of the plasma being used, voices would have been raised. Perhaps, had the foundation known that the companies had the technology but not the will to inactivate viruses sooner, they would have demanded safer products.

There was another letter in the NHF boxes that caught Weinberg's eye. It was written in 1989 to Goldman by Walter Vogel, the father of Weinberg's client and friend, Richard Vogel. Walter, who was president of HANJ, was responding to the NHF's litigation policy: "It is our fear that your statement might discourage an individual from pursuing litigation in appropriate cases. Further, your opinion on the difficulty in proving a cause of action is legal in nature. NHF is not qualified to give such opinions. Finally, we disapprove of the above bulletin/advisory because we perceived it to be favoring the pharmaceutical companies rather than NHF constituents."[8]

Weinberg was on the deposition team with Shrager and Spivey. They considered Goldman's deposition—the first in the class action—a good start, and a victory for their side.

While this was going on, Weinberg did achieve something of a personal victory: Judge Grady finally appointed him to the Steering Committee. At a November 1994 hearing, the judge asked Shrager for a list of lawyers who were doing Steering Committee work who were not on the committee, so he could formally appoint them. Shrager gave him the list, then later walked past Weinberg, leaned down and whispered in his ear: "I told you I would take care of you."

Two weeks later, the plaintiffs and defendants resumed their settlement talks. The activists' community advisory group was not swayed by the state of limitations issue and was determined not to accept too low an offer, especially because of concerns there might be more victims than the 5,600 contemplated in the original settlement proposal. The attorneys for Baxter and Armour were there, along with Jonathan Wadleigh, Corey Dubin, and Ron Niederman, in addition to their lawyers. The companies were still willing to pay $160 million and argued that Judge Grady had derailed a good settlement. They said they would be aggressive in appealing any verdict against them should that occur, a process that could take another five to ten years. They focused on the practical incentives for both sides to settle: getting money in the hands of people who needed it, and allowing the companies to refocus on doing good things for the community. They warned that in another six months, the costs of preparing for trial would have reached such levels that their clients might decide to abandon settlement talks and just try the case. The time to settle was now. The activists and their lawyers agreed to talk it over.

Weinberg, for his part, saw his primary role at this point as passing along to the other lawyers what he was learning in his ongoing searches for documents and experts, before the October 1995 trial date. Between October 1994 and March 1995, he wrote more than two dozen memos, some several pages long, on topics including plasma procurement, the FDA, viral load, and the foreseeability of unknown viruses. He was piecing together a chronology of events that would prove, he thought, that it would have taken any of the companies about two years, start to finish, to develop a virus-free product, if only they had committed the people and money to a serious effort.

In mid-December, Weinberg received a call from a former plasma broker. Weinberg had written to him, asking for his assistance. He agreed to talk about his role in the plasma industry—which he blamed for the hemophilia HIV tragedy—only if Weinberg protected his identity, and the lawyer agreed.

The picture he painted in great detail during their telephone conversation, and in a meeting at his office a month later, solidified Weinberg's opinion that plasma collection was a dirty business. The man said he was not surprised that a new and deadly virus had appeared in clotting-factor concentrates, because the companies were collecting plasma from some populations at higher risk for disease due to their poverty and living conditions—people in Haiti, the Dominican Republic, and Africa; prison inmates in Louisiana, Tennessee, and Florida; drug addicts at skid row plasma centers in cities like Baltimore, Las Vegas, and Los Angeles; and gay men who had been infected with hepatitis. The gay men were recruited specifically because they had hepatitis antibodies in their blood, which could be extracted and used for medicine to prevent or treat the disease. But then, unbeknownst to the donors—who were told that they were performing a vital public service—the remaining material was dumped into plasma pools used for hemophilia medicines.

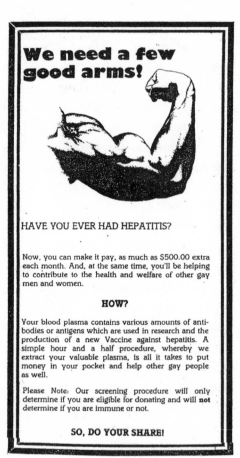

FIGURE 14.2. In the years before HIV was discovered, newspapers aimed at gay audiences often published advertisements such as this one from April 1983, urging those who had been exposed to hepatitis to donate blood plasma. Hepatitis antibodies and antigens were extracted and used in research and for vaccines. What donors and hemophiliacs did not know was that some companies then used the remaining plasma material in the manufacture of hemophilia medicines—with the full knowledge of the U.S. Food and Drug Administration. One month after this advertisement was published, French researchers announced that they had identified a virus they called LAV, later renamed HIV.

Credit: Bill Horn-McGinnis.

The advertisement reads:

We need a few good arms!

HAVE YOU EVER HAD HEPATITIS?

Now, you can make it pay, as much as $500.00 extra each month. And, at the same time, you'll be helping to contribute to the health and welfare of other gay men and women.

HOW?

Your blood plasma contains various amounts of antibodies or antigens which are used in research and the production of a new Vaccine against hepatitis. A simple hour and a half procedure, whereby we extract your valuable plasma, is all it takes to put money in your pocket and help other gay people as well.

Please Note: Our screening procedure will only determine if you are eligible for donating and will **not** determine if you are immune or not.

SO, DO YOUR SHARE!

Later, when they found out what had happened, the gay community would become a strong advocate for the hemophiliacs, helping them organize and advising them on political tactics.

The former broker told Weinberg that there were always adequate supplies for relatively safe plasma in the United States, but plasma could be purchased much more cheaply offshore. The fractionators were able to do this under "short supply" provisions of the Code of Federal Regulations, even though there was no short supply in the United States, he insisted. He said U.S. donors were paid fifteen dollars per donation session while Haitians—identified as one of the original HIV risk groups—received only one dollar.

So the source material, the market, and the clotting-drug companies were all global, which is how AIDS spread among hemophiliacs throughout the world.

There was little incentive for the fractionators to investigate viral inactivation of their products for a couple of reasons, the man told Weinberg. One, any serious efforts might have woken the sleeping government regulators to the notion of improved safety. Two, they would cut into the industry's profit margins, since heating plasma to kill viruses would also destroy most of the clotting proteins, meaning they would have to purchase much more raw material.

The former broker thus confirmed almost all of what Weinberg believed. The lawyer asked if he would agree to testify, but the man said no. He didn't want to ruin his reputation.

Later, however, Weinberg and Grayzel did take a sworn statement from another broker, Joseph Rosen, from neighboring New Brunswick. Rosen, president of Sera-Tec Biologicals, sold plasma to the fractionators.

Rosen confirmed much of what Weinberg and others were learning about the global plasma market. At one point, Grayzel asked Rosen if Sera-Tec had investigated purchasing overseas plasma-collection centers in the early 1970s. Rosen said yes, because the fractionators were buying all the plasma they could get. He also gave an example of some of the people who were getting into this lucrative business: out of the blue, he was contacted by "Mr. Silver," a wig importer from New York who said he had government contacts in South Korea and thought that would be an excellent place to collect plasma. Grayzel did a double take: an importer of what? What did a man who bought and sold hairpieces know about plasma? Rosen said Mr. Silver insisted there was real potential there so eventually, one of Rosen's associates accompanied the man to South Korea. Yes, as it turned out, there was some potential. But a deal was never struck.

Still, it seemed that concerns over the nation's plasma supply were not yet something that could be relegated to history, or lessons learned. On December 15, in Washington, the FDA's Blood Products Advisory Committee met to decide whether to recommend the recall of blood components and plasma products whose source material had come from two donors later identified as suffering from Creutzfeldt-Jakob disease (CJD), a rare, incurable neurological disorder that causes dementia and death. Among those testifying at the hearing were several hemophiliacs.

"I have severe hemophilia, HIV, and, let's not forget, antibodies to hepatitis A, B, C and D," said Richard Colvin, a member of the Committee of Ten Thousand. "For twenty-five years, the manufacturers of AHF have been gambling with my life."

Colvin told the committee that he was among those recently notified that they had received clotting medicine that included blood from a CJD victim.

Another witness, Dr. Craig Kessler, associate medical director of the National Hemophilia Foundation, said that even though little was known about CJD, the foundation felt strongly that "the first and foremost action in addressing this problem is to prevent all blood products manufactured from the donations of CJD-affected individuals from being released back into the market for use."

The committee decided to recommend the recall of the blood components. But in a separate vote, it declined to take a similar stance with plasma products. Nor would it recommend destroying the suspect plasma pools.

In two other votes, the committee recommended that the FDA notify all recipients of blood components containing CJD—but not the recipients of plasma products, since those products wouldn't be recalled. What was the point?

The FDA generally follows the advice of its advisory committees, made up of preeminent experts in their fields. After the hearing, an FDA spokeswoman explained the committee's reasoning: even if contaminated, they believed the plasma was diluted and treated enough to kill CJD.

ON DECEMBER 19, 1994, the defendants asked the Seventh Circuit Court of Appeals to review Judge Grady's class certification and order him to rescind it. Their petition came in the form of a writ of mandamus, an unusual, even provocative action in that it actually named Judge Grady as a defendant. Such petitions—in this instance, an order from a higher court to a lower one—are granted sparingly.

The companies and the NHF contended, among other things, that they would be irreparably harmed, and that the class never should have been certified. They cited, as precedent, similar rulings in other jurisdictions, including New Jersey.

A class action, they said in their petition, would result in "an extraordinarily long and hopelessly complex" set of questions for jurors to answer, and "a tangle" of subsequent legal proceedings "from which the parties and the courts may never extricate themselves."

It was a serious, well-written challenge. If the appeals court agreed, each claim might have to be tried separately, a process that could take years, even decades. Many, perhaps most, of the clients would die before being heard.

It was clear, then, that 1995 would be tumultuous from the start. The plaintiffs' lawyers were learning in great detail what had never been revealed before by anyone outside the offices and laboratories of Baxter, Bayer, Armour, and Alpha. Depositions of industry executives and scientists were commencing on issues they had never had to discuss under oath. Legislative moves to help the hemophilia community would gain more traction. And courts would push the case in directions that few had foreseen.

On January 4, 1995, the Steering Committee filed its opposition to the mandamus petition, defending Judge Grady. The lawyers conceded that some issues might best be resolved on a case-by-case basis, but they argued that for the central issues a single forum was more efficient and made the most sense for the courts and the clients.

Judge Grady ordered the class notices to be sent to the printer. The defendants moved again, asking the Seventh Circuit to stop him. Their concern was obvious: if thousands of notices were sent to everyone with hemophilia and HIV or their survivors, thousands of potential new clients would learn of the legal case.

The Seventh Circuit granted the companies' motion. The notices would not be sent. Oral arguments on the mandamus petition were set to be heard by a three-judge panel on January 30, 1995. It would be led by Richard Posner, chief judge of the circuit, a prolific writer and commentator, and the leading proponent of a school of thinking that believed law should be grounded in economics.

Weinberg called Dr. Shanbrom again. Would he agree to be deposed now? Yes, he replied, as long as he received a subpoena. Again,

Dr. Shanbrom insisted that he and others had recognized by the late 1960s that there was not just hepatitis B in plasma pools, but a new and previously unidentified form of the virus—one that wasn't mentioned in the medical literature until the mid-1970s, and later would be called hepatitis C. Again, Weinberg asked him to produce the documents that he said would prove his claims. Again, the doctor put him off.

15

Of Sheep and Men

The majestic, wood-paneled courtroom in Chicago was filled with lawyers and nearly one hundred hemophiliacs and their families from across the nation. It was January 30, 1995, and three judges from the Seventh Circuit Court of Appeals had a momentous decision to make. Would the industry's petition to decertify the class action prevail? Or would these hemophiliacs, and thousands more like them, be permitted to sue as a group, against the industry that had poisoned them for decades?

Sitting in judgment were Chief Judge Richard Posner and Circuit Judges William Bauer and Ilana Rovner. David Shrager was supposed to present the plaintiffs' argument, but there was an illness in his family and he could not attend, so another Philadelphia attorney, Dianne Nast, took his place. Douglas Fuson, counsel for Armour, represented the defendants.

Among those in the audience was little Roger Holt. Strapped into a special wheelchair that propped his head upright, he barely resembled the nine-year-old Mets fan who had walked into Weinberg's law office less than two years earlier. Roger was dying of AIDS and had difficulty speaking after being stricken by a mysterious neurological and motor-coordination condition the previous summer. The former first baseman was now suffering from muscle spasms, seizures, and blindness.[1] But his mind was still sharp and when he heard something he didn't like, he moaned loudly. Who had the nerve to hush or remove him? Nobody.

Fuson argued that it would be unfair and a waste of court time for the companies to defend themselves in a class action only to be forced to make the same arguments in other cases. He noted that Armour alone was a defendant in 263 individual lawsuits.

Judge Posner asked most of the questions and seemed skeptical of the class certification from the start. The companies, he reminded Nast,

> have won 13 out of 14 cases. They're doing well. You're doing badly. You have a chance with a class action to turn the tables on them in a truly dramatic way. For one thing, you have the chance of upping the number of plaintiffs from 300 or 400 or 1,000 to 20,000. I should think they would be concerned that if this class certification is upheld, they will be forced to settle, because their potential liability is so great, even though their chances of winning are probably better than your chances.[2]

He referred to the viral–inactivation theory as "exotic" and suggested that, while some state courts might support it, others might think it went too far, since the laws on foreseeability varied from state to state.

"I don't think that it is exotic at all," Nast replied. "I think it's almost a textbook question on a law school exam of what foreseeability is about."

Judge Posner, a prominent, much-cited expert on the economic impact of legal decisions, also asked her how much money the plaintiffs would seek in damages. Nast said they did not have a specific number but emphasized that "we don't want to bankrupt these companies. . . . That's not going to help the class that we represent."

As he listened, Weinberg feared the judge was ignoring the value of the MDL, the Multidistrict Litigation. It was obtaining new information that had never been produced before. But he was especially disturbed by Judge Posner's concerns related to potential economic impact, since the companies had not raised the issue in their petition. Indeed, they had done the exact opposite: they had filed financial statements with the U.S. Securities and Exchange Commission asserting that the litigation would have no material effect on their businesses. One of the two basic objectives of the nation's "truth in securities" law is to "prohibit deceit, misrepresentations, and other fraud in the sale of securities," according to the SEC website.[3] So presumably, the companies were truthful in their filings.

Then Judge Posner proceeded to stun the courtroom by comparing HIV-infected hemophiliacs to a flock of sheep swept off the deck of a ship, based on a British legal case from 1874.

"The law required a certain type of fencing on a ship to separate the animals in order to prevent contagion," he explained to the courtroom. "And the defendant failed to put in this required fencing, and there was a storm and all the animals were washed overboard because they did not have the fencing."

But the ship owner was not held liable, Judge Posner noted, because the legal purpose of the fence was only to prevent the spread of disease, not to keep the livestock from drowning.

"There was no duty with respect to this different risk," he said. "Now, isn't it conceivable that a state might say well, there is a duty to act with reference to a risk of hepatitis B, but not with respect to an unknown and even more lethal virus?"

Several audience members gasped. To them, it was bad enough to suggest that the companies had no obligation to sell safe medicines because they did not foresee HIV—even though, for many years before that, they had knowingly sold products contaminated with hepatitis. But was Judge Posner really comparing them to barnyard animals, and was he really suggesting that sheep washed overboard could be compared to the poisoning of thousands of innocent human beings?

Yes. He was.

Roger moaned, his indignant cry ringing through the courtroom.

Judge Posner said the court would take the case under advisement.

ON FEBRUARY 23, 1995, lobbying by what was now a well-organized hemophilia community paid off. The Ricky Ray Hemophilia Relief Fund Act was introduced in the U.S. Congress by Representative Porter J. Goss of Florida, a Republican, who called the HIV epidemic among hemophiliacs a "horrifying" tragedy for which the government was partly to blame. The bill, named for a Florida teenager who died of AIDS in 1992, would establish a $1 billion compensation fund, with each infected person or survivor eligible to receive up to $125,000.

The proposed legislation was sharply critical of the government, stating that it had "failed to fulfill its responsibility to properly regulate the blood-products industry" by not requiring earlier use of available technology to cleanse clotting drugs. According to the bill, which had twenty-two Democratic and Republican cosponsors, this technology had been available before 1980, and federal regulators had allowed contaminated products to remain on the market as late as 1987.

In New Jersey a few weeks later, the statute "window" bill also got a boost when the state senate's Judiciary Committee unanimously backed it. Phyllis Hayes, a Weinberg client and Hackensack resident who had lost her son in 1993, spoke for the dozens of victims and family members who had listened silently, holding aloft photos of loved ones killed by AIDS, as the lawmakers had discussed the measure. "We're not here just for us," she said. "We're here for a whole community. We need your help."[4]

Not long after came the unanimous approval of the state assembly's Health and Human Services Committee. Assemblywoman Loretta Weinberg, a Democrat from Bergen County, said statistics showed that most hemophiliacs born before 1985 had contracted HIV.

"This is a case that . . . involves morality and an expectation of decent health care," she railed. "This is the United States of America."[5]

Such progress in Washington and Trenton fueled a heady optimism. At that point, the annual medical costs for hemophiliacs infected with HIV and hepatitis C were well into six figures. At least seventeen other nations already had established government compensation programs; ultimately, there would be more than twenty, with mean awards ranging from $37,000 to $400,000.[6]

But on March 16, the Seventh Circuit brought the community back to earth: By a 2–1 vote, it overturned the class action, citing the risk of "a monumental industry-busting error." Judges Posner and Bauer, with Judge Rovner dissenting, ordered Judge Grady to decertify the class action.

To Weinberg, the decision seemed ungrounded in any medical or scientific reality. So many of their expert witnesses now strongly endorsed the plaintiffs' arguments. Thousands of documents being handed over by the defendants appeared to back that position. The discovery process was working. It was achieving precisely the goals that were intended by the justice system.

The appeals court, however, seemed to acknowledge none of this, assuming instead that the history of the litigation, and all of the losses in individual cases, defined the new case. And it ridiculed the viral-inactivation theory.

Writing for the majority, Judge Posner said that Judge Grady had exceeded "the permissible bounds of discretion," in part because he was "forcing these defendants to stake their companies on the outcome of a single jury trial, or be forced by fear of the risk of bankruptcy to settle even if they have no legal liability." He added that "preliminary indications are that the defendants are not liable for the grievous harm that has befallen the members of the class."

"A notable feature of this case . . . is the demonstrated great likelihood that the plaintiffs' claims, despite their human appeal, lack legal merit," he said.[7]

So, as he had in court, Judge Posner worried about the economic impact on the companies, even though they had not mentioned it in their briefs. He appeared to have ignored the economic impact on the victims, some of whom were being bankrupted and evicted from their homes.

Judge Rovner cast the dissenting vote, calling the majority decision an "extraordinary step" and noting that "the Supreme Court has consistently cautioned that mandamus is a drastic remedy to be employed only in the most extraordinary of cases."

Regarding the economic issue, she pointed out that "defendants did not offer that rationale in support of their petition. . . . The burden of proving irreparable harm lies with the party seeking mandamus relief, not with the court, and defendants wholly failed to meet that burden here."

This was a devastating loss to the hemophilia community. For most, a class action seemed to be their only hope. In New Jersey it was doubly wounding, given the earlier decision by Judge Hamlin to deny the class there.

Judge Posner recognized this reality in that he offered hope not to the hemophiliacs but to the companies, saying that any additional cases most likely would be dismissed.

"More might be filed," he wrote, "but probably only a few more, because statutes of limitations in the various states are rapidly expiring for potential plaintiffs. The blood supply has been safe since 1985. That is ten years ago."

Weinberg had a vision of that quote being copied into motions to dismiss all over the country.

The Steering Committee filed a motion seeking a rehearing by the full appeals court. It was denied by a 5–3 vote. There was, however, a sliver of hope. The plaintiffs still had their Chicago trial date of October 2, 1995— now, not for the thousands of people they had hoped to represent, but at least for Jonathan Wadleigh, the lead plaintiff in the class action. And there was still the MDL.

Could the plaintiffs ask the U.S. Supreme Court to review the appeals court decision? That, too, was a possibility, but the vast majority of such petitions failed. The community and its lawyers had some deciding to do, but the Steering Committee members were unanimous in agreeing they had to preserve the trial date. Once again, the lawyers would regroup and get ready.

Meanwhile, in neighboring Canada, a new front had opened that would produce even more explosive revelations about the global plasma-products industry, and its relationship with government regulators and blood bankers.

IN THE UNITED STATES, the first report of what later would be named AIDS was published in June 1981 in the *Morbidity and Mortality Weekly Report*, an influential publication widely read by scientists and physicians, issued by the Centers for Disease Control and Prevention. It described the puzzling illness of five young gay men, all from the Los Angeles area, all suffering from pneumocystis pneumonia. Two already had died.[8] The disease officially arrived in Canada with a similar report in March 1982, with one victim, age forty-three, who had reported not feeling well since returning from a trip to Haiti. He also had died.[9] By July and August of that year—just as the CDC was coping with severe budget cuts, staff reductions, and a major reorganization[10]—the symptoms were being reported in hemophiliacs in both countries.

This was the start of what the Canadian government would later call "a nationwide public health calamity"[11] in which approximately one thousand of its citizens were infected with HIV and tens of thousands with hepatitis C, with some then unknowingly infecting others, all because of tainted blood products.

By December 1989, the Canadian government had agreed to award $120,000, tax free, to everyone who had been sickened by HIV-infected blood products. In 1993, Nova Scotia and then Canada's other provinces and territories announced that they, too, would offer financial support, consisting of a $20,000 lump-sum payment and $30,000 per year for life, as well as survivors' benefits. The victims had to agree not to sue any of the parties they believed were responsible.[12]

In the early 1990s, however, Canadians demanded a full investigation. They were angry and afraid that it could happen again. A government committee studied the issue and recommended a public inquiry. Thus was born the Commission of Inquiry on the Blood System in Canada, led by the Honorable Mr. Justice Horace Krever of the Ontario Court of Appeal. His mandate was not to assign blame, or recommend criminal charges. His job was to hold provincial, then national hearings, take testimony, find out what had happened, and issue a full report.

The national hearings launched in March 1995 in Toronto, and Justice Krever's first witness was high profile: Dr. Donald Francis, the onetime CDC epidemiologist who had by now retired from government service to conduct research on a potential vaccine for HIV.

During three days of sworn testimony, Dr. Francis lived up to his firebrand reputation. He said the CDC had made a mistake in not being more forceful in the early days of AIDS, and contrasted its reaction to that of Dr. John Snow, one of the fathers of epidemiology, who in 1854 investigated the cause of a cholera epidemic in London. No one knew about germs in those days, and such outbreaks were frequently blamed on a "miasma," or bad air. But Dr. Snow interviewed family and neighbors of the deceased and was able to determine that all the sick people had drunk water from the same local pump. That helped him stop the epidemic.[13]

"He didn't have proof that the water contained a bacteria . . . but he took the handle off the pump," Dr. Francis said pointedly.

He noted that in 1982, there had been little hesitation among U.S. government officials to issue written warnings to health-care workers about infected blood, even though HIV had not yet been identified. So he was stunned, he said, when the National Hemophilia Foundation issued a newsletter urging people to keep taking their medicine.[14]

The NHF newsletter reported that while a virus might be causing the disease, the risk was minimal and the "CDC is not recommending any change in blood product use." Dr. Francis said that he and his then CDC colleague, Dr. Bruce Evatt, had never said any such thing. They couldn't even remember being asked. And the CDC was pressing for more serious action, but its concerns were consistently minimized, he added.

That testimony was the opening salvo in months of hearings that frequently were front-page news throughout the country. It was far from the only dramatic moment.

The public learned that Canada had a reputation as a major center of the international blood-brokering business, and as a onetime way station for shipments from "vampire shops"—blood collected for little or no payment from impoverished people in developing nations. In the 1970s, one Canadian broker reportedly sold blood from Russian cadavers, labeled as having come from live donors in Sweden.

They learned that Canada's sole fractionator, Connaught, had used an international broker to purchase large quantities of U.S. prison plasma. Krever's final report described how this had been discovered: shipping documents referred to "ADC Plasma Center, Grady, Arkansas." ADC stood for Arkansas Department of Corrections, but Connaught didn't know that until after being notified that a number of the units were contaminated. According to a Connaught memo, the company was informed that "most of the donors in these groups were from a prison population and had not been truthful when their history was taken." Further investigation revealed that the broker also had sold plasma to Connaught that had come from four additional U.S. prisons, all in Louisiana.[15]

They learned, too, that their government and Canadian Red Cross officials had reacted even more slowly than their U.S. counterparts to ensure safe products. During one particularly memorable day of testimony, a physician and blood expert told Justice Krever: "It's safer for a patient to be given a spoon and eat a bowl of sputum than receive untested blood."

Other revelations came from the hundreds of thousands of pages of documents and court transcripts that Justice Krever obtained from industry and health officials, and from U.S. lawsuits.

So Canadians also learned that as HIV was spreading through the blood supply in 1982, U.S. health officials had deleted a warning to hemophiliacs from a CDC article about tainted products. A draft of the article had been sent to the manufacturers before it was published in the

Morbidity and Mortality Weekly Report. Drs. Francis and Evatt had known nothing of the deletion until U.S. lawyers showed the before-and-after versions to Dr. Evatt during a 1995 deposition.

"Do you know why it was omitted?" asked Bob Parks, an attorney for the hemophiliacs.

"I have no idea why it was omitted," replied Dr. Evatt, who headed a CDC division investigating AIDS when he coauthored the article.

"When did you discover that that was omitted?" Parks said.

"Right now," Dr. Evatt said.

A CDC spokeswoman, asked later about the editing, told a reporter that it was "hard to say at what level it was changed."

But one of the biggest stirs erupted when Armour documents, obtained by the Krever commission even though they were sealed from public view by U.S. courts, showed what had happened to the six young hemophilia patients of Vancouver physician Gershon Growe. In the fall of 1987, laboratory tests showed that all six patients, five of them children and two of them brothers, were HIV-positive. Horrified, Dr. Growe had ordered the tests to be redone, since all six had been using heat-treated medicine. Then doctors in Saskatoon and Edmonton reported that they, too, each had a hemophilia patient who suddenly had tested positive for HIV.

An investigation pointed to Armour's clotting drug, Factorate, manufactured in Illinois. The Krever documents, which the company had been compelled to produce in an earlier lawsuit filed by Shrager and Spivey, showed that in the fall of 1985, Armour had been warned by a prominent researcher, Dr. Albert Prince of the New York Blood Center, that its heating process left "detectable virus." Rather than withdrawing their product from the market or notifying anyone, company executives held a meeting that October at which they agreed to "review the relevant agreement" with Dr. Prince on the assumption that he wanted to publish his data. Then they invoked the confidentiality clause of his contract, forbidding him from publishing anything. They decided not to tell the FDA any of this and kept selling Factorate while working on improving their manufacturing process.

The company's own meeting minutes described Armour executive Michael Rodell as saying that "it would unwise to go to the FDA without completing our own work first . . . in Mike's view, the issue is not one of regulation, but rather marketing." The minutes also portrayed the executives' overriding focus as concern about losing ground to other companies. A marketing official "stressed the absolute need to duplicate the data of our competitors because we are in danger of losing a large part of our market share to our competitors," according to the minutes.

The company dismissed Dr. Prince's results as preliminary, but two days after the executives met, the chief of one of their own labs wrote that his staff, too, had found "infectious doses" of HIV in Factorate, the documents showed. Other documents revealed that, even after Armour improved its heating process in early 1987, it continued to sell what remained of the older medicine, much of it going to Canada.

Other documents obtained by Krever showed that between 1985 and 1987, up to fifteen shipments of blood plasma were smuggled out of Africa and sold in Europe to Armour, which made it into products. Armour said it was the victim of fraud, and there was no evidence in the documents to dispute that assertion. Armour said the material was purchased from what it thought was a reputable broker, who had assured the company that it came from Canadian donors.

These latter documents were among the exhibits accompanying testimony by three experts in international plasma trading, including Dr. Barend G. Grobbelaar, who once ran plasma collection centers in the impoverished South African homeland of Transkai and in the kingdom of Lesotho. He acknowledged to Justice Krever that he sometimes sold surplus plasma derivatives in Western Europe but was not asked whether the smuggled plasma, which had been deliberately mislabeled as bovine plasma, came from his centers.

Dr. Grobbelaar, who by the time of his testimony had moved to the Vancouver area, told Justice Krever that AIDS had "vastly and totally" changed what once was his firm belief in paid donors and international trading in plasma products. But the real problem, he asserted, was plasma from the United States, by far the world's largest commercial source. "Let us learn the lessons that the advent of AIDS has presented to us," he testified.

BACK IN THE United States, Duncan Barr, the San Francisco attorney for Bayer's Cutter Laboratories, signaled that his company might be ready to bargain. This was a surprise; when the proposed deal with Baxter and Armour had been presented to Judge Grady, Cutter had been completely unwilling to take part. Barr had represented Cutter since the 1970s; he was a blunt, clever, and very talented man. Of all the industry lawyers, he was perhaps the most formidable, with his deep knowledge from decades of representing the company.

Shrager said Barr told him that the other defendants had been riding Cutter's coattails for years, that Cutter had always been willing to take on all comers, and that the negotiations with Baxter and Armour had been ill considered. If it were up to Cutter alone, it would continue to do battle, but it wasn't. Shrager and Barr thus began secret negotiations, by mutual agreement in complete confidentiality.

The lawyers for the hemophiliacs were also deeply involved in discussing another important issue, communicating almost daily about whether to appeal the Seventh Circuit's ruling that decertified the class. There was no easy answer. Either they would appeal to the Supreme Court, in which case Judge Grady likely would cancel the October trial date, or they would proceed to trial in October, because the Supreme Court almost certainly would not hear their appeal. Duncan Barr's invitation to negotiate seemed to be clear evidence that the trial, now just six months away, was their best leverage to get a deal done.

Judge Grady was a hard read; in a May conference call with Shrager, Spivey, and Barr, the judge wondered aloud whether they had read a recent decision from the Tenth Circuit Court of Appeals that almost completely rejected Judge Posner's opinion in the hemophilia case. Judge Grady called it a "script for certiorari," referring to a writ that orders a lower court to hand over a case record so a higher court can review it. It seemed that Judge Grady wanted them to appeal. Yet he also seemed determined that the case be ready for trial on schedule.

Jonathan Wadleigh, on behalf of the hemophiliacs' unanimous Community Advisory Committee, urged Shrager to go to the Supreme Court. He said the activists understood that the chances of success were very low, but they felt an obligation to exhaust all possibilities on behalf of every community member, not just those who had filed lawsuits. If the appeal was not pursued, and the industry ultimately prevailed in individual trials, the advisory committee and their lawyers would face harsh criticism, he said. Wadleigh also urged the lawyers to keep trying for a settlement. He was very hopeful that Judge Grady might let them appeal and also keep the trial date intact.

So the activists were insisting on inclusion as a matter of principle. Their lawyers wanted to be as inclusive as possible while being realistic. Both parties were in very difficult positions. Each wanted some semblance of justice. But neither the political nor the court systems are really set up for that.

The lawyers' Steering Committee eventually made a decision and it, too, was unanimous. They would not appeal if it meant losing the trial date.

Wadleigh, the Committee of Ten Thousand, and the Community Advisory Committee viewed this as a betrayal. Shrager's dilemma was that he also had an obligation to his clients—those whose cases were pending, and who were entitled to a resolution as promptly as possible. Keeping the trial date would force a settlement that would include everyone, he believed. Again, he asked Wadleigh to consider the consequences, and to support the decision of the Steering Committee. If he and the other activists did not want to do that, Shrager said, they were free to consult with any attorney of their choosing.

This was an invitation that Shrager would come to regret. Rifts were developing over strategy, and they were about to get wider and deeper.

With the appeal controversy heating up, Wayne Spivey gave the Steering Committee a much-needed morale boost. He took a sworn statement from Dr. William Thomas, a former Baxter/Hyland vice president and head of therapeutics research, that, coupled with corporate and government documents unearthed during discovery, was damaging to the defense on several fronts.

The documents showed that, years before Dr. Thomas was hired in 1973—as far back as the 1960s, when factor products were first developed—government regulators already were expressing serious concerns about the hepatitis risks, only to see their concerns curtly dismissed. Some excerpts from the correspondence:

Oct. 5, 1967, from the Division of Biologics Standards to Hyland: "Has there been any follow-up for the occurrence of hepatitis in patients receiving this material?"

Hyland's reply, seven days later: "No follow-up as yet for the occurrence of hepatitis. . . . Since all these patients receive blood, plasma,
or AHF preparations fairly frequently, it would be difficult if not
impossible to connect the appearance of hepatitis with any particular therapeutic episode."

There was this exchange regarding Hyland's product intended to treat
another blood-clotting condition, Factor IX deficiency:

June 19, 1968, from the Division of Biologics Standards to Hyland:
"We are deeply concerned over the risk of hepatitis with this product. Follow-up studies with thorough clinical evaluations should be
done for a period of at least six months."

Hyland's reply on July 23, 1968: "We do not understand the concern
expressed about hepatitis, although we plan to make some follow-
up observations. As with Factor VIII preparations, it seems unlikely
to us that hepatitis virus could be excluded . . . it would be difficult
to name the source of the infection if hepatitis should appear."

The documents also showed that in 1977, Dr. Thomas had proposed an
ambitious project: Developing a method to kill hepatitis without destroying a majority of the clotting proteins. No other company had accomplished that.

At the time, the company funded its research based on whether a
project was on an "A," "B," or "C" list, with "A" defined in company documents as the "most active and significant." The hepatitis project was
placed on the "A" list but, according to Dr. Thomas, it wasn't funded. He
complained in writing to David Castaldi, Hyland's president, that "corporate profitability requirements" seemed to be interfering with him getting
the money and personnel he needed, including a full-time virologist. But
the project was steadily downgraded and by the end of 1978 was relegated
to the "C" list, defined as "projects which have either been shelved, are
inactive . . . or are not considered important at this time," according to the
company documents.[16]

That was the same year that Dr. Van Thiel and his colleagues published their article in the New England Journal of Medicine about the

DEPARTMENT OF HEALTH, EDUCATION, AND WELFARE
PUBLIC HEALTH SERVICE

NATIONAL INSTITUTES OF HEALTH
BETHESDA, MD. 20014
AREA CODE 301   TEL: 656-4000

June 19, 1968
Ref. No. 68-36

RECEIVED
JUN 24 1968
J. W. PALMER

AIR MAIL

John W. Palmer, Ph. D.
Hyland Division
   Travenol Laboratories, Inc.
4501 Colorado Boulevard
Los Angeles, California

Dear Dr. Palmer:

There are several points that we wish to emphasize as a result of
reviewing your application for Prothrombin Complex (Human), Dried,
and the conversations Dr. Aronson has held with Dr. Shanbrom.

3. We are deeply concerned over the risk of hepatitis with this
product. Follow-up studies with thorough clinical evaluations should
be done for a period of at least six months.

Sincerely yours,

Sam T. Gibson, M. D.
Acting Chief, Laboratory of Blood
   and Blood Products
Division of Biologics Standards

July 23, 1968

Sam T. Gibson, M. D.
Division of Biologics Standards
National Institutes of Health
Bethesda, Maryland 20014

Dear Doctor Gibson: Reference No. 68-36

We do not understand the concern expressed about hepatitis, although
we plan to make follow-up observations. As with Factor VIII preparations, it seems unlikely to us that hepatitis virus could be excluded.
Both Factor VIII and Factor IX preparations are used in situations
where the product is needed in spite of its risk, and the labels and accompanying literature call attention to this fact. In either deficiency, the
patient usually receives so many therapeutic infusions of blood or blood
derivatives it would be difficult to name the source of the infection if
hepatitis should appear.

Sincerely,

John W. Palmer, Ph. D.
Vice President and Director of Laboratories

FIGURE 15.1. In these excerpts of 1968 letters exchanged between federal and
Hyland officials, the government said it was "deeply concerned over the risk of
hepatitis" posed by one of the company's blood-clotting products. The response
from a Hyland vice president: "We do not understand the concern."

Credit: Graphic by Theresa Bielski.

onset of liver disease in hemophiliacs treated with factor concentrates, and the urgent need for clean products.

In 1979, the company learned that a German competitor, Behringwerke AG, was testing a heat-treated clotting product. Suddenly, hepatitis made it back to the "A" list, and a Baxter marketing manager recommended hiring nine more people for the hepatitis project. Without them, he warned, "the financial benefits" of a hepatitis-free product "will not occur." But there were further delays in hiring and once again, the project lost favor. There was little serious research until 1981, when Behringwerke's product was licensed in Germany, the documents showed.[17]

Now, hepatitis was seen as "a negative effect on sales and profits," according to the Baxter documents. The company expedited its research and prioritized regulatory approval in Germany, with about 6,000 hemophiliacs, not the United States, with an estimated 15,000 to 20,000. At the time, hemophilia medicines commanded a higher price in Germany, which was the company's largest market worldwide for clotting products. German doctors also tended to prescribe much higher doses than their American counterparts. "The business need in Germany is great," Castaldi wrote in a January 1982 memo.

Dr. Thomas testified that he devoted his life to the hepatitis project, working sixteen- and eighteen-hour days until doctors and family feared for his health. They were right: he became seriously ill and never fully recovered. But "this was the thing I was dedicated to doing," he said.

Baxter received Germany's approval for its heated product in December 1982 and, three months later, from the FDA. It was the first heat-treated Factor VIII product in the United States, and it turned out that the process was even more effective against the AIDS virus. But the four years of delays, from 1977 to 1981, were an opportunity lost. By then, thousands of American hemophiliacs already had contracted HIV.

The Baxter/Hyland documents contained several other revelations:

- At the same time Baxter was downgrading its virus-killing research, the company was buying large quantities of plasma in communities at higher risk for blood-borne diseases: U.S. prisons; U.S.-Mexico border towns; skid-row areas frequented by drug addicts and prostitutes; Lesotho, Africa; and Central America. In sworn statements, some of

Baxter's top scientists said they were unaware of that, because they didn't handle procurement.

- Although the company said it did everything it could to ensure that all its pooled plasma was as safe as possible for human use, Baxter separated out "low bio-burden plasma," which contained little or no hepatitis virus, to make heat-treated Factor VIII for testing—on chimpanzees. Baxter did this on orders from the FDA, which wanted the company to seed the plasma with known amounts of virus. But by segregating this cleaner plasma, Baxter executives recognized that the main pools would have even more concentrated virus levels, the documents made clear. So they developed standards for how much of the cleaner plasma could be withheld, to keep the hepatitis risk from rising to what they deemed unacceptable levels.

- Once Baxter fast-tracked its research, company scientists found the solution was so straightforward that they might not be able to patent it. An interoffice memo dated March 3, 1981, noted that "the simplicity of this process is both an advantage and a major risk," in that while they could find no record of anyone else filing a patent, Hyland's own application had yet to be acted upon by its corporate patent department. In part, they said, this was because a patent might be unenforceable. "Because the process is relatively simple, Research does not believe that it can be successfully maintained as a trade secret," the memo stated.

- Dr. Thomas testified that he knew Dr. Aronson, the FDA's primary regulator of clotting medicines, so well that they had dinner at one another's homes. It was another example of the closeness between the regulator and the regulated.

In all, the deposition of Dr. Thomas was a tremendous success for the plaintiffs. And it fit squarely with what the lawyers were hearing when they took statements from other industry scientists.

For example, just weeks earlier, Dr. Shohachi Wada, a former Cutter protein biochemist, testified that in 1972, he had conducted viral inactivation experiments, using heat on Factor IX. When he heated it at 60 degrees Centigrade, there was very little destruction of the clotting proteins—an important finding given the conventional wisdom that clotting proteins could not be subjected to heat and retain their therapeutic activity. However, the experiment did not kill the two viruses that had been spiked into his test sample. Had his bosses asked him to turn up the heat, or heat for a longer period, and try again? No, they hadn't. He said he would have tried if they had told him to do it. The results were not shared with government regulators, and it appeared that Cutter did not resume this research for many years.

In another deposition, Dr. Charles Heldebrant, Alpha's director of research and development for pharmaceuticals, said his company never worked on killing viruses until mid-1982, when a directive was received from the marketing department. It took the Alpha scientists only about three or four months to develop a process, Dr. Heldebrant said. It involved heating at 140 degrees Fahrenheit for twenty hours.

"What occurred in technology between '80 and '83 that, had you set your mind to it . . . that you couldn't have accomplished?" asked James Holloran, an attorney for the plaintiffs.

"Absolutely nothing," he replied.

In mid-May 1995, Weinberg flew to Los Angeles to depose Charles Smiley, Baxter/Hyland's retired director of plasma procurement, with whom he had spoken by phone two years earlier. They were to meet at the Hilton Hotel in San Bernardino. Weinberg drove from Los Angeles, through the desert. The smog from LA drifted toward the mountains and then stopped, hovering over San Bernardino. The land as he entered town was ashen. It did not look like a very healthy place to live.

Weinberg arrived early, set up his document boxes and notes in the small meeting room reserved by Baxter, then wandered down to the lobby. Outside, he saw Bob Limbacher, the Baxter attorney, get out of a Cadillac, go to the passenger side of the car, and help an elderly man get out. The man walked slowly, with the aid of a cane, and Limbacher held his elbow and led him into the lobby. Weinberg went upstairs to the meeting room to wait.

Limbacher and the elderly man entered the room, and Weinberg was introduced to Charles Smiley. He was not in good health. His arms were covered with bruises. He was shaven but had missed some spots, and his eyes were very bloodshot. He wore one white glove. He was friendly but hard of hearing, so Weinberg had to speak slowly and loudly. Smiley also had some trouble speaking; he suffered from emphysema, and at times would be wracked by coughing.

But in terms of his testimony, Smiley delivered. They covered nearly all of the issues about plasma collection on Weinberg's list. Smiley held nothing back, and when he wanted to talk, Weinberg let him go. More than once, Weinberg saw Limbacher rubbing his temples and taking deep breaths; he knew this was bad for his client.

Smiley expanded on what he had told Weinberg by phone, confirming that plasma collected from at least six different state penitentiaries in Louisiana and Florida was shipped to Baxter and used to produce products that included clotting factor concentrates VIII and IX. He confirmed that Baxter had collected plasma in Nicaragua, Belize, Costa Rica, El Salvador, Guatemala, Columbia, Puerto Rico, and the Dominican Republic, and along the U.S.-Mexico border. This was important because, other than the Puerto Rican and Dominican centers, the foreign centers were neither licensed nor inspected by the FDA.

Smiley also reviewed some of the documents that Baxter had produced for discovery. Weinberg noted they uniformly confirmed that the plasma centers, including those in poverty-stricken and high-crime areas of major U.S. cities, often failed to adhere to Baxter's policies and FDA regulations.

There were plenty of frightening details in those documents.

- At the Los Angeles center, for example, "many of the donors are in poor health" yet "are routinely approved for plasmapheresis by the center's physicians." Donors' plasma was taken without a physician's approval or proper record review; test samples were improperly documented; donors were not asked if they belonged to high-risk groups; traceability of donor records was in question; and the center was in need of a complete cleaning, including centrifuges, sinks, walls, and countertops.

- The Baltimore center had "gross amounts of dried plasma" on various equipment, and hepatitis-positive units were shipped together with negative units.

- The Cleveland center had "a security guard in the Center during operating hours in response to a holdup a few weeks ago during which several shots were fired; many of the employees were at the center only two to six months and were not fully trained . . . toilets overflowed and required repair . . . dried plasma in gross amounts was noted on the equipment . . . there were several failures in entries in logs including record keeping of hepatitis antibody positive donors . . . a donor on the hepatitis hot list was accepted three times for plasmapheresis."

- The Shreveport, Louisiana, center was "located in a high crime rate area" and many of the donors were "obstinate, cruel, and antagonistic."
- The Las Vegas center had forty areas in need of attention, including donor arms not always inspected for needle marks, untested plasma stored with tested plasma, and physical exams not performed as required. Also, a donor who had tested positive for hepatitis in Los Angeles in 1978 was allowed to give plasma *forty-four* times in Las Vegas because Hyland's "hot file" system had failed. It was noted that there had been "past situations involving similar or analogous circumstances."

It all reminded Weinberg of what Smiley had told him on the phone: every car needs a jack for safety. Maybe you'll never need it, but you'll be mad as hell if you have a flat tire and it isn't there.

Later, reading over these sworn statements and internal documents, Weinberg couldn't help but wonder once again about the corporate mindset. Were executives concerned that once the FDA became aware of its early virus-killing research, it might require it to be completed? Were they worried that a safer process, if established, would subject the company to liability for harm already caused? Were they satisfied with the fact that the products would sell no matter what? Did the profit motive outweigh safety concerns and lead to an epidemic? To him, it seemed obvious that the answer to each question was yes.

ON MAY 22, 1995, Weinberg received a two-page, single-spaced fax from Chuck Kozak, who said that he and Tom Mull, both members of the Steering Committee, had been contacted by the activists, who requested that they take "whatever action is appropriate to stay the decertification of the class by Judge Grady and to apply for writs to the Supreme Court,

**Happiness Is...
Sharing the Gift
of Life**

Make A Date To Give Blood,
Platelets And Plasma Today.
The Clinical Center Blood Bank
Building 10
Room 1E-33
496-1048

FIGURE 15.2. A historical poster from the National Institutes of Health urges people to donate blood, platelets, and plasma. The donors, however, weren't always so wholesome.

Credit: National Library of Medicine.

even if such action results in a delay of the October trial." Kozak said he was therefore preparing "a motion to stay the decertification which I will be filing with the Seventh Circuit on Monday."

The memo strongly suggested that Kozak and Mull were positioning themselves to take control of the litigation, noting that "the negotiating committees of these hemophilia groups also expressed a lack of confidence in the leadership of the Steering Committee," sparked by what they saw as "a dramatic change in position on the part of lead counsel from representation of the hemophilia community as a whole, to pursuing the narrower interests of individual clients represented by certain attorneys on the committee."

Kozak and Mull had participated in Steering Committee meetings and calls and had voiced agreement with the strategy to preserve the October trial date. But now, he wrote, they had to "follow the client's instructions" and file the appeal.

Weinberg received a second fax two days later. Kozak confirmed that they had filed the papers with the Seventh Circuit. He added: "Henceforth, Tom and I will be representing the CAC, COTT and the Hemophiliac Community for whom they speak. . . . We have taken these actions unilaterally, and without consultation with the Steering Committee as a whole, or lead counsel."

It was a declaration of war.

On May 23, the lawyer representing Alpha refused to present his client's employees for depositions set for that day. Shrager, realizing that the split on the Steering Committee was creating factions and putting the schedule in jeopardy, set up a conference call with Judge Grady, who ordered both sides to continue with the pretrial agenda. He set a hearing for May 30 to further address the rupture.

Weinberg wanted to see a settlement that got money for all of the victims, and he had no real problems with either Kozak or Mull. He certainly had had his own difficulties with Shrager. Yet the case was on a good track, and the Kozak-Mull strategy seemed like a bad idea to him.

He called Corey Dubin, who was represented by Mull, and arranged a meeting. They had always gotten along well. Weinberg was already in Pasadena, so he drove from there to Dubin's house in Goleta, about a two-hour trip. They went to nearby Santa Barbara for lunch and then to the wharf for a long, slow walk together.

Dubin was firmly on the side of filing the appeal and was deeply suspicious of Shrager. Weinberg tried to persuade him that it was better to use the trial date to negotiate a settlement for everyone, sooner rather than later. Besides, industry was under additional pressure because of the efforts in New Jersey and New York to extend the statutes of limitation.

Only a couple of weeks earlier, for example, the full New Jersey State Senate had approved the bill there by a 38–0 vote, with no comment or debate. The state assembly vote would come next. If the two state bills were signed into law, it would mean more lawsuits would be filed.

Dubin, for his part, was determined to get his day in court, and Weinberg understood this because he had made the very same commitment to his clients. Anybody who wanted to take on the industry could opt out of a class settlement. But the way to achieve a fair result for everyone, Weinberg argued, was to keep the October trial date. Dubin agreed to think about it and they parted amicably, but nothing was resolved.

Things were getting worse among the lawyers. Shrager, Kozak, and Mull exchanged barbed correspondences accusing one another of ineptitude. Kozak wrote that some of Shrager's former clients "have informed me that you have never tried a case to a jury. Perhaps you could tell us something about your track record in trying cases to successful verdicts, and also your success rate at the appellate level?" Mull said Shrager had "declared war on the community of hemophiliacs you are supposed to represent by not following their express instructions on such an important issue." Shrager was biting in his accusations as well, saying the action taken by Kozak and Mull made no sense, and was a betrayal of their colleagues after participating in the debate and the unanimous vote to save the trial date.

This disarray convinced the companies that the Steering Committee was not capable, at least for the time being, of speaking for the community. The prospects for a deal with Cutter, formerly the most recalcitrant but recently the most aggressive of the group in seeking settlement, faded. Armour and Baxter also pulled back from negotiations.

The Steering Committee met at the end of May, just before Judge Grady's hearing, to figure out what was next. The consensus was to stay the course.

Shrager was not at the hearing—he had been rushed to a hospital for an emergency appendectomy—so Bob Parks spoke for the Steering Committee. He and Jonathan Wadleigh implored Judge Grady to allow the trial to proceed in October even as the appeal moved forward.

Kozak spoke next and asked the judge for a two- or three-month continuance, at least until they could learn whether the Supreme Court would hear their appeal. They could hold the trial in November or December, he said.

Judge Grady replied that now he wondered whether it made sense to hold a trial just for the Wadleigh case, before completion of the MDL. The defendants pounced on that suggestion.

"I do not think that there is any justification for proceeding with the Wadleigh trial, specifically in October or at any other particular date, in the absence of it being a class action," said Douglas Fuson, "because it does not stand on any different footing from any other case that is in the MDL."

Duncan Barr agreed.

"The class is gone, Judge Grady," he said. "It is not here. The huge good that you wanted to do cannot be done. . . . We would like to forget this October trial and get on with the MDL and do the universal good of trying all of these cases in the district courts."

So Judge Grady canceled the trial date, postponing the Wadleigh case indefinitely. The perception of those who had believed that the judge would see things otherwise was wrong.

The Steering Committee was left to regroup, try to settle their differences, and, at the judge's direction, come up with a new pretrial discovery schedule. The lawyers for the defendants took their time on that, with what Shrager said was the obvious intent of stalling the process well into 1996. He began looking for eminent lawyers to help with the Supreme Court appeal, although he said the chances of getting heard were about one in fifty. Kozak responded with a letter asking that the Steering Committee allow Arizona lawyer Roy Spece to handle the appeal. Shrager said he would be "seriously considered." Given all that had occurred, he was exceedingly polite.

16

A Failure of Leadership

Thanks in large part to the efforts of Senator Lynch, Elena Bostick, Joe Salgado, Ron Grayzel, and a fully involved activist community, the statute-extension bill made it through the New Jersey State Senate and Assembly, each of which approved it overwhelmingly. By the last week of June 1995, the final hurdle was for the bill, now known as the Blood Products Relief Act, to be signed into law by Governor Christine Todd Whitman. A year of quiet protests at legislative sessions, plus pleading, handshaking, media interviews, massive letter writing, and telephone calling, was about to pay off.

Perhaps no one found this more satisfying and bittersweet than Dee Crooker, who was there for the final vote. On June 21, the day before passage of the legislation, her grandson Roger had died of AIDS complications. It was one month short of his twelfth birthday.

But New Jersey Attorney General Deborah Poritz, later to become chief justice of the New Jersey Supreme Court, announced that there was a problem. The bill, according to a written opinion from her office, was unconstitutional because it could not "revive causes of actions previously barred by a statute of limitations."

A spokeswoman said the governor would review the bill before deciding but the attorney general's views would have "a great impact" on her decision.

The hemophilia activists asked for a meeting with Governor Whitman. They pointed to testimony from Senator Robert J. Martin, a cosponsor of the state senate bill and a Seton Hall University law professor, who said he believed the law would withstand a legal challenge.

But a report from the state assembly's nonpartisan Office of Legislative Services had concluded that the bill might be unconstitutional as "special legislation" affecting only hemophiliacs with AIDS. It was one of the arguments being made by industry lobbyists.

It was just at this time that Weinberg found himself in the uncomfortable position of being forced to call Crooker to see if she really wanted to fire him as her lawyer.

Working with the activists' Community Advisory Committee, Kozak and Mull had hired a Chicago lawyer named Jerome Torshen to file a motion to discharge Shrager as lead counsel and reconstitute the entire Steering Committee—with Mull and Kozak as lead counsel. The motion also alleged that Dee Crooker wanted Weinberg removed from the Steering Committee. Other class plaintiffs were said to have retained Torshen for the same purpose.

When Weinberg called, Crooker said she had no idea that she was participating in an effort to have him removed, but that she had been persuaded by Ron Niederman to hire Torshen. Niederman, she said, was enraged because he believed Weinberg was party to Shrager's deceptions. Crooker then authorized Weinberg to say that she was renouncing Torshen's motion.

Every lawyer on the Steering Committee, other than Mull and Kozak, also filed affidavits in opposition to the motion, and Judge Grady scheduled a June 29 hearing for testimony. Most of the Steering Committee attended; so did Kozak, Mull, and Torshen, along with some members of the community, including Jonathan Wadleigh and Ron Niederman. The judge said he would allow anyone with something to say to speak.

It was a highly charged meeting, with several people stepping up to talk. Niederman, for his part, accused Weinberg of browbeating and intimidating Dee Crooker while she was in mourning over Roger. Weinberg denied the accusation. When his turn came, Kozak criticized the Steering Committee's trial strategy, saying it would be better to focus on how industry had used blood tests not required by the FDA, tests that would have been unlikely to prevent HIV in the products. There was merit, for certain, in the evidence he described, but to Weinberg, it lacked proper perspective as part of a larger strategy. Judge Grady listened to everyone and advised them that his decision would be forthcoming.

In early July, Judge Grady issued his opinion. He strongly rejected Torshen's motion to dismiss and reconstitute the Steering Committee and suggested that he might remove Kozak and Mull. He endorsed the work of Shrager and the Steering Committee.

A few days later, Judge Grady set the new pretrial schedule. All discovery, depositions, and identification of experts would be concluded by June 15, 1996.

Thus, the dispute among the lawyers and their clients had cost their cause at least eight months and had allowed the defendants more time to develop responses to their experts.

While the lawyers were wrestling in Chicago, about 150 hemophiliacs and family members, Dee Crooker among them, gathered outside New Jersey's State House in Trenton for a prayer vigil, organized in response to the growing concern that Governor Whitman would veto the Blood Products Relief Act. A choir from Newark sang while group members took turns placing five hundred blood-red carnations in a basket in the governor's outer office—one for each New Jersey hemophiliac who had contracted HIV. Teddy DePrince, a fourteen-year-old hemophiliac with HIV whose two brothers had already died of AIDS, said he hoped the governor would soften her heart. The group was told that Governor Whitman was still reviewing the bill.

IT TURNED OUT that the Institute of Medicine's Committee to Study HIV Transmission Through Blood Products wasn't so toothless after all.

After a year-long study, on July 13, 1995, it issued a 313-page report that blasted the nation's public-health system for what had happened to users of blood products, blaming a "failure of leadership" for "less than effective donor screening, weak regulatory actions, and insufficient communication to patients about the risk of AIDS."[1]

Had industry been given "appropriate incentives" by government and the National Hemophilia Foundation, "heat treatment processes to prevent the transmission of hepatitis could have been developed before 1980, an advance that would have prevented many cases of AIDS in individuals with hemophilia," the committee summarized. "Treaters of hemophilia and Public Health Service agencies did not, for a variety of reasons, encourage the companies to develop heat treatment measures earlier. Strong incentives to maintain the status quo, and a weak countervailing force concerned with blood product safety, combined to inhibit rapid development of heat-treated products by plasma fractionation companies."[2]

There was much more. The committee made fourteen recommendations. Among them, it said that, as had been done in so many other countries, Congress should establish a no-fault compensation system "for individuals who suffer adverse consequences from the use of blood or blood products," and that a single, high-ranking federal official should be put in charge of ensuring blood safety, along with a Blood Safety Council.[3]

The committee lashed the four major manufacturers of plasma products, noting that they had continued to sell unheated medicines even after heated versions were available, and that the FDA did not order them off the market. Instead, the committee said, the FDA allowed the companies to be "substantially self-regulating," to the point that they dominated membership of the agency's Blood Products Advisory Committee (BPAC), with little or no representation by consumers or other nonindustry people. It noted as well that there was evidence "from internal, nonpublic correspondence that some BPAC members deemphasized the risk to the blood supply in their public remarks but were very concerned in private."[4]

There also was harsh criticism of the National Hemophilia Foundation. The committee noted that, because of its tenuous financial situation, NHF relied heavily on industry funding and concluded that this relationship "seriously compromised the NHF's credibility."[5] And physicians had not pushed for safer products or adequately explained the risks to their patients.

In its other recommendations, the IOM panel endorsed smaller plasma pools and double-treating of products.[6] It said the FDA should no longer regulate "by expressing its will in subtle, understated directives."[7] And it endorsed the role of the CDC, noting that CDC experts had been ignored when they had sounded the alarm in 1982 and 1983. "Other federal agencies must understand, support and respond to the CDC's responsibility to serve as the nation's early-warning system," the IOM report stated.[8]

For the hemophilia community, the overwhelmingly positive report was a delightful surprise. Perhaps most important in terms of the litigation, the IOM fully endorsed the central theory of the case—that there was unnecessary delay in achieving viral inactivation. This element of the report would become a centerpiece in the litigation.

No one was more shocked than Weinberg. He had been contacted by the IOM study director and interviewed extensively for the report. She had asked him for documents, and Weinberg had referred her to some of his sources. He had taken her request to the Steering Committee. But Shrager had been cautious; his sense was that IOM reports generally were the product of compromise, rarely controversial, and the likelihood was that it would not be favorable to the litigation. Even though some of the lawyers, like Judy Kavanaugh and Bob Parks, had lobbied hard for the IOM investigation, the Steering Committee had followed Shrager's lead and had not cooperated, so if the report was unfavorable, the lawyers could have disavowed it. Now, they embraced it.

A couple of weeks later, the hemophiliacs' appeal was filed with the U.S. Supreme Court. Shrager said their Supreme Court experts were guardedly optimistic. The legal team also filed a new national class-action complaint, this time in state court in Florida. Surely, all of the new evidence that was being amassed, plus the IOM report, would make a difference.

THE LATE SUMMER and fall of 1995 were a mixed bag of good and bad news. Weinberg felt whipsawed.

The best came on August 11, when two U.S. senators, Mike DeWine and Bob Graham, introduced a companion to the House version of the Ricky Ray Hemophilia Relief Fund Act, which would pay $125,000 in a lump sum to each infected hemophiliac. The Senate specifically cited the IOM report in saying that the federal government had "failed to fulfill its responsibility to properly regulate the blood-products industry" by not requiring industry to sterilize its drugs sooner.

On the same day—a coincidence, perhaps—the FDA took the rare step of rejecting the advice of its industry-dominated Blood Products Advisory Committee and recommended the recall of any blood products that might contain Creutzfeldt-Jakob disease. The industry warned that it could create shortages. The FDA replied that, should this occur, the products could be released with warning labels.

The FDA also overruled BPAC on whether plasma collection centers should use a new HIV screening test that was about to gain regulatory approval. The committee had argued that it would be too expensive to justify the five or ten lives it might save each year.

For Weinberg, the worst came as very personal, combination punches. First, Mickey Mantle died. This was a big deal to him in many ways, because of the vivid, happy memories Mantle raised. As a child, Weinberg's father had taken him to his first Yankees game. It was in 1964, against the St. Louis Cardinals; Mickey had played right field, and father and son had sat alongside the right field foul line. Mickey had hit a home run to win the game.

Then Weinberg's dog and best buddy, Spike, died at the age of thirteen. Spike had been with him longer than his own family, back when he was just embarking on his career. With his shiny black hair and mischievous sense of humor, Spike also connected him to memories of his father. He cradled Spike in his arms while he died, and cried for him.

More than ever, Weinberg wanted to spend time with his family. He had been traveling regularly, and his sons, Jake in particular, were having a hard time dealing with his absences. One day, Weinberg flew home, landing in Newark and taking a cab home just in time for breakfast with Diane and their sons. Then he had another cab pick him up and take him back to the airport. Jake, who was in elementary school, started to cry, and continued as Diane drove him to school. As she walked him into the building, where he was scheduled to take some standardized tests, Jake suddenly blurted out, "Why can't my father get a good job like all the other fathers?" The principal, a decent man, told Diane to take him home and spend the day with him.

On August 17, as feared, Governor Whitman vetoed the statute of limitations bill, citing her attorney general's opinion that it was illegal. She offered what she said was a compromise: each HIV-infected hemophiliac would be permitted to go before a judge and explain why he or she had not sued within the two-year window of the state statute. As described by Stephen Barr in the September/October 1996 edition of the *New Jersey Reporter*: "A conditional veto announced August 17 made Whitman's opposition official and tried to make it sound as if she were doing the hemophiliacs a favor."

Indeed, it was no compromise at all—it was current law.

"She gave us absolutely nothing," said Elena Bostick, and several New Jersey newspapers agreed in editorials.

The community took some small comfort in signs that the governor wanted to find a way out. Bostick, Joe Salgado, Weinberg, Grayzel, and others continued to lobby legislators, seeking to negotiate or, if necessary, override her veto. Senator Lynch issued a press release, accusing Governor Whitman of "caving in to big-money special interests," and he contacted editorial writers across New Jersey. At one point, the state senate even scheduled an override vote, but the governor's office persuaded the leaders to extend their talks, so the vote was called off.

But even as Grayzel worked tirelessly on the legislative issues, the lawyer they had hired to help them in New York had not filed any cases. Weinberg brought in a new lawyer to serve as cocounsel in New York.

The depositions in the MDL, at least, were producing more positive news for the plaintiffs. One of the more notable was with Dr. W. Thomas London of the Fox Chase Cancer Center in Philadelphia, whom Weinberg had contacted earlier in the year. He was one of the world's leading authorities on hepatitis, and a surgeon, clinician, and longtime collaborator with Dr. Baruch Blumberg, who won a Nobel Prize for discovering the hepatitis B virus. The bulk of Dr. London's research from 1968 to 1995 was devoted to human hepatitis viruses and determining whether they caused liver cancer. At that point, Dr. London was the lead author or coauthor of more than 150 articles published in peer-reviewed medical journals on this topic, including top-tier publications like the *New England Journal of Medicine, Nature, Science*, and the *Annals of Internal Medicine*. In short, he was a superstar.

In his deposition, Dr. London said that new or previously unknown hepatitis viruses were discovered in the 1970s, and that it was entirely foreseeable that they would continue to appear on a regular basis. He said even the best donor-screening tests could not have prevented contamination of the plasma pools, so the manufacturers had a duty to inactivate viruses in their products. He also said the medical community had believed the industry had been researching methods of viral inactivation much earlier than it actually did, since the technology had existed since World War II. He was dismayed when he found out they hadn't.

Dr. London's deposition proved to be an embarrassment to the industry in more ways than one. The corporate lawyer who was questioning him thought he had come armed with some of Dr. London's own studies that seemed to cast doubt on what he was saying under oath. Dr. London was presented with the first article and took his time reading it. Then he chuckled.

"Oh, this is not me," he explained. "There's another Tom London, and he wrote this."

The lawyer, taken aback, handed Dr. London another article. He examined it. That one was written by the other Tom London, too. So much for that line of questioning.

That wasn't the only dark moment for a defense lawyer in the fall of 1995. Another lawyer, in a conversation with Weinberg, boasted that time was on the industry's side. His client, he said, could pay six million dollars to settle the cases in New Jersey, by then over one hundred in number. If Weinberg refused, he said, the companies would simply keep litigating, stretching out appeals for twenty years, and by then all his clients would be long dead. He said he could fund annuities for his children and maybe even his grandchildren from the fees he would earn in all of these cases. Weinberg was getting accustomed to being outraged but this was well over the line. He wrote the lawyer a harsh letter, repeating everything he had said, and sent copies to Shrager, Grayzel, and Ron Niederman. In no time, the letter was posted online, along with a note that encouraged victims to express their outrage in letters and calls to the corporate presidents. Weinberg heard that the lawyer received death threats. Later, he wrote to Weinberg and denied saying any of those horrible things.

ON OCTOBER 2—the very day the class-action trial had been scheduled to begin in Judge Grady's Chicago courtroom—the Supreme Court rejected, without comment, the Steering Committee's attempt to reinstate the class.

"The Supreme Court has denied us our day in court. It's a real tragedy," Wadleigh said. He added that, while he knew that the Supreme Court heard appeals in only a small percentage of cases, "there were several compelling reasons to hear this one."

The rejection meant that perhaps only a few hundred people might ever receive compensation from the blood-products industry. Most cases would be barred by statutes of limitations and other legal impediments, such as AIDS victims not wanting their names to be made public in court documents. And, unlike officials in a number of other countries, U.S. Justice Department officials seemed to have little interest in prosecuting anyone. Community members approached them, carrying files full of incriminating documents, imploring them to file criminal charges, but got nowhere.

Wadleigh, for his part, said he would pursue his civil case with a new attorney. He and the other activists had taken a principled stand and lost, just as Shrager and the Steering Committee majority had feared. Now, not only was there no class action, there was no October trial date, or any other trial date for him in the foreseeable future.

But no one could say that the activists, many of them now physically and emotionally exhausted, had not tried. They could have taken the money and run but decided instead to fight for everyone. And there was still the Ricky Ray bill, which would not exist without them.

Plus, Corey Dubin was not done fighting. He had an ace up his sleeve that no one knew about yet.

Shrager, too, was backed into a corner. He wrote to the plaintiffs, and his point was short and simple: now that there was no class, the Steering Committee would continue to work on the liability issues, but their individual lawyers would be responsible for working on each client's personal medical history, so they could establish how each client had been harmed and when. Shrager's implicit message was, you got what you wanted, and now it's done. Weinberg could not fault him for it.

Shrager's memo to the Steering Committee was equally brief, dealing mostly with the practical matter of how they would be paid. He proposed an assessment against litigated cases, plus $5,000 per case to defray the likely total costs incurred by the committee, which were estimated to be in excess of $2.5 million. Even so, he was still holding out hope that there might be a settlement that would include the entire class.

The Steering Committee met to hammer out the details and agreed to finish collecting the liability evidence and testimony by the end of 1996. Members also agreed to ask Judge Grady to assess a 15 percent fee on all individual cases that settled, plus the $5,000 per case for expenses.

Finally, Shrager sent one more memo to every hemophiliac or family member who had ever contacted his office, advising them to think about their legal options and to discuss them with a competent attorney. He included the list of Steering Committee members but said there were other lawyers who were handling such cases.

Many in the hemophilia community saw no choice but to give up on the civil and criminal courts and shifted their attention to Washington, to work for passage of the Ricky Ray legislation. Ever since the IOM report, their political cause, at least, was gaining ground.

Indeed, on October 12, in response to the report, Secretary of Health and Human Services Donna Shalala ordered sweeping changes in the way the nation regulated blood safety, and she vowed that the federal government would never again allow an AIDS-style tragedy. Her comments came during a congressional subcommittee hearing chaired by Connecticut Republican Representative Christopher Shays, one of a series he was holding on blood safety.

"It is clear that the history is a sorry history that we do not want to repeat," she testified.

For one thing, she appointed a blood-safety director to oversee and coordinate all Public Health Service programs on blood. That might have seemed like an empty, bureaucratic response, but the lack of a single administrator with authority to make decisions was a key factor in the government's slow response to AIDS, she noted.

The man she appointed, Dr. Philip Lee, an HHS assistant secretary, had a sister who had contracted hepatitis from a tainted blood transfusion and then died from liver disease.

She also announced that the FDA would have a new Blood Products Advisory Committee—one with no voting members from industry or even members with "the appearance of a conflict of interest resulting from their connection to the blood industry." Instead, industry members would be nonvoting advisers, Shalala said.

A few weeks later, the Shays subcommittee heard testimony from Dr. David Satcher, director of the Centers for Disease Control and Prevention, who warned that "we are faced increasingly with new and reemerging infectious-disease challenges" that require the nation to be vigilant about blood safety.

Another witness, Fred Feldman, Armour's vice president of technical development, insisted that the companies were better prepared than ever to ensure product safety. Then, in one of the more ironic statements made during the hearings, Feldman asserted that "research conducted by companies and by the government should be published to the greatest extent possible to elicit peer review . . . so that nobody has a blind spot in what can be accomplished in the critical areas I have discussed today." He seemed to have forgotten that his own company had been caught withholding such research and threatening to sue the scientist who wanted to publish it. Later, when a reporter pointed this out to a company spokeswoman, she said Feldman's remarks were not a reference to that incident, but to the need for peer review and consensus in current and future research.

The roller coaster year of 1995 closed much as it had begun, with some victories, many losses, and still some hope. It seemed impossible, but there would be more of everything—litigation, legislation, sorrow, joy, and hard work—in the new year.

17

From Prime Chuck to Dogeza

The first week of 1996 opened with a monster blizzard that dumped more than two feet of snow in New Jersey. It was so bad that the state's blood centers issued urgent appeals, saying their supplies were at critically low levels because of the recently ended holiday season, a flu outbreak, and several December snowstorms that had forced them to cancel dozens of blood drives.[1] Forecasters warned there could be several more inches on the way.

As a result of the storm, the final day of the state legislature's term was pushed back one day, to January 9. On that day, Governor Whitman's conditional veto of the Blood Products Relief Act would be overridden by votes in the senate and assembly, or the override would fail, or the bill would not be posted for a vote in one or both of the houses and would die. For it to be revived, backers would have to start the process all over again, in the next term.

Before the governor's veto, the bill had passed the senate by a vote of 38–0, and the state assembly by a vote of 73–1. But Governor Whitman had never been overridden before.

The decision about whether to post the bill for override votes was left to the leaders of each house. In the state senate, Donald DiFrancesco, a Republican ally of the governor, would make the call. He was an original sponsor of the senate version of the bill, along with Senator Lynch, who was the strongest legislative voice for the hemophilia community. In the assembly, Speaker Garabed "Chuck" Haytaian was the original sponsor, but he had given up his seat to run, unsuccessfully, against Frank Lautenberg for the U.S. Senate. This would be the final day of Haytaian's fourteen-year legislative career. He had a new, hundred-thousand-dollar-per-year job waiting for him, however—as chairman of the state Republican Party, appointed by Governor Whitman. He was well known as a Whitman loyalist, and she seemed to be sticking by him even though he was embroiled in controversy: A week earlier, a legislative employee had filed suit against him, alleging that Haytaian had sexually harassed her, which he vigorously denied.

As a large crowd of anxious hemophilia families watched, the senate considered the bill first, with Senator DiFrancesco calling for the override vote. Thirty-five of the forty senators had slogged through the snow to the senate chambers in Trenton that morning, and a two-thirds majority, or twenty-seven votes, was needed.

It was a slam dunk for the hemophilia community: thirty-one senators voted to override, and four abstained. Not a single senator voted with the governor.

The bill was then carried by cosponsor Senator Robert Martin, a constitutional scholar at Seton Hall University's School of Law, to the assembly chamber. There were only twenty minutes remaining in the session. Hemophiliacs and their supporters followed him, filling the gallery to overflowing. There was an air of restrained joy, waiting to explode; after the senate vote, it seemed to most of the audience that surely the override votes were there in the assembly as well. After all, Haytaian had assured Elena Bostick that if DiFrancesco allowed an override vote, he would, too.

They had not accounted for the power of backroom politics.

Haytaian refused to post the bill, ignoring the pleas of Senator Martin, who watched, dumbfounded. Assemblywoman Loretta Weinberg, a bill cosponsor, stood and asked to speak. Haytaian told her she was out of order and that she should sit down. When she persisted, Haytaian turned off her microphone and gaveled the session closed. Then he left the podium, brushing past reporters and refusing to answer their questions, telling them, "I am now a private citizen."[2]

John Sheridan, the former co-chair of Whitman's transition team, was there in his new role as a Bayer lobbyist. He told reporters that the senate vote was a case of sympathy that had "overridden basic fairness," in that it singled out HIV-infected hemophiliacs for "special treatment that no other group in New Jersey has ever received."[3]

The community members and their supporters were stunned and outraged. To them, the fact that a single legislator could deny his colleagues the right to vote was a shocking display of New Jersey power politics. Perhaps the headline in the following day's issue of the *Star-Ledger*, the state's largest newspaper, put it best: "Haytaian Closes Out Assembly Career with Some Prime Chuck."[4]

There were other considerations, however, that even the political backroom could not control. Governor Whitman's veto, followed by Haytaian's refusal to allow a vote, was creating negative publicity well beyond the hemophilia community, just as she was thought to be on the national political fast track. The specter of dying children following her to the 1996 Republican National Convention, scheduled for that summer in San Diego, could not be ignored. So, within a week after the Trenton debacle, negotiations with her office began anew, and the legislation was rewritten by proponents, legislative sponsors, and members of Whitman's staff. It was agreed that, rather than offering a one-year extension on the statute of limitations, the new version would link the extension to a specific event: the issuing of the IOM report on July 13, 1995. This date would now be regarded as the first official notice to hemophiliacs that their injuries could have been prevented. So the state's estimated five hundred hemophiliacs and others who had contracted HIV from clotting products would have exactly two years from that date—until July 13, 1997—to file suit.

The bill was swiftly reintroduced, passed in the senate in March and in the assembly in May. Two days later, on May 8, 1996, the governor signed it into law, writing in the margin, "With best wishes, Christie Whitman."

As before, the legislation drew sharp opposition from industry, which vowed to challenge it in court. "We think it's unfair, unconstitutional, and bad public policy, and we would expect the courts to uphold our position," said Douglas Bell, a spokesman for the American Blood Resources Association.

The companies followed through in June, suing the state for allegedly violating their rights to equal protection under the law, and arguing that the window for hemophiliacs was unconstitutional because it benefitted only a "narrow class of persons," and not those who had contracted HIV from blood transfusions. They argued that it was unfair to target the for-profit sector while exempting the not-for-profit blood banks.[5]

Whitman, for her part, said she was satisfied that the legislation—the first of its kind in the nation—"balances constitutional concerns with the need for affected persons to have access to the courts."

Her signature on the bill was a bright spot for American hemophiliacs, whose resentment had been growing since late February, when the industry had announced that it would pay compensation to the approximately 1,800 to 2,000 infected hemophiliacs in Japan, about 400 of whom already had died. This would make Japan the twenty-third nation in which compensation—either from government, industry, or both—was to be paid, and the United States was not among them.

Japanese courts had been pressuring for a settlement for months and urging government and industry to acknowledge their mistakes. The government had responded by expressing regret for failing to protect its citizens from contaminated blood products, many of them imported from the United States either as finished products or as plasma sold to Japanese drug firms.

The Japanese deal, finalized in March 1996 with a combination of government and industry funding, awarded a lump sum equivalent of $420,000, plus monthly payments for life, to each infected person.

A dramatic scene unfolded at the Osaka news conference at which the agreement was announced. The mother of an AIDS-stricken hemophiliac cried out that apologies and money were not enough. She demanded *dogeza*—for the drug company executives to drop to their knees and bow in shame, foreheads to the floor. As news photographers recorded this extraordinary twist, the executives, including the president of Green Cross Corporation, Alpha's parent firm, complied. All of them were men, an additional humiliation in that they had to grovel before women.

Masami Kobayashi, Weinberg's San Francisco contact, explained the symbolism to a reporter: "The most extreme form of apology in Japan is committing suicide. Dogeza is the next most extreme form, the most humiliating form. The man who does it loses his reputation and manhood for the rest of his life."[6]

That photo, transmitted around the world by the Associated Press, coupled with the settlement amounts being paid in Japan, created a furor among hemophiliacs in the United States. Rumors swirled that soon, a deal surely would be offered to them as well. Would it be comparable to what they had seen in Japan?

UNBEKNOWNST TO SHRAGER, Weinberg, or others on the Steering Committee, Corey Dubin had been negotiating since December with his old friend John Bacich, president of Baxter's Hyland division in Glendale, California, about one hundred miles from Dubin's home. As one of Dr. Shanbrom's earliest patients, Dubin had grown up around people at Hyland, including Bacich, who had risen from midlevel management. Dubin had brought his lawyer, Tom Mull, into the negotiations. Mull had hundreds of clients.

At the same time, Bayer's main attorney, Duncan Barr, was separately negotiating a settlement of the filed cases with Wayne Spivey, with Spivey thinking he might get as much as five hundred thousand dollars per case plus total legal fees of up to seventy-five million dollars, given the number of people represented by the Steering Committee. In New York and New Jersey, Weinberg and Grayzel represented more than 150 families, more clients than anyone other than Mull.

But Weinberg, Spivey, and the others were in for a shock. On April 18, 1996, Dubin called Weinberg to tell him about his secret negotiations. Armour's lawyer would soon present an offer on behalf of all four companies. They wanted to settle for six hundred million dollars—about one hundred thousand dollars per person—with another forty million dollars for the lawyers. Bayer had decided to participate in this deal instead of following through with the talks initiated by Duncan Barr.

Weinberg went through a swirl of emotions. On one hand, he felt pride and considerable relief that a viable settlement for every person with hemophilia and HIV in the United States, not just those who had filed lawsuits, was finally on the table. It was what he had wanted ever since the day he had agreed to take Andrea Johnson's case. Yet many questions nagged at him: Was it really enough, given what had happened to these people? Would the money come soon? And how would the decisions of his clients—many of whom he would advise to reject the settlement and continue with their lawsuits—affect the offer, not to mention his standing in the litigation?

Later that day, Weinberg received a formal letter from the companies, confirming the offer and the numbers. The letter said that no more than one hundred victims could opt out. Otherwise, the deal was off.

Perhaps no one was more shocked by these developments than Shrager, but he quickly recovered, telling a reporter that he welcomed the offer as "a responsible beginning." By the next day, he was writing memos to the Steering Committee, the defendants' attorneys, and the clients. The offer obviously was a positive step, four times the twenty-five thousand dollars per person suggested two years earlier, but it was still a fraction of what had just been awarded to Japanese hemophiliacs. Shrager also felt that the victims with filed cases deserved more money than those who had not sued. And there was still the nagging question of whether the U.S. government would do its part. No vote had been scheduled on the Ricky Ray bill, even though a majority of Congress had now signed on as cosponsors.

FIGURE 17.1. Takehiko Kawano, president of Green Cross Corporation, and other high-ranking officials bow down in apology before families of victims who contracted HIV from contaminated blood products. The apology, in Osaka, Japan, in 1996, followed announcement of an out-of-court settlement by the drug makers and Japan's Health and Welfare Ministry.

Credit: AP Photo/Kyodo News, Copyright Associated Press.

Judge Grady held a hearing on April 23 to talk things over and decided to suspend further MDL discovery. He told the lawyers to dedicate their resources to negotiations, even though Shrager pointed out that some clients surely would refuse the settlement, and other cases were nearing trial.

Weinberg had several depositions pending—including, at long last, one with Dr. Shanbrom. He could hardly wait. But all were put on hold until at least May 20, the companies' deadline for hemophiliacs to make the agonizing decision about whether to accept their offer. Should they take the money and try to move on with their lives, or keep fighting?

A week before the deadline, the activists, after considerable discussion, announced that the offer was too low. They wanted to negotiate further. Even Dubin had reconsidered. "Why should the life of an American hemophiliac be worth less than the life of a Japanese hemophiliac?" he asked.[7]

In part, the activists cited newly discovered evidence about the culpability of the government, based on two documents that Weinberg had received from a retired regulator, Sammie Young, a former inspector and later compliance director for FDA's Bureau of Biologics (BoB).

The first memo he provided was from 1981, from Dr. Paul Parkman, the bureau's deputy director, laying out the agency's voluntary compliance strategy—a policy that, in essence, permitted industry to self-regulate.[8] The second was a 1982 memo from Robert Spiller, the associate chief counsel for enforcement, to Dr. Harry Meyer, director of the Bureau of Biologics.[9] Spiller wrote that he had been working on a potential criminal prosecution of the Buffalo Plasma Center Corporation and several of its officers and employees. "In reviewing the Bureau's files, I was startled to realize that the Bureau gives advance notice of some inspections of plasmapheresis centers," Spiller wrote. "When I asked at the Bureau, I was told that this practice was long-established and the result of firm policy at the Bureau. This memo is to urge you to change that policy."

Spiller went on to say that the Buffalo inspections had revealed "a pattern of systematic violations and intentional deception, including instructing employees how to change their procedures when inspectors appeared. Employee affidavits taken in connection with those inspections reveal that at any given time, there was a backlog of original documents awaiting rewriting and falsifications. Such documents could be destroyed and replaced when there were warnings of impending FDA inspections."

Spiller concluded: "The most telling cost of our pre-inspection notification, of course, will never be known, as some sloppy or corrupt centers will, with notice, be able to clean up and cover up their operations just long enough for their pre-license inspection to look good, and we will never know of their violations."

These were extraordinary documents that further revealed the federal government's approach to regulation. What's more, Spiller's complaints had had no effect: advance notifications were still FDA's policy.

Later, in a sworn deposition, Young testified that, in terms of taking regulatory actions, the philosophy expressed by Dr. Meyer, "on more than one occasion, was that the biologics industry was a fragile industry and we should, therefore, be careful."

"And you heard him say that?" Weinberg asked.

"Yep," Young replied.

He said that when it came to the processing of Factor VIII products, Dr. Meyer "didn't allow anybody to inspect those places other than people from the bureau. And those bureau people were scientific types—whether they were qualified or not, I won't pass judgment—but they were not quality-control-type inspectors of the kind that would apply the kind of inspections that would be required under good manufacturing practices."

It was difficult for his people to get "the necessary scientific backup" for product recalls, Young said. Recalls often took "quite a lengthy period of time" because "the scientific people were generally concerned with doing research and . . . this was sort of an administration or regulatory function that went against their grain, and so they dragged their feet on it."

The Justice Department lawyer who was attending the deposition moved to strike Young's comment from the record. One of the industry lawyers objected too.

Young retorted that he was the one who objected.

"I don't want that stricken," he demanded.

Weinberg told Young that the other lawyers just wanted to get their objections on the record, and he could ignore them.

"They really don't want to hear what you have to say," he added.

Weinberg then asked Young about the Bureau of Biologics' attitude when field inspectors requested blood product recalls, compared to the response for drugs regulated by others in the FDA, outside of the BoB.

"They objected to recalls," he replied.

The government's lawyer moved again to strike his answer, further raising Young's ire.

"I object to the objection," he countered, "because you can't spend eight years in an area, as a director of a division, without having a pretty damn good knowledge of what the attitude and the philosophy and the overall tenor was of the group. Thank you."

He wasn't finished.

"Recall is not a scientific issue . . . it is an administrative issue," Young explained. "And I damn well know how recalls were operated because I was the author of the last recall policy the agency had when I left the agency, and I was also involved with it a couple more times because I was in the number-three-man seat, office, in the Food and Drug Administration."

The government and industry lawyers took turns objecting some more. Young told them they were insulting him and his many years of experience.

"You've asked me here . . . and then you refuse to listen to my comments," he said.

"Move to strike as narrative and nonresponsive," the government's lawyer responded.

Despite the revelations from the documents provided by Young, and other objections raised by the hemophilia activists in light of the Japanese settlement, the companies barely budged in further negotiations over the proposed U.S. deal. At a May 13 meeting in Philadelphia attended by lawyers from both sides as well as Corey Dubin, the industry agreed to amend its offer only slightly: They would ease the 100-person limit in terms of how many clients could opt out to at least 150, and each person would be guaranteed $100,000. But the cap was still set at $640 million total.

In a June meeting with the other hemophilia lawyers, Weinberg stuck with his position that the offer was purposefully designed to get rid of the best cases for an insultingly small amount of money for those clients. Shrager accused him of favoring his personal interests over those of the class. Shrager's strategy was to accept the money and fees on the table and then, after everyone was paid, negotiate better terms for the opt-out clients. There would be a number of them, including activists like Corey Dubin. The other lawyers agreed. Weinberg was alone and outvoted.

At least he got some much-needed financial relief that summer. For some time, Weinberg had been representing a little girl who had suffered permanent, extensive paralysis resulting from a single-car accident. The child had been rendered a tetraplegic, a form of body paralysis even worse than quadriplegia, by improperly refinished roadwork which had left a steep drop at the edge of a dangerous road in Middlesex County. Weinberg had retained world-class experts in road engineering, biomechanical engineering, spinal injury, and health care costs. He had carefully researched the police records of accidents on the road, which had produced compelling evidence of the danger. He had deposed every relevant employee of the Middlesex County Engineering and Road departments, which had produced even more evidence.

The county finally offered to settle for $2.5 million plus $300,000 per year, increased 5 percent each year of the girl's life. The total value was $8.4 million, probably the largest single settlement ever offered by the county. Weinberg's clients accepted the deal, but it wasn't finalized until late November 1996, so the county wouldn't have to raise taxes before that month's elections. Weinberg's legal fee was more than $1 million, funds that enabled his law practice and his family to survive economically over the next several years.

But that summer, for the first time in years, the Weinbergs didn't rent a beach house for the entire season. Instead, Diane found a cute little place for three weeks on New Jersey's Long Beach Island. Weinberg stayed there the entire time. With the Middlesex case all but done, he and Diane had a safety net. They felt a great sense of relief. There was no point in going anywhere else, and he needed to think and focus on his family. From the house, they could hear the ocean at night. For a few weeks, at least, there was a sense of peace, deep and blessedly simple.

They also found a small, older Cape Cod home for sale a block from their rental. The whole family loved the beach. The older boys surfed and boogie-boarded; the younger ones wore Speedos, had their blond hair cut short, and ran to the beach, their bellies round and cute. The asking price on the house was low—a prior offer had fallen through—and the Weinbergs made an offer that was accepted. They saw this as a clear and compelling sign that life, difficult as it had been, was going to be wonderful for them and their boys.

WITH THE INDUSTRY settlement moving forward, the U.S. and Canadian governments were progressing on their own responses, seemingly despite themselves.

In Canada, Justice Krever, who by this time had spent more than two years and thirty million dollars in taxpayer money on his investigation of blood-product safety, issued a preliminary report that listed more than three hundred allegations of "potential wrongdoing" against former government health ministers, Red Cross officials, and the drug companies. He did not make the details public. But before his full report could be issued as planned in the fall of 1996, legal actions were filed that challenged his right to lay blame on any individual or institution. They were filed in the Federal Court of Canada by most of the country's provincial governments, the Canadian Red Cross, the drug companies, and several federal agencies. Also suing were more than sixty current or former government and Red Cross officials, including one who had died in 1993.

In other words, the Canadian government had spent all this time and money on the Krever investigation and now was suing itself to keep the results secret.[10]

Lawyers argued that Justice Krever had overstepped his authority by conducting "inquisitorial" proceedings. But ironically, filing the lawsuits meant that the preliminary allegations were now a matter of public record, because they had to submit copies to the Federal Court. The Canadian news media took full advantage, with page-one headlines like "Krever Allegations Revealed" and "Potential Misconduct Findings Surface in Court Bid to Muzzle Tainted-Blood Inquiry."

Why were so many people and agencies so angry at Justice Krever? His report indicated that he believed there had been a broad-based failure by government, industry, and the Canadian Red Cross to respond quickly to the AIDS crisis. It also cited delays in developing and purchasing safer blood products, delays in testing, and a failure to inform the public.

The Red Cross, the government, and the companies denied all the allegations and said Krever had not given them a chance to respond dur- ing the hearings.

In the United States, the congressional subcommittee chaired by Representative Christopher Shays issued its own report that summer, blasting the FDA for the way it regulated blood products and saying the agency, despite promised reforms, was still doing a poor job.[II]

The Shays report, adopted unanimously by the House Committee on Government Reform and Oversight, said the FDA did not move swiftly enough on product-safety innovations and, fifteen years after AIDS emerged, had yet to develop an effective recall system for contaminated blood products. It recommended that a fund be established for people who "suffer adverse consequences" from tainted blood- and plasma-based medicines, but did not mention compensation for the hemophiliacs.

The report and its recommendation were particularly important because the committee had oversight over all federal health agencies.

It described a nation in which physicians and patients were ill informed about the potential risks of blood products, or alternatives to their use. It also called upon the government to tackle a long-simmering public-health problem that had been overshadowed by the AIDS epi- demic: the estimated three hundred thousand people who, before new screening tests were available in 1989, contracted hepatitis C from tainted transfusions. Many of those people were unaware they carried the disease, officials said.

Like the IOM report, the Shays document called for smaller plasma pools and criticized regulators for considering hepatitis a "medically acceptable risk" associated with plasma products, concluding that there had been "available technology" to cleanse them earlier.

Echoing the Spiller memo, the report also demanded that the FDA "immediately cease" providing advance notice of safety and compliance inspections, with Representative Shays noting that "the FDA does not rou- tinely notify other regulated industries in advance of upcoming inspections."[12]

In fact, the FDA had admitted to Shays that it could not say how many companies had received advance notice, because it did not keep records of it. But the policy, rather than being cut back, had recently been expanded to include some medical-device companies, as part of a pilot program. Congressional sources said the program was supposed to include only carefully selected device companies but in some regions local FDA directors were taking it upon themselves to include pharmaceutical firms.

Corey Dubin applauded the report except for the obvious omission: even though it called for compensating future victims, it excluded those already infected. "Once again," he said, "the members of Congress have refused to address the devastation of the hemophilia community. How they can call for a no-fault fund, and pass over the fact that there is legislation pending to compensate HIV-infected hemophiliacs, is appalling. . . . we are really tired of waiting and dying."[13]

Dubin said he and others were being told privately that the Ricky Ray bill had little chance of passage that year if at all, even though more than half of Congress had signed on as cosponsors. But the bill was being held up in committee, even as families affected by the tragedy, including Ricky Ray's mother, were flocking to Washington to demand that it be approved.

They included a hemophiliac who had lost seven family members to AIDS—his four brothers, two of their wives, and an infant born infected.

They included a woman whose hemophiliac husband had died of AIDS and whose brother-in-law, after learning he'd also contracted the disease, hanged himself from a tree behind his parents' home.

What was it going to take to get Congress to act? The answer was unconscionable but simple: at yet another congressional hearing, this one conducted by a House Judiciary subcommittee in September 1996, officials from government and industry insisted that, while they did not oppose government compensation, they did not want the Ricky Ray legislation to contain language that blamed any of them for what had happened. There was no failure of leadership, they insisted. The tragedy, they said, had happened during a period of great scientific uncertainty.

All of this was especially galling because, once again, Japan was ahead of America's curve. Public outrage in Japan was resulting in high-profile criminal charges against government and industry officials. First, police raided Green Cross Corporation—the parent company of Alpha, one of the American defendants that had offered the settlement—and the Ministry of Health and Welfare, seizing boxes full of documents. Then they arrested Dr. Takeshi Abe, a hemophilia expert who, as chair of the government's

FIGURE 17.2. Supporters of the Ricky Ray Act, to compensate HIV-infected hemo-philiacs and their families, rally in Washington, D.C., in support of the measure.
Credit: Dana Kuhn.

HIV advisory committee, had not called for heated clotting medicines to be used until mid-1985, more than two years after the products were approved in the United States. A day later, police arrested the president of Green Cross and two other executives.

But in the United States, it was too late for the Ricky Ray bill to move forward that year. It would have to be reintroduced in 1997.

Judge Grady, meanwhile, had given preliminary approval to the settle-ment, but there still were significant details to be worked out. In particu-lar, lawyers for both sides would have to find a way to protect the Medicaid eligibility of those who wished to settle, since Medicaid is based on finan-cial need. They had to ensure that people could actually keep the money, rather than pay most or all of their hundred thousand dollars to insurance companies and government programs that helped fund their care.

The judge also lifted the stay on discovery. The pace of the litigation quickened once again. Weinberg was back to work, with depositions scheduled across the country and in Europe. Another individual hemo-philia case was coming to trial, scheduled for early 1997 in Indiana. It was known as the JKB case, after the initials of the now-dead child whose par-ents were suing.

Bayer's Cutter unit was the defendant and, as usual, was using its highly successful FDA defense as part of its strategy, saying that it was closely regulated by the FDA, which was aware of all of the risks and science concerning the concentrates. Several of the MDL lawyers, including Weinberg, came together to help. They would need to prove that the overworked and sometimes unwilling FDA was not up to the task. The IOM and Shays report would certainly help with that image, they hoped.

In October, Weinberg drove down to Longport, New Jersey, just south of Atlantic City, to Shrager's vacation home. It was a hundred yards or so north of the inlet, on the bay, with a long dock and beautiful views to the west. Shrager, Spivey, and Weinberg were meeting there to prepare for their deposition with Dr. David Aronson, the FDA's former chief blood-products regulator, for use in the JKB case. Over bagels, coffee, and juice, they set to work immediately. Weinberg had been digging for material on Dr. Aronson for several years and brought the best of what he had found with him. The lawyers were confident that this deposition would be highly successful. The meeting in Longport took all day; Shrager was pumped and ready to cross-examine the witness.

At the deposition days later, Shrager was in top form. It was one of the best depositions in the case. Shrager shredded the FDA defense; Dr. Aronson would never again be an effective witness for the companies. There were many highlights, but three stood out.

First, despite repeated objections by the defense lawyers, Dr. Aronson acknowledged he was aware that his FDA colleague, Dennis Donohue, had gone to the West Coast in early 1982 to inspect plasma centers that targeted donors at high risk for hepatitis.

"Describe to me as conscientiously as you can recall what Dr. Donohue told you in the respect of the results of his trip to plasmapheresis centers on the West Coast," Shrager asked.

"Dr. Donahue pointed out that these were blood donors who were of, who traveled huge amounts, they often had many sexually transmitted diseases, and they rarely gave blood in the same place twice," Dr. Aronson replied.

Second, Dr. Aronson said that, after performing some preliminary experiments in his own lab, he had talked to Cutter in 1972 about the possibility of heating their first licensed hemophilia product, used for

Factor IX deficiency, to remove contaminants and then perhaps kill viruses. He said he was aware that Cutter had followed up by doing some experiments, but he recalled that the experiments had failed because heat killed the clotting proteins.

Shrager knew from the earlier deposition of Cutter biochemist Shohachi Wada, who had done the 1972 experiments, that heat had destroyed very little of the clotting proteins, but it didn't kill the viruses, either. Dr. Wada had said the work was then discontinued.

Shrager asked Dr. Aronson whether he had followed up with Cutter "to learn how far they had gone, what the problems seemed to be, what the next step might be or the like."

"It didn't work. I didn't know what direction. They didn't tell me they had any ideas on where to go, either," Dr. Aronson replied.

Third, Shrager asked about the FDA's infamous revolving door: Dr. Aronson and many of his FDA colleagues eventually left government service either to go into industry or become industry consultants or witnesses, and then in some cases, come back again to the FDA. Many also had gotten grant money from industry in general and Cutter in particular, Dr. Aronson included. He ticked off a long list of former colleagues.

"Well, quite a group," Shrager observed.

To Weinberg, Dr. Aronson seemed pitiful as he testified, sinking lower and lower in his chair until only his head was visible in the camera. Weinberg had to get up and adjust the viewfinder of the video recorder. It was saddening to know that this guardian of the public health, by his own account underfunded and understaffed, had been no match for industry. But Weinberg did not feel sorry for him.

At the end of October, the companies announced estimates of how many hemophiliacs and their survivors wanted to accept the settlement. More than 7,500 people had responded to their offer, and as many as 6,500 appeared to be eligible. But the $600 million they had set aside was enough to pay only 6,000 claimants.

Up to 600 of the 7,500 people who had contacted the companies said they were opting out, a number too high from industry's perspective.

Activists said hundreds of other people had not found out about the offer until after the application deadline, especially those whose loved ones had died early in the epidemic and whose survivors had lost touch with the community. They were inundating hemophilia organizations with phone calls, asking for help, but there was none to give. Under the terms of the settlement, people who had missed the deadline not only would be excluded, they would not be permitted to file lawsuits.

The following month, Judge Grady reluctantly announced that he had to postpone the settlement. No one had yet come up with a way to keep liens from being placed against the payments, or to preserve the victims' Medicare or Medicaid eligibility. Lawyers for both sides said a deal was near with the hemophiliacs' private health insurers. But the federal and state governments, which administered Medicaid with federal funds, were balking, as the annual costs of treatment were so high. It might even require an act of Congress to work things out.

Corey Dubin and his team were working on a plan to create a special needs trust fund to handle the money. Judge Grady was impressed and ordered the Steering Committee to help. But he was getting impatient, and soon gave the companies a deadline: They had until early June 1997 to finalize the settlement details and pay the victims. In his order, Judge Grady also issued a challenge to federal and state officials, saying, "It would be unfortunate indeed if this settlement were to fail" simply because government agencies would not sign off on the deal.

Industry lawyers told the judge that at this point, more than half of the affected hemophiliacs were already dead. Federal health officials estimated that at this point, two more were dying each day.

IN NEW YORK, the statute of limitations bill was moving through the Republican state assembly, but there was trouble on the horizon, in the state senate. Several of Weinberg's clients were engaged in the process, but they needed a skilled lobbyist. Unlike New Jersey, where there had been a tremendous grassroots campaign directed flawlessly by Elena Bostick, in New York there was no solid, well-organized victim constituency that could put together high visibility public events to pressure legislators and the governor. The Hemophilia Association of New York was not as much in the activist mode as HANJ.

Weinberg brought on board some capable New York lobbyists and public relations experts in 1996, after telling them about the case and the successful New Jersey campaign. He put together an information package they could use.

Then Weinberg had to get back home and prepare for one of his most important depositions ever—with Dr. Shanbrom.

As he had insisted, the doctor would not appear without a subpoena, so one had been issued. Weinberg was at home, making final preparations, when he received a fax from Wayne Spivey. It was a transcript of a speech made days earlier by Dr. Shanbrom to hemophiliacs and their lawyers in Japan.

In his speech, Dr. Shanbrom ridiculed the heat-treatment theory and the strategy of the American lawyers representing hemophiliacs. He congratulated the Japanese lawyers for prevailing on the same theory but said he could not understand why they had won.

As Weinberg read, he saw how angry Dr. Shanbrom was with him and the rest of the Steering Committee. They had ignored his breakthrough in developing the detergent-based method to inactivate viruses.

It was true that Dr. Shanbrom's process was the basis of most current inactivation methods used by industry. But heat-treating worked, was the first process finally adopted by the industry, and Dr. Shanbrom had not applied for his detergent patent until 1980, too late to prevent HIV. Dr. Shanbrom's response to this, when Weinberg had asked him about it, was that industry had no interest, so he wasn't motivated to work on it earlier.

Weinberg felt betrayed. He had tired of fighting with this man over what was more important: Dr. Shanbrom's work being recognized or justice for the victims. He had been the potential star witness, the scientist who had played a leading role in developing factor concentrates. But his remarks in Japan now made him unusable as a witness.

The deposition was canceled. After years of effort, Weinberg had failed to deliver him.

But Weinberg had to keep working. Despite this huge disappointment, the JKB trial was about to begin. Testimony opened in February 1997 in Indianapolis. The local lawyers put on an excellent case, demonstrating that Cutter had used plasma from high-risk donors, including those with needle marks in their arms, so long as they claimed not to have injected illicit drugs in the previous six months. The lawyers also showed that

Cutter's clotting factor contained plasma from many donors later diagnosed with HIV and produced a December 1982 memo in which the company's in-house counsel had urged that they put warning labels on their product. The evidence was so overwhelming that Cutter's lawyers actually agreed to stipulate that the company had in fact used high-risk donors.

The trial ended in March, and the jury awarded two million dollars to JKB's parents. The jurors agreed that Cutter was negligent in not warning patients sooner about the dangers of their clotting medicines. They could not agree unanimously on whether viral inactivation should have been done earlier.

This case was only the second in which a jury had sided with the hemophilia plaintiffs—and the verdict in the other one, also for two million dollars, had been overturned on appeal.

Cutter filed an appeal in the Indianapolis case, too.

The verdict had many activists questioning once again the fairness of the proposed national settlement.

"The value of everybody's case just went up," Dubin insisted. He added that victims who were seriously ill or in dire need of the money might still want to participate in the settlement. "But if you're doing pretty good and not heavily in debt, I think people ought to seriously consider hanging on a little longer," he added.[14]

Coincidentally, just hours before the JKB verdict, House Speaker Newt Gingrich held a press conference in Washington at which he vowed to vigorously support the Ricky Ray bill.

"The federal government did not do the right thing," said Gingrich, speaking to a crowd on the Capitol lawn. "This bill is a matter of simple justice."

The new version of the bill contained some significant changes. Among them was a section that would prevent the government from treating the settlement money as income when determining hemophiliacs' eligibility for Medicaid and other benefits.

But the other major change was that the legislation had been recast as "compassionate" rather than "compensatory." Despite the harsh criticism leveled in the IOM and Shays reports, the FDA's backers had prevented the bill from blaming the government for anything.

In fact, those two reports were not even the first to find fault with government regulation. As far back as 1988, the Presidential Commission on the HIV Epidemic, appointed by President Ronald Reagan, had concluded that the FDA relied too heavily on industry for setting standards that should be determined by government.

But the Ricky Ray legislation was going nowhere unless the language was revised.

In separate negotiations, the federal government agreed to accept $12.2 million from the companies as reimbursement for hemophiliacs whose treatment was paid for by taxpayers. That allowed Judge Grady to approve the legal settlement, and industry lawyers announced that their clients could start mailing checks.

This also meant that, other than the $12.2 million, the industry would never have to reimburse the taxpayers for the hundreds of millions of dollars in medical expenses that resulted from the use of their tainted products.

Before the deal was done, Weinberg and Elena Bostick made a last-ditch effort. They met with lawyers from the New Jersey Attorney General's Office and New Jersey Medicaid, trying to persuade them to join in the lawsuits against the companies. They argued that the hemophilia-HIV case was one in which a precedent could be set, in which government could shift the burden of the cost of medical care onto the industry that had caused an epidemic. There would never be a clearer case with which to break this new ground, they said.

Weinberg and Bostick were told that the proposal would be considered. Despite follow-up calls and letters, however, they never got a definitive response.

18

Endings

After Dr. Aronson proved less than effective in his deposition for the JKB case, industry lawyers knew they had to come up with another FDA expert. Until then, he had been part of a very effective one-two punch. First, Dr. Aronson would tell juries that the FDA knew what the industry was doing and approved of it, and that the companies were cooperative and compliant. Or, as Dr. Aronson said in his deposition, when Shrager asked him about his relationship with the top managers of the companies he had regulated, "I think I got along with them pretty well."

Then Dr. Aledort, the former medical codirector of the National Hemophilia Foundation, would explain the case from the perspective of a leading treater of hemophiliacs. He would praise the fractionators' drugs and tell juries how careful the companies were, and how responsive to the physicians' desires for better products.

So while the diminished clout of Dr. Aronson was a disappointment to the defense, in 1997 the industry attorneys found a more formidable witness in Dr. Harry Meyer, who from 1972 to 1987 was director of FDA's Bureau of Biologics, and then the agency's Center for Drugs and Biologics. He was an administrator and scientist well above Dr. Aronson in the hierarchy.

Dr. Meyer previously had served at the National Institutes of Health, from 1959 to 1972, where he was chief of viral immunology. In the 1960s, while at NIH, Dr. Meyer and Dr. Paul Parkman developed a modified rubella virus that prolific Merck researcher Maurice Hilleman used to create and license the first commercial rubella vaccine in 1969. They were heroes: before the vaccine, in 1964 alone, a global epidemic had led to an estimated 12.5 million cases of rubella in the United States, and 20,000 infants had been born with birth defects as a result.[1]

Dr. Meyer's move to the FDA came after Senate hearings on whether the public was being adequately protected by regulators at NIH's Division of Biologics Standards. NIH was being severely criticized for its too-collegial approach to vaccine companies. As a result of the controversy, regulatory authority for biologics was transferred to the FDA. Mostly, though, it was a shuffling of the deck chairs, as employees stayed on the same campus and some, like Dr. Meyer, simply got new positions.

Sammie Young had talked to Weinberg about that history—and how, even after the regulation of biologics moved from NIH to the FDA, Dr. Meyer and his staff still regarded themselves and their industry counterparts as the real scientists. The FDA people were cops and paper pushers in their view.

In April 1997, Weinberg flew to Seattle to take a sworn statement from Dr. Meyer. It lasted nearly four full days, the first two in the city and the last two on picturesque San Juan Island, part of a beautiful archipelago with bald eagles, great blue herons, and pods of orcas. By the time Weinberg arrived there by ferry, he was ill from a cold and fever, and for the first time in his life was diagnosed with hypertension.

He didn't know how upset the scientist was about the IOM report and its conclusion that there had been a "failure of leadership" by the FDA during his tenure. Nor did he know how much Dr. Meyer would object to the notion that he and others in government were too chummy with company scientists.

And Weinberg definitely did not anticipate how closely government lawyers would work with their industry counterparts to establish Dr. Meyer as FDA's top defender of industry, notwithstanding the epidemic that befell thousands of Americans on his watch.

Dr. Meyer, who had been interviewed by the IOM committee—briefly, with little time to prepare—had never publicly challenged the report, until now. He arrived ready for a fight. He and Weinberg spent hours sparring over details, in sometimes tense and combative exchanges.

Weinberg asked whether it was accurate to call his approach to regulation "collegial." Dr. Meyer replied that the biologics and pharmaceutical industries were very different.

"The long history of biologics, both in the U.S. and abroad, has been of intense R&D involvement by government as well as academia, and as well in industry, unlike pharmaceuticals, which is 95 percent industry," he said. "The government's involvement in the development of pharmaceuticals is minimal as compared to biologics."

Dr. Meyer took particular exception to the way the IOM panel had portrayed him and his colleagues as "an old buddies club of us sitting down in Biologics, federal employees with people in industry on an advisory committee and industry dominating our advisory committee."

He described the first meeting of the blood advisory committee after the infamous January 1983 CDC meeting—the one where Don Francis had pounded on the table—as an example of unfairness on the part of the IOM panel. It was at that February meeting that the blood advisory committee had decided there was insufficient evidence to conclude that a virus was in the blood supply.

Dr. Meyer ticked off the credentials of some of those committee members: a Yale medical professor, a future secretary of Health and Human Services, a distinguished epidemiologist, a Nobel laureate and president of the Institute of Medicine, and several more. He did acknowledge that some of them were blood bankers. At one point during his lengthy response he accidentally misstated a detail, and the government's lawyer quickly corrected him.

"I guess I need to back up," he said. "I feel so strongly on this point, I need to be a little calmer."

He listed several other committee members with impressive credentials as evidence that they were some of the country's top experts.

"It grieves me somewhat the Institute of Medicine didn't choose to look at something like that," he said. "I apologize, but that's a subject I'm very sensitive about."

There were no hemophilia lawsuits pending against the government, so Dr. Meyer's testimony would help no one but the companies. Weinberg observed that, during breaks, the government and industry lawyers huddled together, as though they were on the same team. Every time Weinberg tried to join the conversation, they all stopped talking. The collaboration between the regulator and the regulated was still alive and well.

Eventually, Judge Grady would write extraordinary orders limiting Dr. Meyer's involvement and would excoriate the government lawyers for what he said were the worst pleadings and arguments he had ever seen in the case, regarding their need to put this witness forward as an expert. But in April 1997, it was Weinberg against them.

He approached Dr. Meyer with visible disdain and the scientist responded in kind; he clearly felt that this upstart lawyer was not giving him the deference he was due. Weinberg didn't care; in his view, this was a man who had failed in his responsibilities at the FDA and then had been rewarded by being appointed president of the medical research division of American Cyanamid, parent of vaccine maker Lederle Laboratories. Meyer's regulatory team had nullified the government's immunity from being sued in civil court by authorizing the release of vaccines that contained excessive amounts of live virus. Now he was being paid by the taxpayers to testify on behalf of the industry he had once regulated. Weinberg felt ill, and it wasn't just because of his cold.

Some of the corporate documents he used in his questioning of Dr. Meyer included telling examples of how industry viewed government regulations.

In May 1979, for example, Michael Rodell, then a Hyland executive, wrote that, at a recent visit to the Bureau of Biologics, he and an FDA official had discussed "the inadvertent pooling of plasma obtained from donors having a history of hepatitis." The official "indicated that the Bureau is quite concerned at the frequency with which events involving inadvertent pooling occur, and that the Bureau finds itself in the position of violating its own regulations in allowing" this. "He fears that at some point in time, the Bureau may find itself in a position not to be able to continue with this policy."[2]

Weinberg showed the memo to Dr. Meyer and asked if he had ever been aware "that the bureau was in the position in 1979 of violating its own regulations and allowing distribution of some products derived from such pools."

"Not to the best of my memory, no," Dr. Meyer replied.

"I've already indicated that having used the plasma from a donor or drawing plasma from a donor with a history of hepatitis is—I mean, that's a basis for exclusion of the donor," he added.

The practice of using plasma from donors with hepatitis was the same one that an FDA official had told a reporter was not "violative" at all. It might have been unwise, he had conceded.

But Dr. Meyer was describing conduct that had persisted even after concerns were raised about the safety of patients on the receiving end of those contaminated products.

In June 1997, Congressman Shays held another hearing on blood-product safety. By now, the IOM report was two years old, and he was determined to find out if any progress was being made toward reforms by the FDA.

The answer: some, but not nearly enough.

Dangerous blood products, according to witnesses and government reports, were still taking a month to recall, even after they were identified. Patients weren't being notified. And when physicians called the FDA's emergency hotline on weekends or holidays, they got clerks, not people with medical training.[3]

"The number and scope of recent blood-product recalls provides further evidence of a fraying regulatory safety net," said Shays, chairman of the Subcommittee on Human Resources of the House Committee on Government Reform and Oversight.

The reports from the General Accounting Office, the Department of Health and Human Services, and FDA's own Office of Special Investigations cited a long list of lapses. The GAO, for example, noted there was no mandatory notification of donors who tested positive for viruses, allowing them "to unwittingly attempt donation again." Nor was the FDA requiring unlicensed blood facilities—those that did not operate across state lines—to report errors and accidents. FDA's inspections of licensed and unlicensed facilities "appear to be inconsistent in focus, scope, and documentation," the GAO said.

FDA officials conceded that most of the criticism was true but said they were making "substantial progress" toward remedying the problems.

Some of the examples had a frightening but familiar ring. Investigators cited a recent incident in which a hospital patient in Kansas went into septic shock and nearly died after receiving a plasma product contaminated with bacteria. But when the hospital reported the incident to an FDA hotline, the call was handled by data-entry personnel. It was another month before the agency realized the severity of the problem and ordered a product recall. By then, there were thirty-three more reported cases.

A subsequent investigation determined that not once in fifty years had the government inspected the plant, owned by Armour, where the product was made. When it was finally inspected, the FDA found eighty-seven deficiencies. It ordered a production halt and allowed the facility to reopen only after the company signed a consent decree, an order issued by a judge that confirms a voluntary agreement between the government and the company.

"The current recall notification system seems more designed to pass the buck . . . than to pass the word about unsafe blood products," Shays said dryly.

BACK IN NEW JERSEY and recovered from his cold, Weinberg was consumed with preparing for trial in one of his cases, known as *DJL v. Armour*. He had to read dozens of highly detailed Armour depositions, as well as thousands of pages of documents, in order to narrow the field to a hundred or so that could be used to argue that the company was negligent in its research and development program. No one had ever argued a case against Armour based on the viral-inactivation theory.

It helped a little that he had been comparing notes with Canada's Royal Canadian Mounted Police, who had embarked on a criminal investigation of the company, as well as others involved in the HIV-hepatitis C tragedy in that country. But the police were looking more at the incident involving Armour's underheated product, while the client in the DJL case had been infected with HIV years earlier, in 1981 or 1982.

So Weinberg was working sixteen-hour days, trying to get comfortable with the science behind the Armour product. Grayzel was tackling the damages part of the case, which also was complicated. Weinberg hadn't fully appreciated how difficult his part would be, or he might have asked for more help. He lost a week of prep time when Judge Wolfson agreed that Dr. Meyer could testify in the New Jersey case, even though Judge Grady had barred him from testifying in the MDL. Again, Weinberg had to fly to Seattle to take testimony from Dr. Meyer.

At least this time, he had two other lawyers with him for the duration. That was a good thing, because Dr. Meyer was not happy to see him, at one point accusing him of being sleazy. But this deposition went better for the plaintiffs. Weinberg thought Dr. Meyer's testimony was weak and that he came across as bitter and angry. He would not give straight answers to their questions.

In addition to gearing up for the DJL case, Weinberg also had to deal with the New York legislative agenda, where there was complication after complication. A crisis arose in early August. The New York legislature was winding down its work, and there were some issues with the bill. If it did not pass then, chances were it never would.

So Weinberg took a break from the DJL case to rewrite the bill, giving the changes to the lobbyists by telephone. It passed on August 3, 1997, a major victory, but now they had to persuade Governor George Pataki to sign it into law. As Weinberg and the other advocates knew only too well from what had happened in New Jersey, this was no slam dunk, and the political maneuvering by opponents would now concentrate on the governor. Bud Herman wrote to Pataki, since he knew him personally. Weinberg contributed fourteen thousand dollars to various Republican organizations in New York in the months leading up to passage of the bill in August 1997. The lobbyists continued to work the issue hard.

September, October, and November came and went. Finally, in December 1997, Governor Pataki signed the New York legislation into law.

There was a moment of comic relief a couple of nights before passage of the bill. It was past midnight, and one of Weinberg's New York colleagues was getting coffee in the statehouse lounge when he saw, on the lounge TV, Senate Speaker Joseph Bruno bang his gavel. The man mistakenly thought Bruno was gaveling the entire legislative session to a close, meaning the hemophilia bill would be dead. He panicked, running frantically through the marbled halls of the statehouse, to the senate chambers. As he neared the entrance he staggered, then collapsed on the floor, nearly unconscious. He was revived by the brother of a hemophiliac who happened to be an emergency medical technician. As he came around, the man was moaning about the vote—the bill is dead, he said over and over again.

The EMT and others reassured him that the session was not over; Bruno was simply ending for the day, and the senate would be back at work in the morning.

Jury selection for the DJL case started in fall 1997 and took two weeks. Judge Wolfson had scheduled pretrial motions, and Weinberg was in court when he learned that a letter had been sent to all counsel by a law firm representing Robert Wood Johnson University Hospital. The letter, sent in response to a subpoena served by Cutter, advised that there were stored blood samples in a hospital freezer from several of the hemophilia patients that Weinberg and Grayzel represented, including DJL. The samples were from 1980, 1981 and 1982, very important years in terms of trying to determine when patients first tested positive for HIV.

The letter from the hospital brought the trial to a temporary halt, because now there was crucial evidence that had to be tested. Depending on the results, it was possible—perhaps even likely—that they could pin down a more definite time frame for DJL's infection. It even could be that another fractionator ought to be the defendant instead of Armour. It was a disaster, particularly in the very first New Jersey case to be tried.

Weinberg was embarrassed and disappointed in himself. He had hoped to establish a precedent with the DJL case, but the misstep over the untested blood was a huge letdown for the client. DJL was never enthusiastic about going to trial and didn't really want to be the poster boy for the hemophilia cause. He lay down on one of the vinyl couches in the hallway outside Judge Wolfson's courtroom, closed his eyes, and seemed to sleep. He did not want to be there. Weinberg couldn't have felt worse.

To make matters worse, Armour intended to argue that DJL's doctor actually chose not to prescribe heated clotting factor when it was first licensed, because he was unsure of its safety. The company's lawyers had set up this defense during the depositions of several prominent treating physicians in New Jersey: no one knew exactly what effect the heat would have on these products. Yes, it might kill germs, but what if it had some unintended side effect? Weinberg was totally unprepared for that. He never saw it coming until they were in court, with the jury selected.

DJL asked the lawyers to settle his case for whatever they could get; he was willing to simply take the class action settlement. The samples were tested, and one tested positive, then negative on retesting. Armour now had another piece of evidence to confuse the issues, as its lawyers could say that DJL had been infected earlier than he was claiming, and at a time when he was using other companies' products.

Fortunately for DJL, Weinberg and Grayzel did much better for their client than the class-action money: they settled for four hundred thousand dollars. According to Armour's attorneys, it was more than the company had ever paid in a case involving a pre-1983 infection.

IN CANADA, Justice Krever prevailed against those who had tried to use the courts to silence him, and released his final report. It was as bad as the fractionators, Canadian Red Cross, and government health officials had feared.

Working from the testimony of 474 witnesses and 50,011 written pages of evidence, plus 1,303 exhibits consisting of nearly 100,000 pages, Krever produced a sweeping document consisting of 1,138 pages in several volumes. It harshly criticized everyone involved in the tainted-blood scandal.[4]

"The principal actors in the blood system . . . refrained from taking essential preventative measures until causation had been proved," Krever wrote. "The result was a national public health disaster."

Krever called for compensation for the victims of blood products and transfusions tainted with HIV and hepatitis C. He said the total could be as many as 28,000 Canadians. Activists estimated that 3,000 already had died.

"Many witnesses expressed a sense of betrayal by the blood system they had implicitly trusted," Krever wrote. He said mismanagement, lax oversight, penny-pinching, and foot-dragging had occurred at nearly every level of industry and government.

Among the most horrifying incidents, Krever said, were a premature infant who received a tablespoon of AIDS-tainted red blood cells even though his parents had not consented to a transfusion; a middle-aged cardiac patient who wasn't told he received HIV-tainted blood because his doctor assumed he no longer had sex with his wife; and a woman who underwent dental surgery and contracted hepatitis C from a platelet transfusion.

The judge heaped particular scorn on Armour, which by this time had changed its name to Centeon; he accused the company of violating provisions of Canada's Food and Drug Regulations by failing to disclose the results of the studies that showed there could be live HIV in their early heat-treated product—the one that had infected the boys in the Vancouver area. Those regulations required that manufacturers inform the federal government "of any deficiency or alleged deficiency concerning the quality, safety or efficacy of any drug manufactured" by the company, he said.

The Canadian health minister responded to the report by vowing immediate reforms, including additional money for regulating blood safety. The government had to do something quickly; the scandal had infuriated and frightened Canadians, and Red Cross blood donations were dropping precipitously.

As a result, Canada took the dramatic step of ordering the Red Cross removed as the nation's primary blood collector. The duties would be transferred to a new nonprofit agency that had consumers but no government bureaucrats on its board of directors. It was almost unthinkable: the century-old Canadian Red Cross, the nation's premier source of donated blood since the beginning of World War II, was being ousted from the blood business. More than 80 percent of the total funding for the Red Cross came from Canada's federal, provincial, territorial, and municipal governments, but under the plan it would relinquish all funds, facilities, and other assets related to blood services.

Led by Canadian activist groups, there now were widespread demands for a criminal investigation, but there was a catch: under the agreement that formed the Krever Commission, the judge could not recommend criminal charges, and none of the information or testimony he collected could be used in criminal proceedings. That point had been reaffirmed in September, when the Supreme Court of Canada ruled 9–0 in favor of allowing him to release his report. The Supreme Court said, however, that while Krever could not recommend criminal charges, he could issue findings of misconduct.

So if anyone were to be arrested and tried, the Royal Canadian Mounted Police (RCMP) would have to start almost from scratch in collecting evidence.

The RCMP formed a task force, and investigators began fanning out around the globe, essentially tasked with duplicating much of what Krever already had done. In February 1998, they announced they were launching a full-scale criminal investigation, dubbed Project Oleander, after the shrub with beautiful but toxic pink flowers. It was a massive undertaking. They interviewed seven hundred people in nine different countries and collected millions of pages of evidence. "There has never been an investigation like this one," RCMP Superintendent Rod Knecht told the *Globe and Mail*, Canada's largest national newspaper.

In April 1998, there was a mediation effort to settle the New Jersey cases, prompted by Judge Wolfson. The parties hired Justice Robert Clifford, retired from the New Jersey Supreme Court. Three cases were selected to mediate. The first was Andrea and Clyde Johnson's case. Each side made opening statements, and then Weinberg, Spivey, Grayzel, and the others involved in the Johnson case adjourned to a side room while the twenty or so lawyers representing the companies conferred with Justice Clifford. They spent about two hours with him. When the judge finally came to the side room, the first thing he asked was whether the Johnson case might not be better suited to the class settlement. Weinberg and the team were surprised, because Cutter's lead counsel had said they were very ready to do business. Weinberg asked Clifford to get the defendants to make an offer; the number that came back was $225,000. Andrea and her daughter could have gotten $200,000 from the class settlement. Weinberg, Spivey, and the others walked out. So much for mediation.

The next case up for trial in New Jersey was *N.M. v. Cutter*, and Weinberg thought it might be the best case in their inventory. N.M., married with two children, had been infected with HIV in early 1984, having infused only Cutter product. He had read the *Philadelphia Inquirer* stories about the hemophilia case and had called the reporter, who had suggested he contact Weinberg. Weinberg, in turn, referred him to Grayzel for the initial meeting.

N.M. arrived at Grayzel's office with a childhood friend, a lawyer from Atlantic City. The lawyer told Grayzel that he expected a referral fee if there was a successful resolution to the case. Grayzel agreed, not aware that N.M. had called Weinberg directly. So already there was a problem. Spivey balked at paying the referral fee, and when Grayzel realized that N.M had been referred by Weinberg, he told the lawyer there would be no fee. Weinberg tried to negotiate with him and eventually they agreed that he would get 10 percent of the net fee, up to a maximum of $50,000—all for someone who had showed up after there was a nationwide settlement offer.

The N.M. case was scheduled to begin in September 1998. Judge Wolfson continued to encourage negotiations on all the New Jersey cases. He had not given up despite the poor outcome with the Johnson case. Cutter then offered to settle the case with N.M., who had directed Weinberg to settle if he got a certain amount of money. The offer was for more than that, even after the lawyer's fee of one third.

But N.M. didn't want to pay that much, arguing that the lawyers had done nothing extraordinary for him. Then his friend filed a lawsuit against Weinberg, Spivey, and Grayzel, claiming he was extorted into agreeing to the $50,000 cap on his fee. In filing the case, he revealed the full name of N.M., even though N.M. had been very concerned that his identity be protected.

Judge Wolfson asked Weinberg to settle as a favor to him, so he did. N.M.'s friend received $85,000. It was unpleasant to be sued by a lawyer who had done no work on the case, but Weinberg was satisfied to put the issue behind him and move on.

In May 1998, nearly three years after it was first introduced, the U.S. House of Representatives voted unanimously for the Ricky Ray Hemophilia Relief Fund Act, and to establish a $750 million trust fund to pay $100,000 to each affected hemophiliac or survivor. House Speaker Gingrich had kept his promise. Five months later, on the last day of its 1998 session, it was approved by the Senate, and it was signed into law by President Bill Clinton a few weeks later.[5]

The National Hemophilia Association rejoiced but noted that this made the United States one of the last developed countries to establish such a compensation program.

At that point, more than 3,000 U.S. claimants had received their checks from the class action settlement, leaving approximately 2,800 unresolved claims, according to the foundation.

There was still one major problem: No money had been appropriated to fund the Ricky Ray law. It would take another two years for victims to start being paid. Even then, there was enough to pay only 670 of the estimated 7,500 people who were eligible, according to HHS Secretary Donna Shalala. She and President Clinton's chief of staff, John Podesta, urged

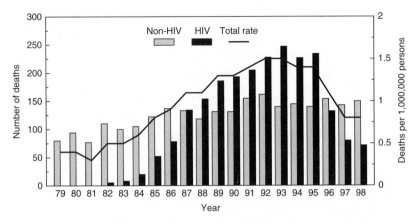

FIGURE 18.1. Deaths among persons with hemophilia A for those with and without HIV-related disease and overall age-adjusted death rate, by year, United States, 1979–1998.

Credit: T. L. Chorba, R. C. Holman, M. J. Clarke, and B. L. Evatt, "Effects of HIV Infection on Age and Cause of Death for Persons with Hemophilia A in the United States," American Journal of Hematology 66 (2001): 229–240, http://onlinelibrary. wiley.com/doi/10.1002/ajh.1050/pdf.

Congress to appropriate the rest of the money. "We must do more," Podesta said.[6]

Congress approved the final funding in 2001, nearly twenty years after the first hemophiliac was infected.

In New Jersey, the industry lawyers had convinced the appellate division of the superior court to consider overturning the statute of limitations law. The appeal specifically involved Joe Salgado but could apply to any of the New Jersey cases. Weinberg knew that if they lost in the appellate division, the cases would, for the most part, be dismissed. He discussed what to do with Salgado and Elena Bostick. They agreed it was time to settle and move on.

Oral argument on the appeal took place in Trenton in January 1999, but before the court could issue its ruling, the New Jersey opt-out cases were settled. The appellate division decided that the law was no longer an issue, and the appeal was withdrawn. The law, and the precedent, for which Weinberg, Grayzel, Bostick, and so many others had fought so hard, would stand.

In New York, too, things were going well at last. Not only had the statute-of-limitations extension been signed into law, but Nicholas

Papain, the lawyer who had taken over the cases there, was doing an excellent job. He asked for a bigger percentage of the fee, and Spivey and Weinberg readily agreed. The lawyers pushed the fractionators to settle, and at first they refused. But the judge overseeing the consolidated New York cases, Associate Justice Karla Moskowitz of the state supreme court's appellate division, ruled that the law extending the statute of limitations was constitutional. Eventually, a settlement was reached.

There was one more major case about to be tried, and that was in New Orleans. Tom Mull and another lawyer, Robert Arceneaux, were representing Kenneth Dixon, who had contracted HIV from clotting products. He died in 1995, and his parents, Leo and Shirley, continued the case after his death. Mull and Arceneaux decided to emphasize a different theory, arguing that there had been a failure to warn patients about high-risk plasma donors.

In preparation for the case, Dr. Meyer was deposed again, this time questioned mostly by Wayne Spivey and Tom Mull. It was much different in tone than the marathon session with Weinberg. After Mull showed Dr. Meyer some advertisements from gay publications, soliciting plasma donors who had been infected with hepatitis, the doctor agreed that use of such donors for clotting drugs was, in his opinion, a violation of federal regulations. He said he had not been aware of such recruiting practices, and there was no requirement or regulation on this subject. Nor, he said, was he aware of the extent to which the industry had used prison plasma.

The Dixons' lawyers also produced two internal industry memos, both summarizing a May 1985 meeting between the FDA and the companies. Both said that Dr. Meyer wanted heated products to replace unheated products in a way that would not attract too much attention. Dr. Meyer "would like the issue quietly solved without alerting the Congress, the medical community and the public," stated one of the memos. "Implicit in the discussion was the concern that the FDA felt that this action was long overdue."[7]

Mull even had something in store for the other half of industry's Meyer-Aledort duo. When Dr. Aledort testified, Mull introduced a letter from the president of Mount Sinai Hospital in New York, advising Dr. Aledort that he was being removed as director of the hemophilia clinic because of his alleged conflicts of interest and the federal investigation. Weinberg was thrilled with that development.

In March 1999, after deliberating for three days, the jury awarded the Dixons an astounding $35.3 million—$56 million with interest. It was the largest amount by far in any HIV-hemophilia case.

But minutes after dismissing the jury and thanking them for their service, the judge opened an envelope that held his decision on the defendants' motion to dismiss the case. He granted the motion, agreeing that the statute of limitations had expired.[8]

The Dixons immediately appealed, arguing that the judge had ignored the jury finding that the companies had fraudulently concealed their wrongful conduct. The Court of Appeal of Louisiana—which quoted Dr. Meyer, Dr. Aledort, and Judge Posner extensively in its written opinion—upheld the trial judge.

Mull and Arceneaux then appealed to the Louisiana Supreme Court. They argued for reversal of the court of appeal based on prescription—the statute of limitations—since the jury had made a factual finding of fraud and misrepresentation. In Louisiana, the doctrine of "contra non valentem" interrupted prescription when a party committed fraud—a finding of fact to be determined by the jury and not the court. Before the state supreme court had a chance to rule, the Dixon family received a substantial seven-figure settlement.

And so the pattern continued: even when U.S. juries ruled in favor of hemophiliacs and their families, they always had to appeal. Not long before the Dixon trial, there had been a similar case in Missouri, where an AIDS-infected hemophiliac was awarded $1.4 million, only to see the verdict reversed.

So, too, continued the Steering Committee's dispute over how to share the legal fees in the MDL. Weinberg felt hopeless; he had been toiling over the litigation for more than six years and, despite multiple recommendations put forward by various lawyers, Shrager hadn't approved a fee schedule. Except for the DJL case, Weinberg had yet to see a dime. Other members of the Steering Committee also were unhappy. One even consulted a lawyer.

Finally, in February 2000, after years of wrangling, the lawyers met for a day in Atlanta and reached a grudging compromise. Weinberg was disappointed in the deal but relieved that it was done. They reconvened in May in Chicago, where Judge Grady approved it. The judge was as good on the

bench that day as Weinberg had ever seen him. There was only one dis-
senter remaining, and Judge Grady's words to him rang true to Weinberg
as well: The fees you earn in these cases, the judge noted, are not the last
fees you will ever earn. There will be more cases, there will be more
work for you, and there is always the opportunity to move on to the
next project.

Weinberg and his clients were paid at last. He helped one of them, his
friend Richard Vogel, close on a new house. And Andrea Johnson bought
a Lexus equipped with hand controls so she could drive.

IN NOVEMBER 2002, the Royal Canadian Mounted Police announced that
they were bringing charges against the Canadian Red Cross Society, a
former Red Cross director, two Canadian government officials, and
Dr. Michael Rodell of Armour. The charges included endangering the
public and criminal negligence causing bodily harm. Armour was charged
with failure to notify under the Food and Drugs Act. More charges of
criminal negligence were added in 2004. That charge alone carried a maximum penalty of ten years in prison if convicted.

It was Dr. Rodell, Armour's vice president of scientific and regulatory
affairs, who had been quoted in the company's meeting minutes as saying
it would be "unwise" to tell the FDA that a scientist had informed them
that Armour's heat-treated clotting drug was likely to contain live HIV.

Weinberg and others in the United States did what they could to help
the RCMP, but the stance taken by Canadian officials that forbade the
police from using Krever's files made things more difficult than they
should have been. It was farcical: the RCMP investigators could read the
Krever documents but for official use were forced to get copies from anyone but Krever. They even enlisted the U.S. Attorney's Office in the Eastern
District of Pennsylvania, which issued a subpoena on behalf of the
Canadian government demanding that Donna Shaw, the *Philadelphia
Inquirer* reporter who had covered the story for years, turn over all of her
work product, including names and materials from confidential sources.
No U.S. journalist would want to set the legal precedent of complying with
such a broad demand from government, much less one filed on behalf of
a foreign country. Instead, she referred the investigators to Weinberg, and
the newspaper hired a top First Amendment lawyer to defend her.

She never handed over a single document. It all seemed especially ironic since the Justice Department had declined to file criminal charges in the United States, despite pleas from many affected families.

In May 2005, the Canadian Red Cross Society pleaded guilty to distributing tainted blood products between January 1983 and May 1990. Six charges of endangering the public were withdrawn. The secretary general of the Red Cross also released a videotaped apology. A month later at sentencing, the Red Cross was ordered to pay the maximum fine—$5,000—as well as to contribute $750,000 each to two scholarship and research funds at the University of Ottawa.

That left the charges against the four individuals and Armour. The trial took a year and a half. Final arguments were scheduled to be heard before Superior Court Justice Mary Lou Benotto at the Court of Justice in Toronto on September 10, 2007.

That morning, spectators walking on University Avenue toward the courthouse couldn't be blamed for feeling a little confused: As they approached the building, they saw a red carpet unfurled on the sidewalk, and an excited crowd with cameras gathering behind velvet ropes. Was the tainted-blood case really that much of an attraction? As it turned out, there was a major international film festival being held in Toronto that week next to the courthouse. The fans were hoping for a glimpse not of lawyers, judges, or victims, but of Brad Pitt and Angelina Jolie.

Inside the courthouse, the proceedings started with the Crown prosecutor, Michael Bernstein, his salt-and-pepper hair standing out against his black barrister's robe, arguing that the defendants had "a duty to disclose a risk of harm" and "a duty not to distribute unsafe blood products."

There was no evidence other than hearsay to suggest that a product shortage made it necessary to use the tainted Armour product, he argued. Armour's competitors could have met the demand. Bernstein also noted that all of his medical experts had testified that the problem was foreseeable.

The defense team went next, each lawyer taking a turn. They scoffed at Bernstein's characterizations, calling them "puffery without substance." The defendants' actions, they told the judge, were completely reasonable, given what science knew at the time. It was wrong, they argued, to judge the defendants based on hindsight. These were fine and good men, careful and responsible, who had devoted their lives trying to help others. If mistakes were made, they were honest mistakes, with the best of intentions.

After the arguments, Justice Benotto said she would need very little time to come to a decision. She would announce it in three weeks, on October 1.

When the day came, Justice Benotto was true to her word. She got right to the point, finding all of the defendants not guilty and saying that they deserved to be exonerated.

"There was no conduct that showed wanton and reckless disregard," she announced, reading aloud from her ruling to a packed courtroom that included a number of victims. "There was no marked departure from the standard of a reasonable person. On the contrary, the conduct examined in detail for over one and a half years confirms reasonable, responsible and professional actions and responses during a difficult time."[9]

She added: "The allegations of criminal conduct on the part of these men and this corporation were not only unsupported by the evidence, they were disproved.

"The events here were tragic. However, to assign blame where none exists is to compound the tragedy."

Six remaining charges against the former Red Cross director were dropped in 2008.[10] The criminal cases in Canada were over.

And so was the chance that any officials would go to prison anywhere in North America for their roles in the tainted-blood scandal.

EVERYTHING I DID, I did for Joe Salgado.

That thought occurred suddenly to Weinberg in July 2010 as he sat in a packed Manhattan theater with his son Michael and they watched the debut of the documentary film *Bad Blood: A Cautionary Tale*, which would be broadcast nationwide on PBS the next summer. Also present was Weinberg's friend and colleague, Donna Shaw.

The filmmaker, Marilyn Ness, was a childhood friend of Matt Kleiner, one of Weinberg's clients. Ness had been inspired by Kleiner's life to make the film, and Michael Weinberg watched, enraptured, as his father appeared on the big screen, a decade younger, telling the story of the epidemic of HIV in the hemophilia community. His son was proud of him.

It was more than Weinberg, the frequently absent father, could have hoped for when he decided in 1991 to take Andrea Johnson's case.

The audience was a reunion of hemophiliacs and their family members from across the country—Corey Dubin flew in from California—as well as activists from the gay community. At the time, some gay activists were embarking on an effort to persuade the government to ease restrictions on gay blood donors. Ness invited them to see her film so they would more fully understand the history; the hemophilia cause for years had gotten strong support from gay and lesbian groups.

By the time the film ended, most audience members were visibly emotional. One gay activist sobbed on a stranger's shoulder. "I didn't know, I didn't know," he repeated.

Dubin, Weinberg, Shaw, and the others mingled before and after, talking, hugging, and reminiscing. Sadly, many more were noticeably absent. COTT alone had lost more than 60 percent of its board of directors, including its two founders, Jonathan Wadleigh and Tom Fahey. HANJ board member Ron Niederman was gone. So was Andrea Johnson. But at last, the nation would see and hear what had occurred to them and their friends.

In 2011, Weinberg, who recently had taught a course about the AIDS litigation at Rutgers University, was invited to speak to medical students at the Wayne State University School of Medicine, in Detroit. The invitation was the idea of a young hemophiliac and medical student who wanted Weinberg to attend a campus screening of *Bad Blood* and then take part in a panel discussion about the film.

After the movie ended, one of the medical students asked Weinberg an excellent question. What, he asked, is the takeaway message from this? What should we learn?

Weinberg had an answer at the ready, though he had not anticipated the question. It had been there for years, just waiting for him to say it.

"Question authority."

The students looked quizzically at Weinberg—earnest, intelligent, idealistic young people, not much older than his own children.

"What I mean is this: When something doesn't make sense to you—like if you're told to inject your patient with a blood product that you think might be dangerous, for example—question authority. Ask the right questions: Is this really the best that can be done? Why can't it be better? Why can't it be safer? Demand to know."

Weinberg was still trying to make sense of what had taken nearly a decade of his life to finish. He had come to feel that the resolution of the hemophilia case had been in some respects a success and in others a failure. In the beginning, when he met Andrea Johnson, he naively envisioned a case in which everyone dealing with hemophilia and HIV would have their day in court—every hemophiliac, wife, child, parent, and survivor.

But the courts are not really designed for that purpose, and when justice happens, it is often more by accident than design. Still, in some real and meaningful ways, his vision came to fruition.

But it took too long, the victims didn't get enough justice or money, and Weinberg knew he'd made mistakes large and small along the way. If he could do it over again, he would try to get the money sooner, before so many died, to pay for AIDS medicines and liver transplants and the other things needed to keep people alive and independent.

Yet, as a colleague had once reassured him, it was a meaningful resolution to a very, very difficult case.

Nothing, ever, is an absolute in life. Nothing works perfectly all of the time, and everyone makes mistakes. The challenge is to learn, and to do better the next time.

EPILOGUE

The line can form as early as 5:30 A.M. outside the Interstate Blood Bank on Broad Street in North Philadelphia, even though it doesn't open for another hour. The center, which pays its donors, is located in a rundown, what you might call in-between section of the city: too far north to be part of fashionable Center City, home of the law firm of Shrager, Spivey & Sachs, and too far south to be affected by the gentrification wrought by Temple University's expansion. Its near neighbors include several vacant store-fronts; a few blocks in either direction, you'll find the Salvation Army, YMCA, homeless shelters, churches, and other social services.

Donors must be at least eighteen years old, weigh at least 110 pounds, and be in good health and well hydrated, according to the center's recorded telephone message. You also need a valid Social Security card, a photo ID, and proof of address that's within 125 miles of the center. No appointment is required.

Interstate's Memphis-based parent company owns thirty whole-blood and plasma collection centers, and was a founding member of the Plasma Protein Therapeutics Association (PPTA), an industry trade association. Its members operate more than 450 collection centers in the United States and Europe and manufacture about 80 percent of the plasma therapies used in the United States, and 60 percent of those manufactured in Europe. The PPTA has voluntary standards that require routine, indepen-dent, third-party auditing of its members' collection centers.[1]

On the bloodbanker.com website, Interstate's Philadelphia patrons offer a variety of comments, ranging from "very professional workers, clean environment" to "the staff is not very polite and talk to people ill mannered."

A visitor can't help but notice, though, that most of the people standing in that line, or sitting inside on the long rows of chairs in the waiting room, appear poor. And paid donors, especially poor ones, continue to be enormously controversial, because they are more likely to be ill and desperate enough for money to lie about their medical history.

As recently as 2007, for example, one of the major plasma-products manufacturers called for collections along the U.S.-Mexican border to end, saying they "compromised the fundamental ethics of our business," according to a story in the *New York Times*. "But the other companies defended the practice and the matter was dropped," the *Times* noted.[2]

During the U.S. litigation, Judge Grady once commented on the broader issue in rejecting the companies' argument that they should not have to produce photos and other records about their blood plasma donors. Grady noted that "we are dealing here with paid if not professional donors" and said he thought that the companies' arguments for preserving privacy were "almost totally disconnected from any genuine concern about confidentiality." He seemed sure there was some other reason.

"The photographs do not show whether these people have infections," he said. "They do not show whether their ears are pierced or whether they are toothless or have gum disease or anything of the kind, or if they do, it would be a rare photograph that does. Most of them do not. . . . They wouldn't help me determine whether that person was a victim of hepatitis, or was a drug user, or was otherwise a person who engaged in the kind of conduct that might cause problems should he donate blood."[3]

So why, the judge wondered, was industry so intent on not giving them to the plaintiffs?

At this point, Judge Grady handed a number of what he said were randomly selected photos to David Shrager, the plaintiffs' lead attorney, and called a ten-minute recess so the lawyer and his colleagues could look at them. When they returned to the courtroom, it became clear why the lawyers saw them as valuable. At least ten of the first handful, Shrager informed the judge, had listed their home addresses as General Delivery, Salvation Army, Salvation Army Mission, or "blank motel."

Also, Shrager said, "Perhaps every single one but two had additionally tattoo marks or scar marks," and "without exception, references to some sort of a medical history."

Is this system of blood and plasma collection the best that industry and governments can provide, for recipients and donors?

The World Health Organization doesn't think so. In 2010 it proposed a global policy of blood self-sufficiency based on "voluntary non-remunerated donation," even as it acknowledged that increasing demand for blood products meant shortages in some countries.[4]

In 2014, a year after a meeting in Italy with representatives from fifty-one nations, WHO followed up by issuing "The Rome Declaration," which formally endorsed the volunteer policy.[5] Among others things, it called upon nations to "introduce legislation to prohibit payment in cash or in kind for the donation of blood, plasma, and other blood components."

Industry strenuously disagreed, with the PPTA quoting a former WHO blood-safety director as saying that if the declaration and similar statements remained unchallenged, "the result will be an inability to provide essential plasma derivatives to more than 80% of the world's population." As a result of its efforts, according to the PPTA, WHO was persuaded to remove its logo from the Rome Declaration, and a disclaimer was rewritten to say that the declaration "does not necessarily represent the decision or policies of the World Health Organization." The PPTA also estimated that 70 percent of the world's hemophilia population had no or insufficient treatment, and said that "an attempt to eliminate private sector industry is outrageous."[6]

The controversy over paid donors—and their role in the AIDS epidemic—erupted again in late 2016 when new research suggested that HIV had first spread to the United States from Haiti, rather than the other way around as long believed. Published in the journal *Nature*, British and American scientists exonerated the French Canadian flight attendant, dubbed "Patient Zero," who for decades had been blamed for bringing the virus to the United States. The team said it tested more than two thousand blood serum samples taken from gay men in the 1970s and estimated that around 1970, "the epidemic moved from the Caribbean to the U.S. rather than from the U.S. to the Caribbean."[7]

How might that relate to plasma products? In an article about the new research,[8] the *New York Times* pointed to findings from Dr. Jacques Pépin, an infectious disease specialist from Quebec. Pépin's 2011 book, *The Origins of AIDS*, [9] theorized that the virus traveled from Africa to Haiti and was spread via a Port-au-Prince plasma center that the newspaper said exported 1,600 gallons per month to the United States. The American-owned center had been the subject of a 1972 *New York Times* article, which had quoted company officials as saying that most of the center's output was purchased by U.S. companies including Armour and Cutter, with the rest going to Germany and Sweden. It also quoted a U.S. health official as saying that it was the companies' responsibility to inspect the operation and verify its quality.[10]

In an October 2016 teleconference with journalists, *Nature* study coauthor Michael Worobey, from the University of Arizona, said that how HIV arrived in the United States remained an open question, according to the *Washington Post.* "It could have been a person of any nationality. It could have even been blood products. A lot of blood products used in the United States in the 1970s actually came from Haiti," he said.[11]

Spurred by factors such as technology and research advances, product development, higher expenditures on health care, and population increases, the market for plasma products has grown rapidly since the era of the hemophilia-HIV epidemic. In 2014, the PPTA estimated the worldwide plasma proteins market at $15.2 billion, with Baxter still holding the biggest share.[12]

This growth is occurring even as the blood industry is shrinking; the number of transfusions is declining due to advances in medical procedures, and recent studies that show that patients often recover more quickly without transfusions.[13]

Besides hemophilia medicines, human plasma is used to produce immunoglobulin, albumin, and other therapeutic proteins. Immunoglobulin, which accounts for about half of all sales of plasma products, is used in patients with a variety of autoimmune and inflammatory conditions; albumin is used to treat burns, shock, and other ailments, and is an ingredient in some vaccines. In short, millions of people use plasma products in some form. The products have saved and improved untold numbers of lives.

But no one is more aware of the potential for disaster than the hemophiliacs who survived the 1970s and 1980s after contracting HIV, hepatitis B, and hepatitis C.

Richard Vogel, one of Weinberg's clients, served from 2011 to 2015 as a consumer representative on the federal government's Advisory Committee on Blood and Tissue Safety and Availability. He's also a board member of the Hemophilia Association of New Jersey.

"Although the products are safe, you still really have to keep your eye on safety and make sure industry doesn't go crazy like they did in the '80s and '70s," Vogel says.

He adds that, at least for U.S. hemophiliacs, "the majority of products are safe today because they are recombinant products"—genetically engineered clotting medicines that contain little or no blood plasma. The Affordable Care Act has made them more available; although many hemophiliacs have health insurance with high co-pays, the law did away with lifetime insurance caps, making it possible for them to switch from the somewhat cheaper plasma-based products, he says.

Today, most Americans who use plasma-based clotting drugs do so because they are much less likely than recombinants to cause "inhibitors"— antibodies formed when the body thinks the medicine is a foreign substance that must be attacked. It's a serious complication, medically and financially, because inhibitors prevent the body from responding to clotting-factor treatment, meaning that the medicine may not stop bleeding episodes. Approximately 30 percent of people with severe hemophilia A develop inhibitors, according to the Hemophilia Federation of America.

The government's Advisory Committee on Blood and Tissue Safety and Availability, as well as the National Hemophilia Foundation, have recommended recombinant clotting factor products as the treatment of choice.[14] But as of this writing, new research, published in May 2016 in the *New England Journal of Medicine*, is making them rethink that advice. The study, done with previously untreated toddlers suffering from severe hemophilia A, found that those who used recombinants were 87 percent more likely to develop inhibitors, compared to those who used plasma-derived Factor VIII medicines.[15]

Still, blood products are safer than ever thanks to increasingly sophisticated donor screening, filtration, and cleansing technologies that go beyond heat—solvent/detergent, ultraviolet irradiation—to eliminate and inactivate a variety of pathogens. Donated blood also undergoes a battery of tests for HIV, hepatitis A and B, Human T-Lymphotropic virus, Chagas disease, West Nile virus, and syphilis.

Do longtime hemophilia activists believe the companies have learned their lesson?

Dana Kuhn, who in the 1990s was the first consumer appointed to the Advisory Committee on Blood and Tissue Safety and Availability, says plasma products are safer today because the committee demanded better screening and collection practices at blood centers. But unless the government continues to be diligent and proactive as "the last line of defense . . . another epic tragedy will reoccur," he says.

"I think they're doing what they are supposed to be doing," Vogel says of the companies. "They have all of these checks and balances with scanning—you know, barcodes and this and that to track the units of blood—but they're always complaining about how much it costs. . . . I think people kind of forget."

In issuing his final recommendations on blood safety, Justice Krever of Canada voiced similar concerns.

"I am confident that if the recommendations are implemented, the likelihood that the tragedy will happen again will be markedly reduced," he wrote. "But in our hope for the future we must not forget that a terrible tragedy did occur."[16]

Memories do indeed fade. Here, for example, is how one fractionation equipment supplier referred to the tainted-blood episode, in an item on its website in 2015: "In the 1980s, it became apparent that viruses such as AIDS were infecting people who had received blood transfusions. There were also a few rare cases of people who were also being infected after receiving plasma products, particularly Hemophiliacs."

As a survivor of that era, Vogel feels a responsibility to educate others. That's why he travels around the country, conducting workshops for others with hemophilia. "People want to know what happened because they don't know," he says.

And the danger isn't over. Scientists are continuously looking for and monitoring new and previously unknown infectious agents. The CDC publishes a monthly online journal called *Emerging Infectious Diseases*, and each issue contains dozens of reports.[17] Since 1998, the CDC has helped organize international conferences on emerging diseases, usually held every two to three years.[18]

Pathogens are identified by a wide variety of vaguely disquieting abbreviations, such as MERS, SARS, and CHIKV.[19] Recent alarms have sounded, too, about the Zika virus, human parvovirus,[20] and hepatitis E, the last of which has been found in patients who used plasma products made from pools that were subjected to the solvent-detergent method of inactivating viruses.[21] Hepatitis E is a non-enveloped virus, meaning it lacks the outer lipid membrane that is attacked by the solvent-detergent process. Prions, the infectious particles that cause ailments such as Creutzfeldt-Jakob disease, also are resistant to solvent-detergent, a method widely used by the plasma industry.[22]

Vogel says the Advisory Committee on Blood and Tissue Safety and Availability also has discussed Babesia, an infection caused by the same ticks that transmit Lyme disease. In July 2015, Dr. Susan Stramer, vice president of scientific affairs for the American Red Cross, called for mandatory Babesia screening, saying that "the fatality rate in transfusion recipients is approximately 18 percent." She said that "although investigational blood donation screening tools are available, they are not in common use," are not required by the FDA, and "many hospitals do not wish to pay for the additional screening."[23]

Vogel agrees. On the committee, especially among the blood bankers, "there's concern with it," he says, "but then there's 'Oh, we'll have to start testing for this and this and this and this and then, you know, our cost of fractionation' . . . so there's always that money issue."

Stramer noted that the PPTA has a list of seventy-seven agents that are known, or have the potential, to be transmitted by transfusions.

The PPTA promises vigilance, saying on its website: "Responding to known and unknown challenges to the safety of plasma protein therapies requires continuous research to develop methods for both the detection of pathogens as well as methods for the elimination of pathogens that could possibly enter the manufacturing process."[24]

These efforts can produce intense debate and discussion. In 2014, the Advisory Committee on Blood and Tissue Safety and Availability voted 16–2 in favor of easing the nation's ban on blood donations from gay and bisexual men, a policy that was enacted as a result of the HIV epidemic. The committee recommended that it be changed to allow donations from men who had abstained from gay sex for one year.

Both of the no votes came from consumer representatives on the committee. Vogel was one of them.

"I understand their point," he says of the gay activists who lobbied for the change. "If you're in a committed relationship for twenty years and you're HIV-negative, I can understand that you want to be able to give blood. The problem that I had, and I still have, is the younger generation who didn't go through the '80s, who now think HIV is a manageable disease and think, 'All I need to do is go out and have sex and take a pill before and after and I'll be fine.'"

"Now, what's going to happen is that the people who lived in Europe for three months or six months who were banned for life from giving blood, now they're going to want to give blood," Vogel adds, referring to the ban that resulted from Creutzfeldt-Jakob disease erupting overseas.

Other members of the committee "were nice about it," he says, but "I have the feeling that sometimes they didn't like to hear me. It was, 'Here he goes again, he's bringing it up again . . . ' but I also thought it was important to be there, just to kind of make them think."

Before the committee's vote, a coalition of groups representing hemophiliacs, HIV/AIDS patients, and gay and lesbian activists issued a joint statement, vowing to continue working together on the issue. They called for "any scientific research that is necessary to allow for the thoughtful consideration of alternative policies regarding donor deferral."[25]

Soon after the vote, the FDA announced its intention to enact the one-year deferral policy, saying that both HHS and FDA advisory committees had carefully reviewed the scientific evidence and believed the change would be safe.[26] It was a carefully measured response that didn't completely satisfy either the pro-safety or pro-gay rights side of the argument.

But after the June 2016 attack by a gunman at a gay nightclub in Orlando, Florida, which killed forty-nine people and wounded fifty-three others, the issue arose again. Gay people were outraged that they were turned away when they tried to donate blood for the victims. A month later, the FDA announced that it would look again at possibly easing the policy.[27]

The FDA's Blood Products Advisory Committee in 2014 also endorsed the agency's plan to ease restrictions on blood donors who previously tested positive for Chagas disease, an often fatal blood-borne ailment that afflicts about 300,000 people in the United States and millions more in Mexico and Central and South America. Testing for the disease began in the United States in January 2007, and the FDA previously had banned such donors. While the committee agreed with the new plan, it was noted that experts may be underestimating the number of people infected with Chagas because most of them are asymptomatic. It also was noted that hundreds of potential donors were classified as "indeterminate"—in other words, the tests couldn't tell whether they were infected.

Hemophilia patients also are left to wonder what, if any, effects they might someday suffer from the rare but fatal variant Creutzfeldt-Jakob disease, linked to eating beef infected with what's popularly known as "mad cow disease." In the late 1990s and early 2000s, v-CJD was detected in plasma products despite all the advances in screening and cleansing technology, and since 2004, there have been several reports of people infected with v-CJD after using blood products.[28] Researchers are studying what this might mean for the future, and are learning more about prions. Meanwhile, hemophiliacs—as usual, the canaries in the coal mine—are being monitored.

Among the most recent published research is an article in the June 2012 issue of *PLOS Pathogens*, an open-access, peer-reviewed medical journal, which states: "It is now clearly established that the transfusion of blood from variant CJD (v-CJD) infected individuals can transmit the disease. Since the number of asymptomatic infected donors remains unresolved, inter-individual v-CJD transmission through blood and blood derived products is a major public health concern."

Says Vogel: "I think it's something to worry about, but nothing has happened since the '90s scare. . . . They haven't really figured it out yet."

Kuhn still remembers when mouse testing revealed that 10 percent were contracting CJD. He was concerned, he says, that it was characterized as "just 10 percent," adding, "I am stunned that a test has not been found for CJD detection in the blood supply for nearly two decades."

Overall, however, there is good reason for optimism in the hemophilia community.

Today, according to the World Federation of Hemophilia, "with proper treatment, life expectancy for people with hemophilia is about 10 years less than that of males without hemophilia, and children can look forward to a normal life expectancy."[29] The medical literature is peppered with articles on how to treat aging hemophiliacs.

"Hemophilia is certainly a manageable disease nowadays," Vogel says, "and with the recombinant factors and prophylaxis, with a lot of people on prophylaxis, they should live a long and healthy life. These kids nowadays get to play any sport they want—maybe not hockey unless they have mild hemophilia, but with prophylaxis you don't have to worry about joint damage."

In addition to the recombinant medicines, scientists also are working on synthetic blood, gene therapy and other cutting-edge treatments and cures.

Once a death sentence, HIV has been transformed into a chronic disease. Hepatitis C is being conquered, too. A small number of hemophiliacs have had liver transplants because of the damage caused by hepatitis C, and the procedure cured their hemophilia as well. More importantly for the larger population, for whom hepatitis C has become even more deadly than AIDS, there are new drugs that cure hepatitis C in 90 to 100 percent of cases, according to the FDA. But these medicines are very expensive; Vogel says he was quoted a price of $90,000 for a full course of treatment. His insurance company would not approve it, however, because the genotype of his hepatitis C does not match the one for which the FDA has approved the drugs. He hopes the agency will expand its criteria soon, so he, too, can be cured.

In summary, "I guess the takeaway is, I think the products are safe nowadays, but we still have to be vigilant," Vogel says.

"Years ago, we put all of our trust in our physicians and the manufacturers, and you saw what happened. So we're a little skeptical of trusting them again."

NOTES

CHAPTER 1   LIQUID GOLD

1. Boudreaux telephone interview with author Shaw, December 7, 1999. Additional details from the interview are throughout this chapter.

2. Department of Corrections, "West Florida Parishes Region," accessed July 13, 2015. http://www.doc.la.gov/wp-content/uploads/statmap/WFPRegion.pdf.

3. Angola Rodeo, "Welcome to the Angola Rodeo," video, accessed July 13, 2015, http://www.angolarodeo.com/.

4. Baxter-Hyland shipping records, in authors' possession.

5. UNAIDS, "Prisons and AIDS: UNAIDS Point of View," accessed July 13, 2015, http://www.unaids.org/sites/default/files/media_asset/prisons-pov_en_0.pdf.

6. American Correctional Association, "Plasmapheresis Centers in Correctional Institutions," 1984, 2–4, accessed July 13, 2015, https://www.ncjrs.gov/pdffiles1/Digitization/99209NCJRS.pdf.

7. Donna Shaw, "In 2 Countries, Tracing a Trail of Tainted Blood; Investigators Find the Traffickers Relied on High-Risk Donors: Inmates, Drug Addicts," *Philadelphia Inquirer,* December 29, 1995, accessed July 15, 2015, http://articles .philly.com/1995–12–29/news/25667549_1_plasma-products-plasma-industry-blood-products.

8. Ibid.

9. Donna Shaw, "Blood Brought from AIDS-Ravaged Africa; Plasma Mislabeled as from Animals Was Sold to an Area Company; There's No Evidence It Knew What Was Happening," *Philadelphia Inquirer,* December 22, 1995, accessed July 15, 2015, http://articles.philly.com/1995–12–22/news/25669483_1_plasma-collection-centers-armour-officials-blood-system.

10. Donna Shaw, "Offer to Be Rejected in HIV Case; the $640 Million Settlement Is Too Low, Say Leaders of Hemophiliacs Infected by Tainted Drugs," *Philadelphia Inquirer,* May 13, 1996, accessed July 15, 2015, http://articles.philly.com/1996–05–13/news/25627399_1_corey-dubin-hiv-infected-hemophiliacs-blood-clotting-products.

11. J. S. Taylor, E. Shmunes, and A. W. Holmes, "Hepatitis B in Plasma Fractionation Workers: A Seroepidemiologic Study," *Journal of the American Medical Association*

230 (6) (Nov. 11, 1974)::850–853, accessed July 15, 2015, http://jama.jamanet-work.com/article.aspx?articleid=358000.

12. Donna Shaw, "On the Trail of Tainted Blood; Hemophiliacs Say U.S. Could Have Prevented Their Contracting AIDS," *Philadelphia Inquirer*, April 16, 1995, accessed July 15, 2015, http://articles.philly.com/1995–04–16/news/25685137_1_hemophil iacs-blood-clotting-products-aids-virus.

13. Donna Shaw, "Efforts to Make Blood Products Safer Tied to Competitive Pressures," *Philadelphia Inquirer*, July 18, 1995, accessed July 15, 2015, http:// articles.philly.com/1995–07–18/news/25677302_1_hemophiliacs-blood-prod ucts-blood-clotting-medicines.

14. Donna Shaw, "Firm Squelched Findings of Risk of AIDS in Its Medicine; the Local Company Was Told of Risks with Its Blood-Clotting Product; It Kept the Product on the Market," *Philadelphia Inquirer*, October 5, 1995, accessed July 15, 2015, http://articles.philly.com/1995–10–05/news/25694624_1_armour-officials-aids-virus-armour-pharmaceutical. Donna Shaw, "Was U.S. Medicine Dumped? Canadians Charge That Armour Sent the Leftover Hemophilia Medicine over Their Border," *Philadelphia Inquirer*, October 6, 1995, accessed July 15, 2015, http://articles.philly.com/1995–10–06/news/25696451_1_aids-virus-armour-pharmaceutical-hemophiliacs. Donna Shaw, "Firm Did Not Act on AIDS Virus Warning; a Scientist Said Armour's Method Did Not Kill All the Virus in Its Plasma; Stricter Steps Waited 2 Years," *Philadelphia Inquirer*, October 23, 1995, accessed July 15, 2015, http://articles.philly.com/1995–10–23/news/25695035_1_armour-executives-armour-pharmaceutical-aids-virus. Walt Bogdanich and Eric Koli, "2 Paths of Bayer Drug in 80's: Riskier Type Went Overseas," *New York Times*, May 22, 2003, accessed July 15, 2015, http://www.nytimes .com/2003/05/22/business/2-paths-of-bayer-drug-in-80-s-riskier-one-steered-overseas.html.

15. Internal corporate documents, in authors' possession.

CHAPTER 2   BEGINNINGS

1. Superior Court of New Jersey, Appellate Division, "State of New Jersey, Plaintiff-Respondent, v. William Grunow, Defendant-Appellant," March 6, 1985, accessed July 15, 2015, http://www.leagle.com/decision/1985440199NJSuper241_1415.xml/ STATE%20v.%20GRUNOW.

2. Rudy Larini, "'Love Triangle' Slayer Paroled after 6 Years," *Star-Ledger*, February 7, 1990.

CHAPTER 3   HOW COULD IT HAPPEN AND NOBODY DID ANYTHING WRONG?

1. U.S. Centers for Disease Control and Prevention, "Hemophilia Facts," accessed July 15, 2015, http://www.cdc.gov/ncbddd/hemophilia/facts.html.

2. American Society of Hematology, "Hemophilia: From Plasma to Recombinant Factors," accessed July 15, 2015, http://www.hematology.org/About/History/50-Years/1524.aspx.

CHAPTER 4   A HISTORY IGNORED

1. Profiles in Science, National Library of Medicine, "The Charles R. Drew Papers," accessed July 15, 2015, http://profiles.nlm.nih.gov/ps/retrieve/Narrative/BG/p-nid/336.

2. Office of the Surgeon General, Department of the Army, "Surgery in World War II, Activities of Surgical Consultants," vol. 1, chapter 4, accessed July 15, 2015. http://history.amedd.army.mil/booksdocs/wwii/actvsurgconvoli/CH06.htm.

3. Douglas Starr, *Blood: An Epic History of Medicine and Commerce* (New York; Knopf, 1998), 101–106.

4. L. B. Seeff, G. W. Beebe, J. H. Hoofnagle, J. E. Norman, Z. Buskell-Bales, J. G. Waggoner, N. Kaplowitz, R. S. Koff, J. L. Petrini Jr., E. R. Schiff, et al., "A Serologic Follow-Up of the 1942 Epidemic of Post-Vaccination Hepatitis in the United States Army," *New England Journal of Medicine* 316, no. 16 (1987): 965–970.

5. Emanuel M. Rappaport, "Hepatitis Following Blood or Plasma Transfusions: Observations in Thirty-three Cases," *Journal of the American Medical Association* 128, no. 13 (1945): 932–939.

6. War Department telegram to JAMA editor, dated March 4, 1946, obtained from U.S. Army Military History Institute, Carlisle Barracks, Carlisle, PA.

7. Emanuel M. Rappaport, "Further Observations on Delayed Hepatitis Following Transfusions and the Role of Asymptomatic Donors in This Syndrome," obtained from U.S. Army Military History Institute, Carlisle Barracks, PA.

8. Office of the Surgeon General, Department of the Army, "Surgery in World War II, Activities of Surgical Consultants."

9. C. K. Kasper, "Judith Graham Pool and the Discovery of Cryoprecipitate," *Haemophilia* 18 (2012): 833–835, accessed July 16, 2015, http://onlinelibrary.wiley.com/doi/10.1111/hae.12042/pdf.

10. Letter dated April 30, 1974, from Judith G. Pool to Dr. Charles C. Edwards, Assistant Secretary for Health, Department of Health, Education and Welfare.

11. Statement from World Federation of Hemophilia, Congress XII, New York, 1977.

12. J. A. Spero, J. H. Lewis, D. H. Van Thiel, U. Hasiba, and B. S. Rabin, "Asymptomatic Structural Liver Disease in Hemophilia," *New England Journal of Medicine* 298, no. 25 (1978): 1373–1378.

13. Federal Register notice of Food and Drug Administration Final Rule, January 13, 1978 (43 FR 2142).

14. N. J. Ehrenkranz et al., "Pneumocystis Carinii Pneumonia among Persons with Hemophilia A," *Morbidity and Mortality Weekly Report* 31, no. 27 (July 16, 1982); 365–367, accessed July 16, 2015, http://www.cdc.gov/mmwr/preview/mmwrhtml/00001126.htm.

15. Sir Macfarlane Burnet, *Natural History of Infectious Disease,* 3rd edition (Cambridge, UK: Cambridge University Press, 1962), 360–361.

16. Robert Massie and Suzanne Massie, *Journey* (New York; Random House, 1975).

17. Ibid., 243

18. Ibid., 243–244.

19. Ibid., 245.

20. J. Scott Armstrong, "The Panalba Role-Playing Case," *American Marketing Association Proceedings,* August 1976, 213–216, accessed July 15, 2015, http://repository.upenn.edu/marketing_papers/129/.

21. Gary T. Schwartz, "The Myth of the Ford Pinto Case," *Rutgers Law Review* 43 (1990–91): 1013.

22. D. A. Marshall, S. H. Kleinman, J. B. Wong, J. P. AuBuchon, D. T. Grima, N. A. Kulin, and M. C. Weinstein, "Cost-Effectiveness of Nucleic Acid Test Screening of Volunteer Blood Donations for Hepatitis B, Hepatitis C and Human Immunodeficiency Virus in the United States," *Vox Sanguinis* 86, no. 1 (January 2004): 28–40.

CHAPTER 5   DIGGING IN

1. Institute of Medicine, *HIV and the Blood Supply: An Analysis of Crisis Decisionmaking* (Washington, DC: National Academy Press, 1995), 48.

2. Richard D. Lyons, "Ousted F.D.A. Chief Charges 'Pressure' From Drug Industry," *New York Times,* December 31, 1969.

3. Institute of Medicine Forum on Drug Discovery, Development, and Translation Medicine, *Challenges for the FDA: The Future of Drug Safety, Workshop Summary* (Washington, DC: National Academies Press, 2007).

4. U.S. Department of Health and Human Services, HHS FY2015 Budget in Brief, Food and Drug Administration, accessed July 17, 2015, http://www.hhs.gov/about/budget/fy2015/budget-in-brief/fda/index.html.

5. Pharmaceutical Research and Manufacturers of America, "About PhRMA," accessed July 17, 2015, http://www.phrma.org/about.

6. Harry Meyer deposition, in authors' possession.

7. Neal Nathanson and Alexander Langmuir, "The Cutter Incident: Poliomyelitis Following Formaldehyde-Inactivated Poliovirus Vaccination in the United States during the Spring of 1955," *American Journal of Epidemiology* 78, no. 1 (1963): 16–28.

8. From testimony of David A. Kessler before the Subcommittee on Oversight and Investigations of the Committee on Energy and Commerce, House of Representatives, July 28, 1993.

9. U.S. Government Accountability Office, "Drug Safety: Improvement Needed in FDA's Postmarket Decision-making and Oversight Process," published March 31, 2006, publicly released April 24, 2006.

CHAPTER 8   ALL FOR BUSINESS

1. National Hemophilia Foundation, "Hemophilia Patient Alert #1," July 14, 1982, in authors' possession.

2. National Hemophilia Foundation, "NHF Urges Clotting Factor Use Be Maintained," Hemophilia Newsnotes Summer 1983, in authors' possession.

3. "Heat Treated Factor VIII Now Licensed by FDA,"*Hemophilia Newsnotes*, Summer 1983, 3–4.

4. Donna Shaw, "Hemophilia Foundation Chief Knew of AIDS Risk in 1984; the 'Risk' of a Recall Was 'Not Worth the Benefit,' the Former Foundation President Said," *Philadelphia Inquirer*, November 3, 1994, accessed July 19, 2015, http://arti cles.philly.com/1994–11–03/news/25868356_1_aids-virus-aids-risk-louis-aledort.

5. "Heat Treated Factor VIII Now Licensed."

6. K. Schimpf, H.H. Brackmann, W. Kreuz, B. Kraus, F. Haschke, W. Schramm, J. Moesseler, G. Auerswald, A.H. Sutor, K. Koehler, P. Hellstern, W. Muntean, and I. Scharrer, "Absence of Anti-Human Immunodeficiency Virus Types 1 and 2 Seroconversion after the Treatment of Hemophilia a or Von Willebrand's Disease with Pasteurized Factor VIII Concentrate," *New England Journal of Medicine* 321 (1989): 1148–1152.

CHAPTER 9   SOMEWHERE HERE, I HAVE THE DOCUMENTS

1. Randy Shilts, *And the Band Played On* (New York: St. Martin's Press, 1987), 220.

CHAPTER 10   MORE LAWYERS, MORE EXPERTS

1. J. A. Spero, J. H. Lewis, D. H. Van Thiel, U. Hasiba, and B. S. Rabin et al., "Asymptomatic Structural Liver Disease in Hemophilia," New England Journal of Medicine 298, no. (25) (1978): 1373–1378.

2. "Baxter Celebrates 50 Years as a Pioneer and Leader in the Biotechnology Industry," Baxter Healthcare Corporation news release, November 10, 2003, http://www.prnewswire.com/news-releases/baxter-celebrates-50-years-as-a-pioneer-and-leader-in-the-biotechnology-industry-72919672.html.

CHAPTER 11   A MEETING WITH ROGER

1. Paul von Zielbauer, "Iraqis Infected by H.I.V.-Tainted Blood Try New Tool: A Lawsuit," *New York Times*, September 4, 2006, accessed July 22, 2015, http://www.nytimes.com/2006/09/04/world/middleeast/04aids.html?ex=1158897600 &en=60d4dd1ca71030bd&ei=5070.

2. Marlise Simons, "France Convicts 3 in Case of H.I.V.-Tainted Blood," *New York Times*, October 24, 1992, accessed July 21, 2015, http://www.nytimes .com/1992/10/24/world/france-convicts-3-in-case-of-hiv-tainted-blood.html.

3. Associated Press, "AIDS-Tainted Blood Scandal Spreads to French Prisons," *Gainesville (FL) Sun*, November 7, 1992.

4. Craig R. Whitney, "Top French Officials Cleared over Blood with AIDS Virus," *New York Times*, March 10, 1999, accessed July 21, 2015, http://www.nytimes .com/1999/03/10/world/top-french-officials-cleared-over-blood-with-aids-virus .html.

5. Sarah Boseley and Alexandra Topping, "'A Horrific Human Tragedy': Report Criticises Response to Blood Scandal," *Guardian*, February 23, 2009, accessed July 22, 2015, http://www.theguardian.com/society/2009/feb/24/haemophilia-contamination-report.

6. National Hemophilia Foundation. "Medical Advisory #409: Signs of Variant Creutzfeldt-Jakob Disease Found in a UK Patient with Hemophilia; No Added Risk Seen for U.S. Patients," accessed July 22, 2015, https://www.hemophilia.org/ Newsroom/Medical-Advisories/Medical-Advisory-409-Signs-of-Variant-Creutzfeldt-Jakob-Disease-Found-in-a-UK-Patient-with-Hemophilia-No-Added-Risk-Seen-for-US-Patients.

7. Lord Penrose. "The Penrose Inquiry," accessed July 22, 2015, http://www.penroseinquiry.org.uk/.

8. BBC News, "Penrose Inquiry: David Cameron Apologises over Infected Blood," accessed July 22, 2015, http://www.bbc.com/news/uk-scotland-32041715.

9. Sheldon H. Harris, *Factories of Death: Japanese Biological Warfare, 1932–1945, and the American Cover-up* (New York and London: Routledge, 2002).

CHAPTER 12   AN ACT OF MAN

1. T. L. Chorba, R. C. Holman, M. J. Clarke, B. L. Evatt, "Effects of HIV Infection on Age and Cause of Death for Persons with Hemophilia a in the United States," *American Journal of Hematology* 66 (2001): 229–240, accessed July 23, 2015, http:// onlinelibrary.wiley.com/doi/10.1002/ajh.1050/pdf.

CHAPTER 13   THE TROUBLE WITH TORTS

1. John T. Nockleby and Shannon Curreri, "100 Years of Conflict: The Past and Future of Tort Retrenchment," *Loyola of Los Angeles Law Review* 38 (2005): 1.

2. David Shrager memo dated March 18, 1994, in authors' possession.

3. David Shrager memo dated March 22, 1994, in authors' possession.

4. David Shrager memo dated May 13, 1994, in authors' possession.

5. Donna Shaw, "2 Firms to Pay HIV-Infected Hemophiliacs; Blood Products Were Tainted with the AIDS Virus," *Philadelphia Inquirer*, August 3, 1994.

6. Hearing testimony, U.S. District Court for Northern District of Illinois, Eastern Division, August 5, 1994.

7. Judge John F. Grady, written opinion, August 17, 1994.

CHAPTER 14   I MURDERED MY CHILD, BUT NOT ALONE

1. Peter Jones, Correspondence, *British Medical Journal* (June 21, 1980): 1531–1532.

2. Michael Rodell to Peter Jones, August 14, 1985, in authors' possession.

3. Armour document, in authors' possession.

4. Armour corporate memo, in authors' possession.

5. National Hemophilia Foundation financial records, in authors' possession.

6. Donald Goldman letter to the World Federation of Hemophilia, 1986.

7. Donald Goldman deposition, September 1994.

8. Walter Vogel letter to Donald Goldman, August 3, 1989.

CHAPTER 15   OF SHEEP AND MEN

1. Dolores Crooker, prepared statement before the Subcommittee on Human Resources, Committee on Government Oversight and Reform, U.S. House of Representatives, July 31, 1997.

2. From the Seventh Circuit Court of Appeals transcript, January 30, 1995.

3. U.S. Securities and Exchange Commission, "The Laws That Govern the Securities Industry," accessed July 24, 2015, http://www.sec.gov/about/laws.shtml.

4. Donna Shaw, "N.J. Senate Panel OKs Bill for HIV-Infected Hemophiliacs; Many Contracted the Virus from Medicines," *Philadelphia Inquirer*, March 14, 1995.

5. Donna Shaw, "N.J. Committee OKs Bill Giving Hemophiliacs More Time to Sue," *Philadelphia Inquirer*, March 28, 1995.

6. C. Angelotta et al., "Legal, Financial, and Public Health Consequences of Transfusion-Transmitted Hepatitis C Virus in Persons with Haemophilia," *Vox Sanguinis* 93, no. 20 (August 2007): 159–165.

7. Chief Judge Richard Posner, Seventh Circuit Court of Appeals opinion, March 16, 1995.

8. M.S. Gottlieb, H.M. Schanker, P.T Fan, A. Saxon, J.D. Weisman, I. Pozalski, "Pneumocystis Pneumonia—Los Angeles," *Morbidity and Mortality Weekly Report* 30, no. 21 (June 5, 1981): 1–3, accessed July 24, 2015, http://www.cdc.gov/mmwr/preview/mmwrhtml/june_5.htm.

9. J. Doherty and S. King, "Case Report: Pneumocystis Carinii Pneumonia in a Homosexual Male—Ontario," *Canada Diseases Weekly Report* 8, no. 13 (March 5, 1982): 65–68.

10. Bruce Evatt, "The Tragic History of AIDS in the Hemophilia Population, 1982–1984," *Journal of Thrombosis and Haemostasis* 4 (2006): 2295, accessed July 24, 2015, http://www1.wfh.org/publication/files/pdf-1269.pdf.

11. Horace Krever, "Final Report [the Commission of Inquiry on the Blood System in Canada]," part I, "Introduction," 1997.

12. Ibid.

13. John Snow, "The Cholera near Golden-Square, and at Deptford," *Medical Times and Gazette*, September 23, 1854, accessed July 24, 2015, http://www.ph.ucla.edu/epi/snow/choleraneargoldensquare.html.

14. National Hemophilia Foundation, "Hemophilia Patient Alert #1," *Hemophilia Newsnotes*, July 14, 1982, in authors' possession.

15. Krever Report, chapter 14, "The Risk in Factor Concentrates," 389–395.

16. Baxter/Hyland documents, in authors' possession.

17. Ibid.

CHAPTER 16   A FAILURE OF LEADERSHIP

1. Committee to Study HIV Transmission Through Blood and Blood Products, Division of Health Promotion and Disease Prevention, Institute of Medicine, *HIV and the Blood Supply: An Analysis of Crisis Decsionmaking* (Washington, DC: National Academy Press, 1995), executive summary.

2. Ibid., 4–13.

3. Ibid., executive summary.

4. Ibid., 5–18.

5. Ibid., 7–22.

6. Ibid., 8–14.

7. Ibid., 8–19.

8. Ibid., 8–16.

CHAPTER 17   FROM PRIME CHUCK TO DOGEZA

1. Angela Stewart, "Blood Centers Press the Quest for Donors," *Star-Ledger*, January 10, 1996.

2. Kathy Barrett Carter, "Haytaian Closes Out Assembly Career with Some Prime Chuck," *Star-Ledger*, January 10, 1996.

3. Tom Johnson, "Hemophiliac Bill Dies Despite Senate Rebuff of Veto by Governor," *Star-Ledger*, January 10, 1996.

4. Carter, "Haytaian Closes Out Assembly Career with Some Prime Chuck."

5. Robert Schwaneberg, "Blood-Clot Drug Makers Challenge Suit Deadline for AIDS Hemophiliacs," *Star-Ledger*, June 22, 1996.

6. Donna Shaw, "Japanese Government, Firms Agree to AIDS Compensation; Japanese Victims Who Contracted HIV through Tainted Blood Products Will Receive $420,000 Each," *Philadelphia Inquirer*, March 15, 1996, accessed July 26, 2015, http://articles.philly.com/1996–03–15/news/25636750_1_hemophiliacs-aids-virus-blood-products.

7. Donna Shaw, "Offer to Be Rejected in HIV Case. the $600 Million Settlement Is Too Low, Say Leaders of Hemophiliacs Infected by Tainted Drugs," *Philadelphia Inquirer*, May 13, 1996, accessed August 12, 2016, http://articles.philly.com/1996–05–13/news/25627399_1_corey-dubin-hiv-infected-hemophiliacs-blood-clotting-products.

8. Government document, in authors' possession.

9. Government document, in authors' possession.

10. Donna Shaw, "Legal Battle under Way over Canadian Inquiry into Blood Products," *Philadelphia Inquirer*, May 23, 1996, accessed July 26, 2015, http://articles.philly.com/1996–05–23/news/25626581_1_blood-products-drug-companies-red-cross-officials.

11. Donna Shaw, "Report Blasts FDA's Blood Regulation; Doctors and Patients Are Ill-Informed, It Says. A House Panel Wants a Fund for Future HIV Victims," *Philadelphia Inquirer*, July 26, 1996, accessed July 27, 2015, http://articles.philly.com/1996–07–26/news/25622554_1_blood-products-fda-new-congressional-report.

12. Representative Christopher Shays, "Protecting the Nation's Blood Supply from Infectious Agents: The Need for New Standards to Meet New Threats," adopted by the Government Reform and Oversight Committee on July 25, 1996.

13. Ibid.

14. Donna Shaw, "Verdict Clouds a Deal on Blood. A Hemophiliac's Family Was Awarded $2 Million. Other Victims May Now Reconsider Their Pact," *Philadelphia Inquirer*, March 27, 1997, accessed August 12, 2016, http://articles.philly.com/1997–03–22/news/25572808_1_corey-dubin-hemophiliacs-committee-of-ten-thousand.

CHAPTER 18   ENDINGS

1. Andrew Cliff and Matthew Smallman-Raynor, *Oxford Textbook of Infectious Disease Control: A Geographical Analysis from Medieval Quarantine to Global Eradication* (Oxford: Oxford University Press, 2013), 122. The College of Physicians of Philadelphia, "The History of Vaccines," accessed July 28, 2015, http://www.historyofvaccines.org/content/articles/rubella.

2. Industry memo, in authors' possession.

3. Donna Shaw and Josh Goldstein, "FDA Cited over Safety of Blood Products. There Have Been Delays in Recalls and a Lack of Information for Patients; the Agency Said It Was Making Progress," *Philadelphia Inquirer*, June 6, 1997, accessed Aug. 12, 2016, http://articles.philly.com/1997–06–06/news/25528367_1_plasma-products-blood-products-hospital-patient.

4. Justice Horace Krever, "Final report. Commission of Inquiry on the Blood System in Canada," accessed July 28, 2015, http://epe.lac-bac.gc.ca/100/200/301/hcan-scan/commission_blood_final_rep-e/.

5. Ricky Ray Hemophilia Relief Fund Act of 1998, accessed July 28, 2015, https://www.congress.gov/105/plaws/publ369/PLAW-105publ369.pdf.

6. "HHS Begins Notifying Ricky Ray Hemophilia Relief Fund Recipients of Payments," *HHS News*, accessed July 28, 2015, http://archive.hhs.gov/news/press/2000pres/20000828.html.

7. Industry memos, in authors' possession.

8. "Jurors Award Family of AIDS Infected Hemophiliac $35.3 Million," PRNewswire, accessed July 28, 2015, http://www.prnewswire.com/news-releases/jurors-award-family-of-aids-infected-hemophiliac-353-million-75346352.html.

9. Peter Small and Tracy Huffman, "Accused in Tainted Blood Trial Exonerated," *Toronto Star*, February 10, 2007, accessed July 28, 2015, http://www.thestar.com/news/canada/2007/10/02/accused_in_tainted_blood_trial_exonerated.html.

10. Canwest News Service, "Charges Dropped Against Former Director of the Canadian Red Cross," Canada.com, accessed July 28, 2015, http://www.canada.com/story.html?id=787f5e8e-e119–4805-aa37-aa23a710b764.

EPILOGUE

1. Plasma Protein Therapeutics Association, "About PPTA," accessed July 28, 2015, http://www.pptaglobal.org/about-us/about-ppta.

2. Andrew Pollack, "Is Money Tainting the Plasma Supply?" *New York Times*, December 5, 2009, accessed July 28, 2015, http://www.nytimes.com/2009/12/06/business/06plasma.html?pagewanted=2.

3. Judge John F. Grady, during U.S. District Court hearing on December 13, 1995, in Chicago.

4. World Health Organization, "Blood Transfusion Safety," accessed July 28, 2015, http://www.who.int/bloodsafety/transfusion_services/bts_high_level_forum/en/.

5. World Health Organization, "The Rome Declaration on Achieving Self-Sufficiency in Safe Blood and Blood Products, based on Voluntary Non-Remunerated Donation," accessed July 28, 2015, http://www.avis.it/userfiles/file/Rome DeclarationSelf-SufficiencySafeBloodBloodProductsVNRD.pdf.

6. Jan M. Bult, "Meeting Patient Need for Plasma Protein Therapies," paper presented to Singapore Plasma Protein Therapeutics Association, Singapore, accessed July 28, 2015, http://www.pptaglobal.org/images/presentations/2014/JMB_Singapore_2_Patient_Needs_1.pdf.

7. M. Worobey, T. D. Watts, R. A. McKay, M. A. Suchard, T. Granade, D. E. Teuwen, B. A. Koblin, W. Heneine, P. Lemey, and H. W. Jaffe, "1970s and 'Patient 0' HIV-1 Genomes Illuminate Early HIV/AIDS History in North America," *Nature* 539 (2016): 98–101.

8. Donald G. McNeil Jr., "H.I.V. Arrived in the U.S. Long Before 'Patient Zero,'" *New York Times*, October 26, 2016.

9. Jacques Pépin, *The Origin of AIDS* (New York: Cambridge University Press, 2011).

10. Richard Severo, "Impoverished Haitians Sell Plasma for Use in the U.S." *New York Times*, January 28, 1972.

11. Ariana Eunjung Cha, "Mythology of 'Patient Zero' and how AIDS virus traveled to the United States is all wrong." *Washington Post*, October 26, 2016.

12. Ibid.

13. Ibid.

14. National Hemophilia Foundation, "MASAC Recommendation Regarding the Use of Recombinant Clotting Factor Products with Respect to Pathogen Transmission," accessed July 31, 2015, http://www.hemophilia.org/Researchers-Healthcare-Providers/Medical-and-Scientific-Advisory-Council-MASAC/MASAC-Recommendations/MASAC-Recommendation-Regarding-the-Use-of-Recombinant-Clotting-Factor-Products-with-Respect-to-Pathogen-Transmission.

15. F. Peyvandi, P. M. Mannucci, I. Garagiola, A. El-Beshlawy, M. Elalfy, V. Ramanan., P. Eshghi, S. Hanagavadi, R. Varadarajan, M. Karimi, et al., "A Randomized Trial of Factor VIII and Neutralizing Antibodies in Hemophilia A," *New England Journal of Medicine* 374 (2016): 2054–2064.

16. Justice Horace Krever, "Final Report. Commission of Inquiry on the Blood System in Canada," accessed July 28, 2015, http://epe.lac-bac.gc.ca/100/200/301/hcan-scan/commission_blood_final_rep-e/.

17. U.S. Centers for Disease Control and Prevention, *Emerging Infectious Diseases*, accessed July 28, 2015, http://wwwnc.cdc.gov/eid.

18. U.S. Centers for Disease Control and Prevention, "International Conference on Emerging Infectious Diseases," accessed July 28, 2015, http://www.cdc.gov/iceid/.

19. Mary Gustafson, "MASAC Update," paper presented to Plasma Protein Therapeutics Association, accessed July 28, 2015, http://www.pptaglobal.org/images/presentations/2014/MASAC_September_20_Mary_Gustafson1.pdf.

20. S. A. Baylis, P. W. Tuke, E. Miyagawa, and J. Blümel, "Studies on the Inactivation of Human Parvovirus 4," *Transfusion* 53 (2013): 2585–2592.

21. A. Adonov, G. Rock, L. Lin, J. Borlang, J. Hooper, E. Grudeski, and J. Wu, "Serological and Molecular Evidence of a Plausible Transmission of Hepatitis E Virus through Pooled Plasma," *Vox Sanguinis* 107 (2014): 213–219.

22. Susan Stramer Q&A, "The Potential Threat to Blood Transfusion Safety of Emerging Infectious Disease Agents," *Clinical Advances in Hematology & Oncology* (2015), accessed July 31, 2015, http://www.hematologyandoncology.net/files/2015/07/Stramer1.pdf.

23. Ibid.

24. Plasma Protein Therapeutics Association, "About PPTA," accessed July 28, 2015, http://www.pptaglobal.org/about-us/about-ppta.

25. Committee of Ten Thousand, "Joint Statement," accessed July 28, 2015, http://www.cott1.org/cott-news/2014/8/23/joint-statement.

26. U.S. Food and Drug Administration, "Blood Donor Deferral," accessed July 28, 2015, http://www.fda.gov/forpatients/illness/hivaids/safety/ucm117929.htm.

27. U.S. Food and Drug Administration, "Blood Donor Deferral Policy for Reducing the Risk of Human Immunodeficiency Virus Transmission by Blood and Blood

Products; Establishment of a Public Docket; Request for Comments," *Federal Register*, July 28, 2016, accessed Aug. 12, 2016, https://www.federalregister.gov/articles/2016/07/28/2016–17804/blood-donor-deferral-policy-for-reducing-the-risk-of-human-immunodeficiency-virus-transmission-by.

28. S. McCutcheon, A. R. Alejo Blanco, E. F. Houston, C. de Wolf, B. C. Tan, A. Smith, M. H. Groschup, N. Hunter, V. S. Hornsey, I. R. MacGregor, et al., "All Clinically-Relevant Blood Components Transmit Prion Disease Following a Single Blood Transfusion: a Sheep Model of vCJD," *PLOS ONE* (2011), accessed July 28, 2015, http://www.ncbi.nlm.nih.gov/pubmed/21858015.

29. World Federation of Hemophilia, "About Bleeding Disorders," accessed July 28, 2015, http://www.wfh.org/en/page.aspx?pid=637#Life_expectancy.

INDEX

Note: Page numbers in italics refer to images.

275

ABOUT THE AUTHORS

ERIC WEINBERG is the principal of the Weinberg Law Firm, which he founded in New Brunswick, New Jersey, in 1984. He has successfully represented thousands of victims in complex civil cases involving defective pharmaceutical products and medical devices, medical malpractice, vehicle negligence, product liability, premises liability, and construction matters. He has tried approximately thirty jury trials and more than two hundred bench trials, obtaining verdicts and settlements for his clients in excess of $800 million. He was instrumental in obtaining a $670 million settlement for HIV-infected hemophiliacs, and the settlements he negotiated for his hemophilia clients in New Jersey and New York totaled an additional $30 million. He served for several years as a trustee of the Hemophilia Association of New Jersey. Weinberg graduated from Rutgers College, New Brunswick, New Jersey, and from Boston University School of Law. After law school, he worked for the Somerset County, New Jersey, Prosecutor's Office before going into private practice. He and his wife live in Highland Park, New Jersey, and have four sons.

DONNA SHAW is a professor at The College of New Jersey in Ewing, where she serves as chair of the Department of Journalism and Professional Writing. Before that, she spent most of her career as a journalist, for newspapers including the *Philadelphia Inquirer,* where she worked for seventeen years, and then at WedMD as an editor. Her time at the *Inquirer* included ten years on the business news staff, where she covered pharmaceuticals, biotechnology, and health care. At WebMD, she developed a nationwide network of news bureaus and worked closely with other managers to help make WebMD the nation's premiere website for health and wellness information. She has bachelor's degrees in English and journalism from the

Pennsylvania State University, and a master's degree from Columbia University, where she was a Knight-Bagehot fellow in economics and business journalism. She also studied biotechnology as a journalism fellow at the University of Maryland's Knight Center for Specialized Journalism, and at Virginia Commonwealth University. She and her husband have two children and live in Philadelphia.